Props

READINGS IN THEATRE PRACTICE

Series Editor: Simon Shepherd

Published:

Ross Brown: Sound

Jon Davison: Clown

Penny Francis: Puppetry

Alison Maclaurin and Aoife Monks: Costume

Eleanor Margolies: Props

Scott Palmer: Light

Simon Shepherd: Direction

Forthcoming:

Jane Boston: Voice

Joslin McKinney: Construction

Readings in Theatre Practice
Series Standing Order ISBN 978–0–230–53717–0 hardcover
Series Standing Order ISBN 978–0–230–53718–7 paperback
(*outside North America only*)

You can receive future titles in this series as they are published by placing a standing order. Please contact your bookseller or, in the case of difficulty, write to us at the address below with your name and address, the title of the series and the ISBN quoted above.

Customer Services Department, Macmillan Distribution Ltd, Houndmills, Basingstoke, Hampshire, RG21 6XS, UK

Props

Readings in Theatre Practice

Eleanor Margolies

First published 2016 by
PALGRAVE

Palgrave in the UK is an imprint of Macmillan Publishers Limited, registered in England, company number 785998, of 4 Crinan Street, London, N1 9XW.

Palgrave Macmillan in the US is a division of St Martin's Press LLC, 175 Fifth Avenue, New York, NY 10010.

Palgrave is a global imprint of the above companies and is represented throughout the world.

Palgrave® and Macmillan® are registered trademarks in the United States, the United Kingdom, Europe and other countries.

ISBN 978–1–137–41336–9 hardback
ISBN 978–1–137–41335–2 paperback

This book is printed on paper suitable for recycling and made from fully managed and sustained forest sources. Logging, pulping and manufacturing processes are expected to conform to the environmental regulations of the country of origin.

A catalogue record for this book is available from the British Library.

A catalog record for this book is available from the Library of Congress.

Printed in China

Contents

Series Preface

This series aims to gather together both key historical texts and contemporary ways of thinking about the material crafts and practices of theatre.

These crafts work with the physical materials of theatre – sound, objects, light, paint, fabric, and – yes – physical bodies. Out of these materials the theatre event is created.

In gathering the key texts of a craft it becomes very obvious that the craft is not simply a handling of materials, however skilful. It is also a way of thinking about both the materials and their processes of handling. Work with sound and objects, for example, involves – always, at some level – concepts of what sound is and does, what an object is and does … what a body is.

For many areas of theatre practice there are the sorts of 'how to do it' books that have been published for at least a century. These range widely in quality and interest but next to none of them is able to, or wants to, position the *doing* in relation to the *thinking about doing* or the thinking about the material being used.

This series of books aims to promote both thinking about doing and thinking about materials. Its authors are specialists in their field of practice and they are charged to reflect on their specialism and its history in order, often for the first time, to model concepts and provide the tools not just for the doing but for thinking about theatre practice.

The series title 'Readings in Theatre Practice' uses the word 'reading' in the sense both of a simple understanding or interpretation and of an authoritative explication, an exegesis as it were. Thus, the books first gather together people's opinions about, their understanding of, what they think they are making. These opinions are then framed within a broader narrative which offers an explanatory overview of the practice under investigation.

So, although the books comprise many different voices, there is a dominant authorial voice organising the material and articulating overarching arguments. By way of promoting a further level of critique and reflection, however, authors are asked to include a few lengthy sections, in the form of interviews or essays or both, in order to make space for other voices to develop their own overviews. These may sit in tension, or indeed in harmony, with the dominant narratives.

Authors are encouraged to be sceptical about normative assumptions and canonical orthodoxy. They are asked not to ignore practices and thinking that might question dominant views; they are invited to speculate as to how canons and norms come into being and what effects they have.

We hope the shape provides a dynamic tension in which the different activities of 'reading' both assist and resist each other. The details of the lived practices refuse to fit tidily into the straitjacket of a general argument, but the dominant overview also refuses to allow itself to fragment into local prejudice and anecdote. And it's that restless play between assistance and resistance that mirrors the character of the practices themselves.

At the heart of each craft is a tense relationship. On the one hand there is the basic raw material that is worked – the wood, the light, the paint, the musculature. These have their own given identity – their weight, mechanical logics, smell, particle formation, feel. In short, the texture of the stuff. And on the other hand there is theatre, wanting its effects and illusions, its distortions and impossibilities. The raw material resists the theatre as much as yields to it, the theatre both develops the material and learns from it. The stuff and the magic. This relationship is perhaps what defines the very activity of theatre itself.

It is this relationship, the thing which defines the practice of theatre, which lies at the heart of each book in this series.

Simon Shepherd

Acknowledgements

I have had the good fortune to discuss objects, props and puppets with many thoughtful and imaginative people over the years this book has been fermenting: with teachers at the University of Glasgow and the London College of Printing; with students at the Central School of Speech and Drama, and Rose Bruford College; with fellow members of the London College of Printing semiotics seminar, the University of Roehampton theatre research seminar and the Object Theatre Network at Nottingham Trent University; and with friends and colleagues in audio description, theatre design, puppetry and stage management.

I am especially grateful to Dick McCaw for the opportunity to document the practice of extraordinary theatre-makers under the aegis of the International Workshop Festival, and to Pamela Howard and Theo van Leeuwen, the most generous and inspiring of PhD supervisors.

Some of the ideas discussed here were first developed in conference papers and in essays for journals including *Visual Communication, New Theatre Quarterly, Performance Research* and *Animations Online* – my thanks to the conference participants and editors for many helpful comments and suggestions of new areas to explore.

I am indebted to all the theatre-makers who have spoken to me about their work and allowed me to observe or participate in workshops. They include: Dot Young, Fraser Burchill, Guy Dartnell, John Wright, Julian Crouch, Pamela Howard, Phelim McDermott, Rachel Riggs, Rene Baker, Sean Myatt, Steve Tiplady, Tim Hatley, and the late Clive Barker. My understanding of props has been hugely enriched by working with directors – particularly Lee Lyford (Theatre Royal Bath), and Helen Stanley and Cath Beckett (Lewisham Youth Theatre) – who have invited me to play with stuff for real.

My warm thanks to Aoife Monks, Claire Corniquet, Marion Rhéty, Tobias Hoheisel, Judith Flanders and Nina Raine who have generously allowed me to include substantial extracts of their work, and to Carolin Karrer for sharing her unpublished thesis on prop-making. A residency at the library of the Institut International de la Marionnette in Charleville-Mézières and a grant from the Society for Theatre Research enabled me to carry out research on object theatre.

I'm grateful to Jenni Burnell, Lucinda Knight, Nicola Cattini and Clarissa Sutherland at Palgrave, and to series editor Simon Shepherd and the anonymous reviewers for their suggestions. Heartfelt thanks to the friends who read work in progress and who helped with translations from French, in particular Claire Doucet, Paul Piris and Brigitte Lambert.

This book is dedicated to my sister and brother, who endured my first experiments with papier mâché and brown paper tape, and to my parents, who have always encouraged me both to make things and to think about making.

Chapter

1   Introduction

While props are often treated as a discrete category for the purposes of the production process – with their own workshops, directors and makers – many theatre designers argue that there is no hard and fast distinction between scenography, costume and props in their work, nor in the audience's perception. There are, however, good reasons to look at props separately. As objects often familiar from the world outside the theatre, props engage the performer's body in the stage world (States 1985: 44). They also, as I will argue, engage the spectator's body. Props are of special interest when thinking about how performance represents the world. The attitude adopted in performance towards a small portion of reality, such as a newspaper, may stand for an attitude to vaster realities which are harder to conceive, such as forests. As Phelim McDermott and Julian Crouch of Improbable Theatre write, in 'watching a puppeteer animating materials, we see her attitude to the world she inhabits. How a performer interacts and treats her materials will be a good indication of how she will treat other performers and also herself during the creative process' (McDermott and Crouch 2000: 13).

The aim of this book is to bring together theoretical writing on objects and things with the practical knowledge of those involved in theatre as actors, makers and spectators. This first chapter looks at the theoretical background to objects in performance, ending with an extract from the influential essay 'Man and Object in the Theatre' by Jiři Veltruský. Chapters 2 and 3 consider the object from the performer's point of view, in training, rehearsal and as part of the devising process. Chapters 4 and 5 look at props from the point of view of the dramatist and director, focusing first on the period when the conventions of realism were established, and then considering other approaches. Chapters 6 and 7 are based in the prop workshop and rehearsal room, discussing practical questions about materials and making as well as spectators' responses. Chapters 8 and 9 bring together roles which have been distinct in the earlier chapters, looking at theatre-makers who dissolve the boundaries between director, designer and playwright and, in doing so, frequently give the prop a starring role as an autonomous object. The final two chapters examine the existence of the prop without actors – in the museum, immersive set, touch tour or props store. In these settings, the prop is a remnant of past performance, but also offers the potential for future animation. This book looks at props almost entirely within the European and North

American context and does not discuss performance in Africa, Asia or South America. For each of these continents, the significant and diverse roles that objects play in performance deserve a fuller consideration – and far greater expertise – than I can offer here.

PROP, OBJECT, THING OR PUPPET?

A reader's first question might be whether we should speak of 'props' at all, or rather of the wider category of 'objects'. After all, many props are objects before they enter the theatre, although some are born as props. Perhaps props should be considered alongside 'puppets' as examples of objects deliberately made for performance. Or are props just 'things', miscellaneous examples of the 'stuff' that surrounds us? Daniel Miller, in his book of that name, resolutely refuses to define 'stuff', celebrating the variousness of material culture: 'Does an email or a fashion count as stuff, a kiss or a leaf or polystyrene packing?' (Miller 2010: 1). For many, the 'prop' has a musty smell, redolent of cupboards and store rooms, and they choose to avoid the word to avoid the negative connotations of theatricality and artifice. Others delight in the craft skills embodied in the 'prop sword' or 'fake food'. The long history of props in performance, and the contemporary apparatus of specialist staff and departments in theatres, opera houses, film studios and universities, all mean that the term cannot be abandoned without further consideration.

Prop

The Oxford English Dictionary defines the word 'prop' as 'theatrical slang', short for 'property', in the sense of 'any portable article, as an article of costume or furniture, used in acting a play; a stage requisite'. The earliest usage cited by the OED is from *A Midsummer Night's Dream*: Quince promises to 'draw a bill of properties, such as our play wants'. A recent practical handbook, *The Prop Building Guidebook*, defines a prop as 'a physical object that an actor uses during a performance', although some of the items that could be provided by a props department may not be handled in performance, such as plants and crockery used for set-dressing (Hart 2013: 2). In *The Stage Life of Props* (2003) Andrew Sofer defines a prop as 'a discrete, material, inanimate object that is visibly manipulated by an actor in the course of performance'. He draws attention to the 'portability' of the prop: 'By definition, a prop is an object that goes on a journey; hence props trace spatial trajectories and create temporal narratives as they track through a given performance' (Sofer 2003: 2). *The Stage Life of Props* thus traces the 'journeys' of five iconic objects – skull, handkerchief, fan, communion wafer and gun – through the plays in which they appear. In practical terms, the idea of moveability is often what distinguishes a prop from an element of the set, although in performance the boundaries are more fluid.

Being derived from 'property', the word 'prop' originally referred to an object that belonged to a theatre company or the actor. For Jonathan Harris and Natasha Korda this means that props are especially vibrant examples of material culture, found at the intersection of business interests (investments and assets), daily life (many props move back and forth between everyday use and onstage life) and artistic decisions (props can suggest how history, other countries or mythological figures, for example, have been represented in particular productions). Nevertheless, as they point out, the term has some negative associations, or at least a sense of something 'subsidiary':

> the term has also acquired some of the connotations of 'prop' in the sense of 'an object placed *beneath or against* a structure' [emphasis added]. The latter meaning certainly resonates with the tendency to regard stage properties as theatrical prostheses, strictly ancillary to and "beneath or against" the main structure, the play-text.
>
> (Harris and Korda 2002: 1)

The distinct etymologies of the terms used in various European languages are suggestive of slightly different attitudes to the object in performance. In French, *accessoire* implies something secondary and supportive, while the German term *Requisit* suggests that the object is necessary to the performance. (The German term has been adopted by many Slavic languages – in Polish, it becomes *rekwizyt*.) In Spanish, one word, *utileria*, denotes both 'tool' and 'prop' – perhaps suggesting the possibility of a fluid movement between daily life and performance. But, as in English-language theatre, many theatre-makers avoid these terms and refer to the moveable items on their stages otherwise: in French, as an *objet* (object) or *chose* (thing) – *objet trouvé* or *théâtre d'objet*; in Polish, as a *przedmiot* (object) or *rzecz* (thing) – as in Tadeusz Kantor's references to the *przedmiot biedny* – 'poor object'.

Object

Discussing 'objects' rather than 'props' allows a connection to be made between the theatrical object and the object of attention in other disciplines including fine art, philosophy, psychoanalysis, anthropology, semiotics and actor-network theory. It makes it possible to think about the overlaps between everyday and performative use, rather than remaining within the domain of the theatre. But a preference for 'objects' rather than 'props' can also express a wholesale rejection of 'theatricality', with its associations with tawdry costumes, wobbly sets, papier mâché food, artificiality and illusions. Michael Fried's 1967 essay 'Art and Objecthood', which criticised minimalist art for its 'theatricality', is often in the background when 'theatre', 'acting' and 'props' are rejected by contemporary artists (including performance artists).

However, the Latinate etymology of 'object', and its role in philosophical discourse, can evoke a chilly, academic tone that seems at odds with the

unpredictability of live performance. Even the practitioners of 'object theatre' have expressed doubts about the word. Christian Carrignon recalls that
when Katy Deville proposed the phrase *théâtre d'objet* to describe the new
theatrical form – storytelling accompanied by assemblages of small objects –
that they were making, 'we all grimaced', because the word 'object' was
'cold, lifeless' (Carrignon and Mattéoli 2009: 25). Sculptor and puppet-maker
Peter Schumann, founder of Bread and Puppet Theatre, warns against using
the word 'object' in order to define the non-human world as a collection of
undifferentiated non-subjects:

> We who think of ourselves as subjects don't even know donkeys well enough, not
> to speak of fence posts and rocks, to which we assign the job of object, because
> we haven't discovered their individuality yet. As a donkeyman – which means:
> related to donkeys and therefore also to fence posts and rocks – I shy away from
> that particular definition: object.
>
> (Schumann 2001: 48)

Schumann defends everyday 'things' and their metaphorical place at the
'heart of things', with a warning against objects which 'proselytize objectiv-
ity and objectification'. Yet the etymology of 'object' can tell a different story:
an object is a thing 'thrown before' the mind. Every reference to an 'object'
thus potentially embodies a miniature performance: a material thing thrown
by someone or something into view of a spectator.

Thing

How are things? Is this thing we're talking about now, like, 'a thing'? A
'real thing'? In everyday language, we talk about 'things' to mean not just
concrete objects but also vaguer issues, matters, topics and even entities
coming into being. Literary and cultural critic Bill Brown discusses the paradoxical ways in which we use the term 'things': 'On the one hand, then, the
thing baldly encountered. On the other, some thing not quite apprehended'
(Brown 2004: 5). He wonders whether 'things' represent the amorphousness
of matter out of which 'objects' are constituted by the perceiver. As a consequence, things could be imagined as

> what is excessive in objects, as what exceeds their mere materialization as
> objects or their mere utilization as objects – their force as a sensuous presence or
> as a metaphysical presence, the magic by which objects become values, fetishes,
> idols and totems. Temporalized as the before and after of the object, thingness
> amounts to a latency (the not yet formed or the not yet formable) and to an excess
> (what remains physically or metaphysically irreducible to objects).
>
> (ibid.)

Brown's essay plays with the paradoxes of the thing, near to hand but hard
to theorise: 'Things lie beyond the grid of intelligibility the way mere things

lie outside the grid of museal exhibition, outside the order of objects.' Thus, while we might spend time in rehearsal talking about whether this thing or that is the 'sort of thing' that the actor or designer is looking for, the term is too all-gathering for most of the discussion in this volume. It has however been productive for companies such as The Ding Foundation, who make their wordless 'visual narratives' by taking materials or specific objects as their starting point.

For art critic W. J. T. Mitchell, the distinction between objects and things lies in their relation to subjectivity and agency: 'objects are the way things appear to a subject – that is with a name, an identity, a gestalt or stereotypical template…Things, on the other hand…[signal] the moment when the object becomes the Other, when the sardine can looks back, when the mute idol speaks, when the subject experiences the object as uncanny…' (quoted in Bennett 2010: 2). The relevance of this formulation to performers is obvious, but as Tim Ingold suggests, the distinction reflects – and reinstates – a failure to understand objects in their relation to their surroundings: in setting 'things aside in order to focus on their "objectness", they are cut off from the flows that bring them to life' (Ingold 2010: 7).

Ingold returns to Heidegger's essay 'The Thing', which argues for a vital distinction between the object of attention and the 'thing' (*Ding*), by looking at a common household vessel.

> Near to us are what we usually call things. But what is a thing? Man has so far given no more thought to the thing as a thing than he has to nearness. The jug is a thing. What is the jug? We say: a vessel, something of the kind that holds something else within it. The jug's holding is done by its base and sides. This container itself can again be held by the handle. As a vessel the jug is something self-sustained, something that stands on its own. This standing on its own characterizes the jug as something that is self-supporting, or independent. As the self-supporting independence of something independent, the jug differs from an object. An independent, self-supporting thing may become an object if we place it before us, whether in immediate perception or by bringing it to mind in a recollective re-presentation. However, the thingly character of thing does not consist in its being a represented object, nor can it be defined in any way in terms of the objectness, the over-againstness, of the object.
>
> (Heidegger 1971: 166–7)

What, Heidegger wonders, defines the jug? Is it the base and sides that allow it to hold liquid? Or the void they contain? Or the act of outpouring itself – a gesture that brings a particular material configuration into existence?

The etymology of 'thing' has further performative associations. In Old High German, the word *thing* means a gathering: specifically, 'a gathering to deliberate on a matter under discussion, a contested matter. In consequence, the Old German words *thing* and *dinc* become the names for an affair or matter of pertinence'. Heidegger confronts the accusation that his investigation of 'the nature of the thingness' might be 'based on the accidents of an etymological game', but argues that there is a substantial connection between the two aspects, the material object and the social and deliberative gathering: 'Thinging gathers' (174).

Ingold asks readers to consider first the furnishings of an ordinary room – table, chair, pen and pad – and then a living tree.

> Is the tree, then, an object? If so, how should we define it? What is tree and what is not-tree? Where does the tree end and the rest of the world begin? These questions are not easily answered – not as easily, at least, as they apparently are for the items of furniture in my study. Is the bark, for example, part of the tree? If I break off a piece in my hand and observe it closely, I will doubtless find that it is inhabited by a great many tiny creatures that have burrowed beneath it and made their homes there. Are they part of the tree? And what of the algae that grow on the outer surfaces of the trunk or the lichens that hang from the branches?
>
> (Ingold 2010: 5)

Ecologists have described the mutual dependence of trees, insects and the symbiotic relationship of plants and fungi in mycorrhizal partnerships; Ingold asks if the insects 'belong' to the tree as much as the bark does, then why should birds or squirrels not be considered part of the tree? The setting of the tree, 'the way it responds to the currents of wind, in the swaying of its branches and the rustling of its leaves', also defines its character. Ingold writes: 'These considerations lead me to conclude that the tree is not an object at all, but a certain gathering together of the threads of life. That is what I mean by a thing' (ibid.). For Ingold, every object considered properly is a 'gathering'.[1]

Puppet

Through performance, a prop can become a 'thing', with – in Bill Brown's terms – a sensuous or metaphysical presence that compels the spectator's attention. Does it then become a theatrical subject? In that case, how is it distinguished from a puppet? The theorist of puppetry Henryk Jurkowski distinguishes actors from objects, props and puppets as follows: 'Actors are human beings fulfilling theatrical functions; objects are things made by human beings not for theatrical use; props are things made for theatrical use; puppets are objects made to be theatre characters' (1988: 80). This is a useful definition when thinking about the range of contemporary Western performances that use puppetry techniques. Jurkowski helps to pin down the difference between a puppet (designed and made to move in particular ways), and an object (transformed into a theatrical character by exploiting features designed for non-theatrical purposes). Thus the puppet horses designed by Adrian Kohler of Handspring for the National Theatre's production of *War Horse* have joints that mimic equine anatomy and sophisticated controls that allow the horse to swivel its ears. In contrast, in the object animation show *Pinocchio* by Indefinite Articles, the talking cricket is an ordinary wooden clothes peg – it is appropriated without any decoration or adaption, the spring mechanism becoming the cricket's moving jaw. The distinction between 'puppet' and 'object' is important when thinking about how puppeteers animate everyday objects. When thinking about props more generally, however, Jurkowski's definition is misleading. Props have never just been 'things made for theatrical use' – the word encompasses a whole range of objects designed and made for non-theatrical contexts. A prop may have been used outside the theatre for years, changing its appearance and acquiring shared and personal meaning, a patina of age and even an 'aura' or 'charge', before it is appropriated by the theatre and used in ways the original designer never intended.

It can be argued that any ordinary object becomes a 'prop' once it has been selected for use on stage, in a process similar to the 'framing', by which an object placed in a gallery becomes a 'found object'. For Bert States, in the theatre 'we are, technically, within the museum: all that is on stage is art' (States 1985: 39). However, while objects that become 'found objects' in galleries rarely return to the street or supermarket, a 'prop' can move back and forth between stage and world. This is a reflection of the different market conditions that apply to art and theatre. If art collectors and galleries tend to preserve the traces of actions and performances, theatre objects are typically destroyed, re-used, remodelled or returned to the outside world once they have served the performance. Material studies of props and costumes in early modern theatre have been particularly revealing in this regard – see, for example, Harris and Korda (2002), Jones and Stallybrass (2001).

Mnemonic by Theatre de Complicite (1999) draws attention both to the evocative power of everyday objects and the potential for objects to cycle between theatre and daily life. In the opening speech, Simon McBurney addresses the audience directly, as if making a spontaneous introduction. He speculates about why his father is coming into mind, and then points out a chair beside him on the bare stage. He tells us that the chair belonged to his father, who sat on it, as did his grandfather. He tells us that the chair has been used in several Complicite shows, including *The Chairs*. The intertextual joke suggests that, like the performer, this object not only has a life history of its own but also a notable theatrical career. (McBurney had directed a production of Ionesco's *The Chairs* at the Royal Court Theatre two years before *Mnemonic*.) Then McBurney sits on the chair. It collapses. He calls into the wings, asking for another chair, and admits to the audience that it's a 'fake' chair, a 'joke' chair.

One spectator reported that at the moment of the chair's collapse she thought with sympathetic concern: 'Oh no, he's broken the chair, his *grandfather's* chair.' For her, the chair was no longer just a 'prop' chair – it had been 'animated' with personal significance, emotional meaning by McBurney's words. Later in the same performance, the chair is further 'animated' as a puppet. (In fact, it is another 'fake' chair, made to look exactly like the

Richard Katz holds the 'broken' chair that becomes the Iceman in *Mnemonic* by Complicite.
Photo: Sarah Ainslie.

first one.) Carefully constructed to resemble a functional chair when folded up, the puppet chair opens up to reveal arms and legs that are jointed like human limbs. The performers move the limbs and give the chair breath and intention. But even before this act of puppetry took place, the chair had become a 'performing object': it moved out of the realm of the 'prop' when McBurney pointed it out on stage and began to weave a story around it. McBurney recalls the decision-making in rehearsal:

> In *Mnemonic* we had to represent a 5000 year old corpse that emerges brown and wrinkled out of a glacier in 1992. It became clear to us that any literal representation would be more than faintly ludicrous. The words alone that described his appearance were stronger than any banal prop.
> But something had to stand in for his presence.
> So we used a chair.
> But the chair was more evocative if broken.
> So we used a broken chair.
>
> (Ainslie 2010: 99)

Frank Proschan defines 'performing objects' as 'material images of humans, animals, or spirits that are created, displayed, or manipulated in narrative or dramatic performance' (cited in Bell 2008: 2). For John Bell, Frank Proschan's term is 'a most useful concept for an expanded sense of the world of puppets', taking in 'the stuff, junk, puppets, masks, detritus, machines, bones, and molded plastic *things* that people use to tell stories or represent ideas' (ibid.).

This book refers to 'props' in the context of performance practice but these critical distinctions between props, objects, things, puppets and performing objects should remain in mind.

THE 'ACTION FORCE' OF A PROP

The Prague School semiotician Jiří Veltruský describes props as having an 'action force' of their own, contrary to the usual view:

> The prop is usually designated the passive tool of the actor's action. This does not, however, do full justice to its nature. The prop is not always passive. It has a force (which we call the action force) that attracts a certain action to it. As soon as a certain prop appears on the stage, this force which it has provokes in us the expectation of a certain action.
>
> (1964: 88)

Veltruský's term 'action force' is related to the concept of 'affordances' first developed by Jakob von Uexküll (1864–1944). Affordances can be defined as the physical properties that provide possibilities for action – for example, a handle makes it possible to hold something in the hand. In Donald A. Norman's book *The Design of Everyday Things* he glosses the notion of affordances as follows: 'Knobs are for turning. Slots are for inserting things into. Balls are for throwing or bouncing' (Norman 1998: 9).

Thus a chair on stage could be said to 'invite sitting'. A performer could decide instead to balance it on the forehead – but this action would play off the audience's unspoken expectation of 'sitting'. Some objects have narrowly defined affordances in everyday life: for example, a hat might seem to offer fewer potential 'ways of using' than a large scarf. In the case of a pistol, the association with firing a shot is so strong that it has become shorthand for dramaturgical expectations about verbal as well as physical objects. The playwright and director Vladimir Nemirovich-Danchenko describes how the dramatic principle now sometimes referred to as 'Chekhov's gun' developed in a discussion about an early draft of *The Seagull*. The first act ended with the revelation that Masha was Dr Dorn's daughter, but this was not mentioned again in the play. Nemirovich-Danchenko recounts:

> I said that one of two things must be done: either this idea must be developed, or it must be wholly rejected, all the more so if the first act was to end with the scene. According to the very nature of the theatre, the end of the first act should turn sharply in the direction in which the drama is to develop.
>
> Chekhov said: 'But the public likes seeing a loaded gun placed before it at the end of an act!'

'Quite true,' I said, 'but it is necessary for it to go off afterwards, and not be merely removed in the intermission!' It seems to me that Chekhov more than once repeated this rejoinder. He agreed with me. The end was changed.

(quoted in Innes 2000: 143)

Similarly, in object improvisation workshops, teachers often draw attention to the affordances of everyday objects, pointing out that an audience may bring an expectation that objects will behave in particular ways: for example, that a pair of scissors will open, rather than remain closed. Performers may choose to develop or reject this potential, but always with awareness that every object is 'loaded' with past experience and anticipation.

In discussing affordances, Donald Norman focuses on 'perceived affordances' – a concept of particular relevance to theatre. Norman argues that users' goals, beliefs and past experiences (of handles, mugs, etc.) will affect the range of affordances they perceive in any object. In a similar way, audience members may see a prop as a familiar object extracted from common reality, and at the same time bring an awareness of its theatrical history and previous use. In *The Stage Life of Props*, Andrew Sofer cites Marvin Carlson's concept of theatrical 'ghosting' to describe theatre as 'a vast, self-reflexive recycling project':

The same elements – stories, texts, actors, props, scenery, styles, even spectators – appear over and over again. Our pleasure in seeing the relic revived, the dead metaphor made to speak again, is the very reason we go to the theater to see a play we already know well.

(Sofer 2003: 2–3)

For Veltruský, the existence of objects' action force can also be demonstrated by the way that they can give an impression of continuing 'life', even when no actor is on stage:

Even then, the action does not stop. The action force of the object comes to the fore in all its power. The objects on stage, including perhaps also their mechanical movements such as that of the pendulum of a clock, exploit our consciousness of the uninterrupted course of events and create in us the feeling of action. Without any intervention of the actor, the props shape the action. They are no longer the tools of the actor, we perceive them as spontaneous subjects equivalent to the figure of the actor. For this process to occur, one condition must be met: the prop must not be the mere outline of an object to which it is linked by a factual relationship, because only if it preserves its reality can it radiate its action force and suggest action to the spectator.

(Veltruský 1964: 88)

An example of the power of props to evoke a reality is suggested by the opening scene of Ena Lamont Stewart's play *Men Should Weep* (1947). The stage directions describe a cramped Glasgow tenement room, full of clutter, with nappies strung across the fireplace. Two young children are asleep behind a curtain, and are heard but not seen in the play. The theatrical presence of the children is created both through their voices and through the objects associated with them. As well as the drying nappies, there is a constant flow of props – a slice of bread and jam, a spoon and bottle of cough mixture – from the visible area of the stage to the unseen region of childhood, sickness and sleep, suggesting a reality that might have been difficult to portray directly within realistic conventions.

Veltruský's description of the way a prop 'attracts a certain action to it' is susceptible of a narrow interpretation: a gun is for firing, a shoe is to wear. But in theatre as in everyday life, the value of a shoe is also found in its design, colour and sound qualities. A painted outline of a shoe would serve as an 'icon', to communicate the idea of 'a shoe' – like a larger-than-life boot hanging above a cobbler's – but a theatrical prop 'must not be the mere outline of an object', Veltruský says, for 'only if it preserves its reality can it radiate its action force and suggest action to the spectator'.[2]

Semiotics is sometimes discounted as an approach to theatre on the grounds that its underlying 'linguistic analogy' disqualifies it from treating non-linguistic areas of experience. For example, Bert States argues that

> in addressing theater as a system of codes [semiotics] necessarily dissects the perceptual impression theater makes on the spectator. And, as Merleau-Ponty has said, 'It is impossible to decompose a perception, to make it into a collection of sensations, because in it the whole is prior to the parts.' Moreover, the more one treats theater as a language, the more like *all* languages it becomes.
>
> (States 1985: 7)

Several separate points can be distinguished in these comments. Merleau-Ponty's comment captures theatre's power to make a 'synergetic combination' building up a 'force greater than that generated by the sum of all constituent parts taken individually' (Melrose 1994: 7). He makes a useful distinction between discrete 'sensations' and the whole 'perception' (which presumably may draw on several sensory channels at once). This suggests the importance of considering each perception as a whole, however vague or inexplicable it seems. But 'a performance' is not 'a perception'; the interacting sensations have been deliberately organised by theatre-makers, and are capable of separate consideration. States' second objection is that semiotic analysis treats experience 'as a language' and thus 'as a system of codes'. This might have been true of Saussurean semiotics but is no longer true of all semiotics – nor of all linguistics.[3]

In the past, studies of signs have tended to disregard matter, 'production' and the material differences between different performances of musical scores, plays or texts, resulting in 'a linguistics which treated the handwritten and the printed sentence, the sentence written in sand and the sentence carved in stone, as identical for the purposes of linguistic analysis' (Kress and van Leeuwen 2001: 69). Work in 'social semiotics', however, drawing on the approaches taken by Michael Halliday, explicitly rejects the 'code book' model. According to Theo van Leeuwen, a semiotics of Western sound, for example, might

> not take the form of a code book, but the form of an annotated catalogue of the sound treasures Western culture has collected over the years, together with the possible uses to which they might be put, as gleaned from past and present experience.
>
> (Van Leeuwen 1999: 6)

Semiotic practices drawing on the work of the members of the Prague School, and of Roland Barthes and Michael Halliday are also concerned with the meaning of 'unsemiotised' experience, and perceptions that have not yet become part of a system: systematic description and analysis of an object in all its sensory dimensions might reveal areas that have been neglected because of the habitual blind spots of observers, and open up new possibilities for making meaning. Important examples of this approach would be Roland Barthes' discussions of the 'grain' of the voice and the 'punctuum' of a photograph (Barthes 1977, 1982). Susan Melrose asks whether, for example, a chair on stage ceases to be a 'theatre sign' if she, as a spectator, 'loses her gaze' in the 'richness of its fabric, in its pleasing curve of frame' – without 'translating' it into another sign. Without this 'translation', does it cease to be part of theatre communication? (Melrose 1994: 26). She concludes that

> what in part makes theatre work is its capacity for creating those events which enable us to experience the blur where one system insinuates itself into another, with which it might be logically at odds; the blur where two options – and not one – from a given system, are simultaneously made available.
>
> (27–8)

This recalls Veltruský's suggestion that rather than trying to translate matter into speech, the theatre 'should be considered as laboratory of "contrastive semiotics"' (Veltruský 1964: 107).

THE PROP AS TEXT AND CONSTRAINT

How does Veltruský's notion of the 'action force' of the prop work for the performer – and what are the implications for those who find or make props? One can think of material objects as offering performers two contrasting aspects – serving as either 'texts' or 'constraints'.

Any object can be 'read' as a 'text for performance' by becoming aware of its physical properties and of the meanings that are attributed to these properties. Bertolt Brecht showed a vivid appreciation of the work of designers and actors in selecting props that already showed the signs of use. A poem by Brecht from about 1932, 'Of all the works of man', expresses a view of the found object as embodying social history. Objects that show evidence of wear and tear – dented cooking pots or cutlery with wooden handles smoothed by years of use – seem to Brecht, he says, the 'noblest' of forms (Willett 1984: 139). In a similar reflection, Michel de Certeau describes a village museum in Vermont that displays old tools. The display 'includes innumerable familiar objects, polished, deformed, or made more beautiful by long use; everywhere there are as well the marks of the active hands and labouring or patient bodies for which these things composed the daily circuits' (de Certeau 1984: 21). The worn places in a knife's wooden handle not only reflect the past usage – they can also instruct us how to hold it. For an actor, these instructions can serve as a score for improvisation or performance.

The sometimes obsessive work of the designer, stage manager or props team in sourcing objects that function correctly and evoke the right feelings is captured in a letter from Nemirovich-Danchenko to Chekhov, reporting back on the first London production of *The Cherry Orchard*. The two régisseurs had worked hard, he writes, to 'intensify' the 'astonishing moods of the play':

> We had three dress rehearsals, we examined every corner of the stage, we tested every electric-light bulb. For two weeks I lived in the theatre with the decorations, the properties; I made trips to the antique shops, seeking out objects which would give the necessary touches of colour. But why dwell on this? I am speaking of a theatre in which not a single nail has been overlooked.
>
> (quoted in Innes 2000: 162)

Scenographer Pamela Howard describes how this research process can be shared with a whole company, discussing a workshop for her production of Martinů's opera *The Marriage*. Everyone involved in the production was asked to join in, contributing photos, images and memorabilia to create a 'huge visual collage' on a wall. As the participants rearranged items under thematic headings 'a point of view and an aesthetic emerged'. This

> informed our final selection of furniture and objects that would describe the different locations of the opera. It could be some small detail that sparked off an idea – a picture of an old refrigerator, the colour of period graphic type in a magazine, a hair ribbon, a pair of gloves. All these objects served to inform us about a world that no longer exists, but which we were seeking to recreate.
>
> (Howard 2009: 83–4)

This process of carrying out and sharing visual research by establishing a wall of source material is widely used. The research can then be referred to by directors, actors and members of the production team wondering, 'What kind of teacup is right? What sort of shoes would that person wear? What colour sums up a young girl's bedroom in 1950?' (Howard 2009: 84).

In his discussion of the 'aura', Walter Benjamin finds it both in the personal object and the utilitarian object: 'if we designate as aura the associations which, at home in the *mémoire involuntaire*, tend to cluster around the object of a perception, then its analogue in the case of a utilitarian object is the experience which has left traces of the practised hand' (Benjamin 1970: 188). The access to memories and emotions – in Proust's case, recalled by the taste of a madeleine dipped in lime-blossom tea – has a parallel in the access to practices of work and use. The work an actor does on an object when using it as a source for character or historical research is close to Benjamin's imaginative reconstruction of the life of consumer items in the Paris arcades.

Benjamin aimed, writes Susan Buck Morss, to bring the 'mute object' to speech. He proceeded 'as if the world were language. The objects were "mute". But their expressive (for Benjamin "linguistic") potential became legible to the attentive philosopher who "named" them, translating this potential into the human language of words, and thereby bringing them to speech' (Buck Morss 1989: 13). For the actor, what they 'read' in an object may be translated not into speech but into gesture, expression, tempo – and these are in turn 'read' by the audience.

In Stanislavski's early work, objects are primarily seen as texts that can be read by actors to access an emotional or social history. In *An Actor Prepares*, the student actor Kostya relates with some embarrassment how he became lost in contemplation of a chandelier during a concert. His acting teacher, Tortsov, reinterprets this distraction as valuable research:

> You were trying to find out how and of what the object was made. You absorbed its form, its general aspect, and all sorts of details about it. You accepted these impressions, entered them in your memory, and proceeded to think about them. That means that you drew something from your object, and we actors look upon that as necessary. You are worried about the inanimate quality of your object. Any picture, statue, photograph of a friend, or object in a museum, is inanimate, yet it contains some part of the life of the artists who created it.
>
> (Stanislavski 1980: 195)

While objects can serve as rich texts for performers, they can also serve as constraints, chosen to restrict the performer's freedom. Interaction with a specific object produces specific kinds of movement. A game played by a group aiming to keep a ball in the air, for example, changes when played with different kinds of ball. The quality of the players' movement will reflect the ball's physical characteristics – a small football requires more force than a balloon and players will probably make faster, more direct movements. A player could deliberately work against the given qualities to discover other movement possibilities – to smash a balloon downwards, for example – but the potential of an object is not infinite. It is almost impossible to use a balloon to break a window. The physical constraints are similar to the rules of a game – they encourage certain kinds of action and discourage others.

Paradoxically, constraint can be a means of liberating the actor. It makes some of the decisions, suggesting certain kinds of gesture, rhythm and structure. Referring to non-European performance traditions such as Noh, in which individual performers can only make small – if significant – variations from a fixed form, Eugenio Barba claims that 'the actor who works within a network of codified rules has a greater liberty than he who – like the Occidental actor – is a prisoner of arbitrariness and an absence of rules' (Leabhart 1989: 56). Barba wished to liberate the actor who is paralysed by the obligation to choose between infinite options, like a dazed shopper in a hypermarket. Other writers, including Keith Johnstone and Enrique Pardo, have also suggested that a constraint can free the actor both from the pressure to perform and the pressure to conform. A physical constraint, such as the aim of keeping a ball in the air, can make it impossible for actors to give any energy to the activity of demonstrating that they are clever, charming or imaginative.

These two aspects of work with an object – as text and as constraint – depend on investigating and responding to what has been invested in the object through its construction and subsequent use. They tend to have been separated in actor training through artificial divisions between 'movement' and 'acting'. For an actor, both aspects can come into play, depending on the context of the production.

THE NEGLECT OF MATERIALITY

Given that objects offer such rich resources to the actor and spectator, why is there so little written on the materiality of theatre? Numerous books and articles deal with practical questions of finding, making and adapting props but there is a surprising lack of discussion of materiality from a spectator's point of view. Andrew Sofer suggests that literary critics are 'trained not to see' objects as 'material participants in the stage action' and ignore 'the *spatial* dimension (how props move in concrete stage space) and the *temporal* dimension (how props move through linear stage time)' (Sofer 2003: 2–3). These dimensions, Sofer suggests, 'allow the object to mean in performance'. Nevertheless, by focusing on generic categories such as the skull and the fan, *The Stage Life of Props* neglects materiality and the senses or, in John Bell's view, 'eschews the messiness of actual performance for the sureties of literary criticism' (Bell 2005: 161). Sofer doesn't discuss the details of particular performances and thus excludes questions about materials and construction, and how these might affect both the actor's work and the spectator's response.

Jonathan Gil Harris and Natasha Korda found in 2002 that props 'have barely rated more than a passing mention' in most studies of Shakespeare and his contemporaries. They suggested that the erasure of props from theatrical history can be partly traced to the Puritan anti-theatrical writers:

'Protestant iconoclasm and antipathy to the theatre operated in tandem with a pronounced hostility to *objects*: the props of religious and dramatic ritual alike served – as did the paltry Eucharist biscuit – to distract attention from more godly, hidden truths, by virtue of their very visibility' (Harris and Korda 2002: 5). Although the critical balance is being redressed, with several recent journal issues on objects and performance (for some further reading, see the list at the end of this chapter) the neglect of materiality in performance studies reflects a wider cultural preference for abstraction over embodiment and has profound environmental and ethical consequences.

The material world may be the privileged domain of knowledge in modernism, the place where scientific truths can be found (see Askegaard and Firat 1997), but it is also dismissed in quite contradictory ways: characterised as at once base and superficial, both recalcitrant and empty, both intrinsically meaningless and capable of being filled with arbitrary meanings. A range of explanations for the neglect of material culture in other disciplines have been proposed. Writing on museum studies, Susan Pearce notes that academic history 'has been characterized by a lack of interest in material culture and a corresponding lack of a theory about the place objects hold in the production of historical narrative' (Pearce 1992: 196). Historian Raphael Samuel, arguing for increased attention to the productions of popular culture, suggests that 'official historians' see materiality as 'vulgar', 'superficial' and too easily commodified (Samuel 1994). Jennifer Bloomer sees a contrary but related impulse in architecture: a drive towards the 'New' (which is 'always bright, sparkling clean, light, full of promise, devoid of weight') in an attempt to 'escape from Materia, the old, generative soil, the origin' (Bloomer 1996: 19). And although the most seemingly abstract disciplines, such as science and mathematics, have 'fully embodied roots in modes of measurement, perception, and instrumentation', practical experimentation has a much lower status than theorising (Leder 1990: 134). The philosopher of science, Robert P. Crease, who draws on Husserl, Dewey and Heidegger to support an analogy between scientific experimentation and performance as embodied thinking, notes that the 'move away from action as a philosophical theme was practically contemporaneous with Western philosophy itself, and was at work when Plato began using the Greek word for knowledge, *episteme*, which for Homer and others had meant practical skill and ability, with an emphasis on its ideational content' (Crease 1993: 22).

The desire for liberation from materiality restates classical oppositions between male and female, spirit and matter, subject and object, which can be perceived at work in Aristotle's analogy between architecture and procreation: 'the timber (material) with which the builder constructs is passive and receptive to the form (idea) that lies in the soul of the builder, and is inscribed in the material by the activity of his tools in the same way that the material of a female body is inscribed by Nature with mammalian form via the active, moving tool of semen' (quoted in Bloomer 1996: 20–21). The specific character of an individual's interaction with the material world has also been used to define social class. As Hegel stated in his 1803–6 lectures:

> Social stratification is explained by reference to the various forms of labor. The peasantry represents 'immediate familiarity with raw, concrete labor' in nature. Concrete labor is elementary labor, [the] material means of sustenance.... This materiality changes into the abstraction of labor and knowledge of the general: the class of commerce and law. The labor of the bourgeois class is the abstract trade of the individual; its disposition is uprightness.
>
> (Asendorf 1993: 2)

Thus materiality and material labour are characterised as belonging to the female half of the population, to the lower classes and to 'undeveloped' or 'primitive' cultures. Material production and consumption are separated – at first within communities, and later between countries – as concrete labour is exported or hived off to an underclass.

In theatre, concerns that materiality might distract from a play's true meaning are often traced back to Aristotle, although recent writers have disputed the view that Aristotle's *Poetics* entirely dismisses *opsis*, the materiality of the stage – props, costumes and so on (see Harrison and Liapis 2013). Elizabethan dramatist and pamphleteer Thomas Dekker complains in *The Magnificent Entertainment* that "the Soule that should giue life, and a tongue" to plays is breathed "out of Writers pens," but that "the limnes of it ly at the hard-handed mercy of Mycanitiens [i.e. mechanicals]... Carpenters, Ioyners, Caruers, and other Artificers sweating at their Chizzells" (quoted in Harris and Korda 2002: 6). The author is at the mercy of the craftspeople responsible for creating the material reality that appears on stage.

CRAFT KNOWLEDGE

It is clear that different kinds of work or material interaction make available specific ways of knowing the world. Even among the woodworkers that Dekker mentions, the carpenters, joiners and carvers will each use a different set of tools and have different priorities in assessing the qualities of their materials. A carpenter making a carcass, the concealed frame of a cupboard, would use a soft wood such as pine, while a 'carver' would need a closer grained hardwood, such as lime, to achieve fine details. This kind of practical expertise can be related to the interaction of 'lay' and 'expert' knowledge, as described by Brian Wynne (1996). He analyses the 'highly dynamic systems of knowledge involving continuous negotiation between "mental" and "manual" labour, and continual interpretation of production experiences' found in craft-based agriculture (Wynne 1996: 68). He claims that a 'multidimensional and adaptive' complex of knowledge and experience is frequently mistaken for a lack of theoretical content when compared with scientific knowledge. Wynne argues that local forms of knowledge also involve the 'reflection and sustenance of important cultural and material values'; scientific knowledges are not neutral but 'correspond with particular cultural and epistemic principles – instrumentalism, control and alienation' (ibid.: 70).

Wynne's account of the continuous 'negotiation between "mental" and "manual" labour', and 'interpretation of production experiences' also captures the operation of practical knowledge in the props workshop – or in the rehearsal room. The performer of a speech or a piece of music is using both mental and physical resources (voice, body, instrument), while responding to and interpreting the qualities of the sounds they produce; designers, prop-makers and stage managers are also negotiating between material and immaterial values. In a short account of an incident in the everyday work of the lighting operator, printed alongside their essay on the 'mastercraftsperson', Nick Hunt and Susan Melrose (2005) describe how an individual sitting at the lighting desk during a plotting session or technical rehearsal might have to deploy several kinds of knowledge at once: technical knowledge (for example, which channel controls which lantern), emotional-affective knowledge of the production (what the designer and director are trying to achieve with the lighting) and knowledge of the interpersonal relationships (how an idea can be suggested tactfully). A stage manager and props team also have to operate within these three domains of knowledge: technical (construction techniques), emotional-affective (the function of the prop in the production) and interpersonal (how the actor feels about the prop).

Decisions about props and 'stage business' that fall into the 'emotional-effective' or 'asethetic' domain have a wider significance because they always embody specific attitudes or forms of relationship to matter. Teemu Paavolainen suggests that 'an ecological approach' to props gives the performance analyst 'ease in recognizing that a singular object onstage may equally afford manipulation, sitting on, masking, costuming, or even puppetry' (Paavolainen 2012: 6). This expanded notion of 'affordances' connects to the work being done in environmental philosophy to expand the notion of 'use value'. For example, a local council's Tree Officer might assess the value of a tree when considering whether to give permission for a property developer to fell it. An economic value can be assigned to the living tree, based on its ability to improve drainage (and so reduce the risk or extent of flooding) or provide shade (mitigating the effects of heat). The tree captures carbon and provides food and habitat for wildlife. In addition, an urban tree typically has many social functions – as a landmark, meeting place, memorial or support for a swing. In Tim Ingold's description of the tree as a 'gathering', all these elements can be considered together. As the 'environmental services' provided by the tree become less easily converted into financial value, they move closer to the concerns addressed in theatre. How do people live together? How do specific environments, buildings, objects and social structures enable or discourage specific kinds of interaction?

BEYOND THE VISUAL AND AURAL: PHENOMENOLOGICAL APPROACHES

A significant consequence of the neglect of materiality has been the sidelining of the sensory experience of performers and spectators. If props often move between everyday life and the stage, this exchange is found on the interpretative level too. Spectators deploy their knowledge of the 'off-stage' existence of objects – both how they behave physically and their cultural associations – in order to interpret the meaning of objects that appear on stage, and draw upon more than visual or aural perceptions. As Merleau-Ponty suggests:

> The form of objects is not their geometrical shape: it stands in a certain relation to their specific nature, and appeals to all our other senses as well as sight. The form of a fold in linen or cotton shows us the resilience or dryness of the fibre, the coldness or warmth of the material... One sees the weight of a block of cast iron which sinks in the sand, the fluidity of water and the viscosity of syrup. In the same way, I hear the hardness and unevenness of cobbles in the rattle of a carriage, and we speak appropriately of a 'soft', 'dull' or 'sharp' sound.
>
> (Merleau-Ponty 1976: 229–30)

Phenomenological approaches promised to consider all the sensory aspects of the physical world, and their interaction. Simone de Beauvoir describes how Jean-Paul Sartre was introduced to phenomenology in 1932 – with the help of an apricot cocktail:

> Aron said, pointing to his glass: 'You see, my dear fellow, if you are a phenomenologist, you can talk about this cocktail and make philosophy out of it!' Sartre turned pale with emotion at this. Here was just the thing he had been longing to achieve for years – to describe objects just as he saw and touched them, and extract philosophy from the process.
>
> (de Beauvoir 1976: 112)

Sartre called for a 'psychoanalysis of *things*' in *Being and Nothingness*, praising Bachelard's work on the 'material imagination' of vague substances like fire and clouds (Sartre 1969: 600). Yet Sartre's writing has not so far proved very productive for the study of objects in performance. One reason might be that indicated by David Trotter in his investigation of 'mess' in literature and art; he comments on this foundational scene in a Paris café: 'If Aron had only tipped the glass over, we might actually have got somewhere by now' (Trotter 2000: 15). For Trotter, Sartre's writing is overly dependent on the visual, tending to examine neatly bounded objects. (An important exception is his discussion of the *visqueux* (sticky or viscous) – see Chapter Six on papier mâché.) Similarly, Merleau-Ponty criticises Sartre for 'skyscraper thinking', and developing a philosophy installed in vision, in the reductive overview, and in a conception of the other's gaze as hostile. Merleau-Ponty calls instead for a dialectic that would involve a 'refusal of panoramic thinking' (Merleau-Ponty 1968: 91).

In his turn, Michel Serres claims to have 'laughed a lot' at the 'austere and meager' character of the examples given by Merleau-Ponty in *Phenomenology of Perception:*

> From his window the author sees some tree, always in bloom; he huddles over his desk; now and again a red blotch appears – it's a quote. What you can decipher in this book is a nice ethnology of city dwellers, who are hypertechnicalized, intellectualized, chained to their library chairs, and tragically stripped of any tangible experience. Lots of phenomenology and no sensation – everything via language.
>
> (Serres and Latour 1995: 131–2)

This caricature of the disembodied phenomenologist hardly applies to the later Merleau-Ponty of *The Visible and the Invisible* but is a challenge to any desk-based writing on performance. Serres calls for phenomenology to address 'tangible experience', and the senses neglected by most philosophy. His book *Les cinq sens* (1985) opens with his experience of saving himself from a fire on board a ship. He describes how the decisiveness of his body, acting without his conscious control, revealed to him the meaning of the phrase: *sauvez nos âmes.* He learned, he says, that the *âme* (soul or spirit) can move about the body as attention or intentionality is moved. Gymnasts and performers train the spirit to 'move and surround them'; in some collective games, the players 'lose their soul in conferring it to the object they have in common, the ball, around which they organise themselves, balance themselves, having become a collective' (Serres 1985: 18, my translation). Dancers are practised in directing their intention into particular parts of the body, yet a discussion of the mind–body awareness as trained by sport, dance or performance has been curiously absent from phenomenological writing until recently.

Even when watching performances which are confined behind a proscenium arch, spectators use information gleaned by the distance senses to deduce something about a character's bodily experiences. Fight directors have developed techniques which employ sound (vocalisation, and displaced contact such as a slap on the highly resonating chest to represent the sound of a punch in the solar plexus) and movement (the attacked person mimicking reflex actions) to induce sympathetic reactions in the spectator's body. Similarly, the prop department's techniques of illusion (distressing upholstery, constructing a delicate antique vase that can be shattered nightly) are designed to give spectators visual and aural clues so that they 'know' what the sofa feels like, or how delicate the vase is. Theatrical sound designers can give plastic objects resonance, or make a zinc bucket 'ping' when mimed berries are dropped into it. For spectators, the sight and sound of material interactions can induce sensations in the senses of proximity – the impression of 'feeling' the texture of an object or 'smelling' a silk rose through the stimulation of memory or imagination. Barthes wrote:

> As signifying site, the gaze produces a synesthesia, an in-division of (physiological) meanings which share their impressions, so that we can attribute to one, poetically, what happens to another ... Hence, all the senses can 'gaze' and, conversely, the gaze can smell, listen, grope, etc. Goethe: 'The hands want to see, the eyes want to caress'.
>
> (quoted in Melrose 1994: 215)

There is increased interest in performance studies in *introception* (the perception of sympathetic and parasympathetic processes through changes in pulse rate, digestion etc.) and *proprioception* (the sense of balance and position in space) alongside the five senses as commonly understood.[4] Examples in performance might include food presented on stage affecting the body's chemistry and provoking hunger or nausea, or site-specific or promenade performance heightening spectators' awareness of their position in the space. Through a combination of empathy and sensory stimulation, a spectator may *feel* the imbalance of a tottering Lear, or the muscular effort of someone picking up a heavy suitcase. If a spectator seems to share the vertigo or exuberance, the vulnerability or aggression, of the characters on stage, is this sympathy of the muscles and solar plexus a purely idiosyncratic reaction? When this sympathetic response is discussed, it is usually in the context of violence. Stanton Garner writes:

> Even in its dramatised forms, pain violates the perceptual demarcations and the differential spheres of 'otherness' essential to representation, including the spectator within its discomfort through a kind of neuro-mimetic transferral (the impulse to close one's eyes during simulated blindings on-stage reflects, not simply an aversion to the *sight* of pain, but also a deeper defense against its sympathetic arising within the field of one's own body).
>
> (Garner 1994: 180–1)

This sensory involvement is not limited to one character with whom the spectator immediately identifies, or to familiar emotions. The following examples from *Hamlet* suggest how performance might be understood to affect spectators both conceptually and viscerally.

Hamlet contains three non-verbal 'performances' – a dumbshow, a mad scene and a duel – and commentaries on how these performances work on spectators. The visiting players address hearing and sight separately: a dumbshow precedes the performance of 'The Murder of Gonzago'. The first (silent) enactment of a murder passes without a reaction from the audience, but at the second, which is accompanied by the murderer's

description of his own actions, Claudius stops the performance. Is it
the repetition or 'upon the talk of the poisoning' that the performance
becomes unbearable? The scene seems to imply the superior power of verbal drama when compared to tableaux. In contrast, the 'distract' Ophelia
reveals the power of non-verbal communication: she 'hems, and beats her
heart', her 'winks and nods and gestures' give the impression of a muted
thought process:

> Her speech is nothing,
> Yet the unshaped use of it doth move
> The hearers to collection; they yawn at it,
> And botch the words up to fit to their own thoughts.
>
> (IV. v. 7–10)

Ophelia's communication is no longer primarily through words but through
song and symbolic objects; the hearers 'repair' her words, filling in the gaps.
Lastly, in his commentary on the duel between Hamlet and Laertes – 'A hit,
a very palpable hit' – the courtier Osric suggests the visceral immediacy of
a sword fight for spectators.

The shift in the meaning of 'palpable' from literally 'tangible' to 'perceiv-
able by any sense' is an example of the metaphorical transfer between the
senses. Joseph Williams identified a 'directional flow' in the transfer of adjectives across a number of languages – the flow runs 'from touch to taste to
smell, but never in the other direction', while sight and sound only receive
adjectives from touch, as in 'warm' colours or 'soft' sounds (Watson 1999:
189). There are potential implications for thinking about how audiences
'read' non-visual physical properties through an image. Merleau-Ponty
suggests that even colour is not perceived as an abstract or pure quality.
Rather it is mingled with other material properties such as texture, 'bound
up with a certain wooly, metallic or porous configuration or texture'. Thus
a red dress is 'a punctuation in the field of red things, which includes the
tiles of roof tops, the flags of gatekeepers and of the Revolution, certain ter-
rains near Aix or in Madagascar' (Merleau-Ponty 1968: 132). The designer or
stage manager who selects a red chair (say) for a performance thus engages
an awareness of how a specific compound of shade/texture/weight/design
positions this object in a field of other objects; the actors, designers and directors who work with the chair further activate or suppress these meanings by
the choices they make about positioning/lighting/manipulation; and finally
audience members bring their own understanding of the chair's properties
and its place in their own personal field of sensory associations. One way to
consider all these engagements with the object is to look at them as forms of
'animation', drawing on the suggestion made by Jiři Veltruský in his 1955
essay 'Man and Object in the Theatre'. It is important to note that 'animation'
does not refer in this essay to 'giving an object the illusion of independent
life', as in puppetry, but is a much wider term.

THE SPECTRUM OF ANIMATION

In this influential essay, Veltruský discusses props in terms of actors' inter-action with them. He describes a range of possible interactions along a continuum: at one end, the object is a lifeless element of scenic décor; at the other extreme, the object is a protagonist.

> In a period when the theorists had in mind only the realist theatre, the opinion arose that only a human being can be the subject, just as is the case in everyday life. All other components were considered mere tools or objects of human action. The development of the modern theatre and the increasing familiarity with the theatre of non-European culture areas, however, led to the contradiction of this opinion, and later it turned out that it did not quite apply even to the realist thea-tre. The purpose of this study is to show that the existence of the subject in the theatre is dependent on the participation of some component in the action, and not on its actual spontaneity, so that even a lifeless object may be perceived as the performing subject, and a live human being may be perceived as an element completely without will.
>
> (Veltruský 1964: 88)

Veltruský describes a gradual transition between the spheres of man and object. This is glossed by Keir Elam as 'a subjective-objective *continuum* along which all stage sign-vehicles, human and inanimate, move in the course of the representation' (Elam 1980: 15). The analysis of performance shows how objects move along that spectrum: at one end, spoken words, light or sound give subjective 'life' to a prop by bringing it to the audience's attention; at the other extreme, manipulation can give a prop the illusion of having independent life. The 'spectrum of animation' provides the under-lying structure for this book, as chapters move from 'realist' or 'everyday' interactions with props through 'improvising' with props as equal partners, to a framing of the prop as protagonist in 'object theatre'. The following extract comes from the conclusion of Veltruský's essay:[5]

THE RELATIONSHIP BETWEEN MAN AND OBJECT

We have followed the different degrees of participation in the action by the various components, degrees different by the extent of activeness. It became clear that the transition between them is quite gradual, so that they can not be considered sealed-off spheres. The function of each component in the individual situation (and in the drama as a whole) is the resultant of the constant tension between activity and passivity in terms of the action, which manifests itself in a constant flow back and forth between the individual components, people and things. It is therefore impossible to draw a line between subject and object, since each component is potentially either. We have seen various examples of how a thing and a man can change places, how a man can become a thing and a thing a living being. We can thus not speak of two mutually delimited spheres; the relation of man to object in the theater can be characterized as a *dialectic antinomy*. We have seen in the above examples that the dialectic antinomy between man and thing occurs in the most varied structures and is thus not the exclusive property of the modern theater. In some structures, of course, it is emphasized, and in others suppressed and minimized.

The view that man in the theater is exclusively the active subject and things are passive objects or tools of the action arose, as has already been mentioned, at a time when the theorists had in mind only the realist theater. But not even in the realist theater was the fluctuation between men and object removed completely, it was only suppressed to such an extent that the error which we have already spoken of could occur. The realist theater attempted (though it never really succeeded) to be a reflection of reality not only in its individual components, but also in their integration. And in daily life we are of course used to differentiate very exactly between man and thing as far as their spontaneous activity goes, but again only in terms of our present-day epistemological horizon as determined by civilized life. In other horizons, for instance in the mythical world views of primitives or children, personification and the fluctuation between man and things play a very important part indeed. Although civilisation is progress as compared to the primitive way of life, it can not be denied that its forms so far have by the most varied conventions broken up the direct relationship between man and his environment. On the example of action in the absence of the subject we have seen how precisely these conventions can be used to link together unconventionally various aspects of reality. We are perhaps not exaggerating if we claim that this is one of the most important social objectives of the theater. This is precisely where the theater can show new ways of perceiving and understanding the world.

(Veltruský 1964: 90–91)

As Veltruský points out – and it remains true nearly 80 years later – much thinking about props has been dominated by a realist model of theatre. Our 'present-day epistemological horizon' makes a division between 'man and thing', and between 'dead' and 'alive'. A shift in our horizons is needed to understand the mutual interaction of inanimate and animate elements. In her book *Vibrant Matter: A Political Ecology of Things*, Jane Bennett sets out to 'highlight the active role of nonhuman materials in public life' (Bennett 2010: 2) and describes the ethical task of cultivating 'the ability to discern nonhuman vitality, to become perceptually open to it' (14). Readers interested in developing the approach of 'new materialism' might want to look at the work of Tim Ingold, such as *Perception of the Environment* (2000) and, making a more explicit connection to theatre practice, Teemu Paavolainen's *Theatre/ Ecology/Cognition: Theorizing Performer-Object Interaction in Grotowski, Kantor, and Meyerhold* (2012). Paavolainen's definition of ecology as 'organism-environment interaction' is specifically intended to undo the dichotomy between subject and object.

A paradigmatic prop – though not made for theatrical performance – is described by Tim Ingold. With a group of students, he made kites:

We did this indoors, working on tables. It seemed, to all intents and purposes, that we were assembling an object. But when we carried our creations to a field outside, everything changed. They suddenly leaped into action, twirling, spinning, nose-diving, and – just occasionally – flying. So what had happened? Had some animating force magically jumped into the kites, causing them to act most often in ways we did not intend? Of course not. It was rather that the kites themselves were now immersed in the currents of the wind. The kite that had lain lifeless on the table indoors had become a kite-in-the-air. It was no longer an object, if indeed it ever was, but a thing. As the thing exists in its thinging, so the kite-in-the-air exists in its flying. Or to put it another way, at the moment it was taken out of doors, the kite ceased to figure in our perception as an object that can be set in motion, and became instead a movement that resolves itself into the form of a thing.

(Ingold 2010: 8)

The object in performance similarly becomes immersed in the currents of performance, sometimes 'animated' by a performer, sometimes by light, sometimes by a spectator's attention.

Veltruský's concept of a 'spectrum of animation' allows us to escape the assumption that realism, invisibly dominating mainstream theatre, film and television, is the 'natural' approach to objects in performance. Considering instead where objects sit on the spectrum of animation opens up a diachronic view of the simultaneous existence of different modes of being in relation to matter. If a prop can be more than just a 'support' to the actor, how exactly does it become an autonomous performing object, or draw the audience's attention in the way that an art object does? Bearing in mind a spectrum of animation, in which objects can be actants and people can be things, opens up a space in performance studies for considering how matter and people mutually influence each other.

FURTHER READING

On new materialism:

Jane Bennett, *Vibrant Matter: A Political Ecology of Things* (2010); Karen Barad, 'Posthumanist Performativity: Towards an Understanding of How Matter Comes to Matter' (2003); Fiona Candlin and Raiford Guins, *The Object Reader* (2009); and Tim Ingold, *The Perception of the Environment: Essays on Livelihood, Dwelling and Skill* (2000).

On objects in performance:

There have been three recent issues of theatre journals dedicated to objects and materials: *On Objects: Performance Research* 12: 4 (2007), *Theatre Symposium*, 18: *The Prop's The Thing: Stage Properties Reconsidered* (2010); and *Theatre Journal: Theatre and Material Culture* 64: 3 (2012). Significant volumes include *Theatre/Ecology/Cognition: Theorizing Performer-Object Interaction in Grotowski, Kantor, and Meyerhold* by Teemu Paavolainen (2012) and *Performing Objects and Theatrical Things*, a collection of essays edited by Marlis Schweitzer and Joanne Zerdy (2014).

On the object in visual arts and craft:

Anthony Hudek (ed.), *The Object* (2014) includes short extracts from significant writings on objects by theorists and artists; *The Real Thing* (2015), a collection of Tanya Harrod's incisive essays on craft; *Thinking Through Craft* (2007) by Glenn Adamson; and Hal Foster, *The Return of the Real* (1996). Harrod's essays in *The Real Thing* are particularly attentive to discussions of tacit knowledge, and in this regard she praises the depth of the National Sound Archive's interviews with craftspeople. The NSA also has significant holdings of interviews with theatre designers.

On semiotics and phenomenology:

Ric Knowles, *Reading the Material Theatre* (2004); Gay McAuley, 'Objects in Performance' in *Space in Performance* (1999); Susan Melrose, *A Semiotics of the Dramatic Text* (1994); Frank Proschan, *Puppets, Masks, and Performing Objects from Semiotic Perspectives* (1983).

On particular objects and their material and cultural history:

Daniel Miller studies material culture from an anthropological starting point in his many publications including *The Comfort of Things* (2008) and *Stuff* (2010). Galen Cranz, *The Chair* (1998) and Henry Petroski, *The Pencil* (1989) are two of the most interesting cultural and material studies of single objects; Steve Connor's *Paraphernalia* (2011) includes short essays in cultural phenomenology on bags, batteries, buttons, combs, glasses, handkerchiefs, keys, newspaper, rubber bands, sticky tape and so on. *Things* (2004) edited by Bill Brown includes his influential essay 'Thing Theory' alongside essays drawing on diverse fields including physics, art history and anthropology.

Chapter

2 The Object in Actor Training and Rehearsal

The work that actors do with objects in training and rehearsal shapes their handling of props in performance. The way actors work with props in performance, in turn, defines an attitude (implicit or explicit) towards the material world that audiences pick up on. For example, one can characterise underlying attitudes such as: the world is a shared fiction, constructed by agreement between the people in the room; the world is solid, a reliable support for my life; the world is fragile and liable to collapse; the world is strictly divided into things that are mine and things that belong to other people, and so on. In *Metaphors We Live By*, George Lakoff and Mark Johnson gather speech formulas that are structured by underlying concepts such as 'time is money' or 'life is a journey'. For example, the concept that 'life is a container' is expressed in phrases such as 'I've had a *full* life', 'Life is *empty* for him', '*Get the most out of* life' and 'Her life is *crammed* with activities' (Lakoff and Johnson 2013: 51). I suggest that dramatic structures and modes of performance can also express underlying concepts, and that this is particularly clear in the performer's work with props.

Work with physical objects in actor training or rehearsal can have various purposes:

a) to develop actors' sensitivity, powers of recall and analysis of emotion. The object here is treated as a **text** or **score**: its physical features (shape, smell, material, texture etc.) encode cues for the memory. This view of the object is found in the writing of both Stanislavski and Brecht – although, of course, they put the knowledge to work for different purposes.

b) to develop physical coordination, speed of reaction, attention and peripheral vision. The object here is a form of physical **constraint** which challenges the actor. As in children's games with simple objects such as balls and jacks there is an iterative process of learning, mastering and transforming the game, increasing complexity to make it more interesting. Individuals and groups can devise their own variations, that is, improvise within the constraints. Clive Barker describes the rules of acting exercises as constituting 'a resistance against which the players struggle to raise the skill to a higher level' (Barker 1989: 233). Exercises can also be made specific to the skills needed by actors: developing kinetic skills in handling material objects, integrating movement with words, interacting with others.

c) to develop relationships between members of a group, including building trust and non-verbal communication. It might be useful to think of the object here as a **toy** – it may also have aspects of text and constraint, but it is most important as a shared object, a way of enabling collaborative play. As Miranda Tufnell and Chris Crickmay write in their handbook for improvisation, when an object exercise develops into 'direct interaction with others', the objects become 'common property' (Tufnell and Crickmay 1990: 119).

d) to develop material for performance through improvisation or devising. Here the object is primarily a **text** or **score**, but actors may work with objects that eventually become props.

The first two aspects of the object are discussed in this chapter; the latter two are discussed in the following chapter as they move into rehearsal and devising. Many object exercises used in actor training also reappear in rehearsal, transmitting a shared attitude to the material world to members of a company who may have very different backgrounds. In some contexts, rehearsal can be a form of continuing training; in the case of Brecht, who founded no school of acting, we rely largely on his comments on rehearsal to discover his thoughts on training.

Underlying their ostensible purpose in developing the skills of the individual actor and of the company, different types of work with objects also produce distinctive attitudes towards the material world. These attitudes have an impact on the actor's view of the theatre and/or performance – what it is and may be – and also on the audience. This idea of an underlying attitude expressed through object play can be illustrated by looking at two contrasting strands of training that both make use of objects. Both trace their origins back to Stanislavski, but with quite divergent results. Stanislavski's earlier writing, and the writing of those practitioners who drew on them (including North American acting teachers Lee Strasberg and Uta Hagen who developed their own systems of 'object exercises') focused on training the actor's 'emotional memory', while Stanislavski's later writing on the 'method of physical actions' influenced practitioners such as Vsevolod Meyerhold and Michael Chekhov who developed exercises that made use of simple, generic objects such as sticks and balls. The starting point for the latter approach was the physical interaction, with the view that this could produce or provide insight into psychology or interpersonal interactions. The chapter ends by looking at objects in the teaching of two contemporary practitioners: Jacques Lecoq and John Wright.

How did it happen that such different approaches claim common source in Stanislavski? The reception and transformation of Stanislavski's ideas in the United States was complicated by delays in the publication of his writing but also by the intricacies of transmission between teachers and students. The chapters that were published in English as *An Actor Prepares* were intended by Stanislavski to be published in a single volume together with the chapters that were subsequently published as *Building a Character*.

Political and editorial complications meant that while *An Actor Prepares* was published in an abridged English translation in 1936, *Building a Character* was not published until 1948 (in Russian) and 1949 (in English).[6] This delay had important implications for the reception of Stanislavski's work in the United States, where his first volume was often treated as his final word.[7] Alongside the books, students played a very important role in the diffusion of Stanislavski's ideas. Two of Stanislavski's former students, Richard Boleslavsky and Maria Ouspenskaya, founded the American Laboratory Theatre in 1925. One of their students, Lee Strasberg, was a co-founder of the Group Theatre (with Harold Clurman and Cheryl Crawford). Uta Hagen was directed by Harold Clurman on a production in 1947 and in *Respect for Acting* (1973) she mentions this as the experience which crystallised her own theory of acting. Actor and acting teacher Stella Adler was a member of both the American Laboratory Theatre and the Group Theatre; in 1934 she and Clurman studied with Stanislavski for five weeks. Though there are similarities between Adler, Hagen and Strasberg in the vocabulary they use in relation to objects, their approaches have very different implications.

OBJECT AS TEXT: EMOTIONAL MEMORY

The most prominent exponent of the use of objects in actor training to develop observation, memory and analysis of emotion is Stanislavski. His early acting theory places great stress on the importance of props and the actor's emotional response to them. This emphasis grew out of his work as a director of Chekhov's plays. As he writes in *My Life in Art* (1926), it was Chekhov who

> discovered to us the life of things and sounds, thanks to which all that was lifeless, dead and unjustified in the details of production, all that in spite of our desires created an outward naturalism, turned of itself into living and artistic realism, and the properties on the stage took on an inner relationship with the soul of the actor. Chekhov, like no one else, was able to create inward and outward artistic truth.
>
> (quoted in Innes 2000: 139)

Chekhov and Stanislavski may have at times disagreed about how to represent 'things and sounds' (see Chapter 4) but they agreed that the object in performance was a text for the actor to read as much as the spectator.

Stanislavski's appreciation of the power of objects to carry emotional memory developed not only in relation to the plays he directed but also through a reading of nineteenth-century fiction, as his detailed notes on the contents of Ranevskaya's handbag in *The Cherry Orchard* suggest. Her handbag might contain, he imagines, a scarf, a French novel, a purse, perfumes and sal volatile. Yet, as Jovan Hristic has commented, apart from the purse, 'all the objects Stanislavski so carefully enumerates will remain forever hidden in her handbag' (Hristic 1995: 178).[8]

In Stanislavski's fictionalised account of actor training, *An Actor Prepares*, exercises using props move from observation to mimed interactions to interactions with real objects. In the first place, they are intended to help actors to become aware of their environment – the classroom and their homes, the city and the natural world – and of the connections between the senses, memories and emotions. The narrator of *An Actor Prepares* describes the acting classes taught by the school's Director, Tortsov, in great detail. The narrator also takes 'movement classes', but these have a secondary status, being taught by the Assistant Director, Rakhmanov, and tend to take place outside the pages of the book. However, one day Tortsov is absent and Rakhmanov takes the acting class instead, performing what is described as 'drill'. He says to the students:

> I shall select an object for each of you to look at. You will notice its form, lines, colours, detail, characteristics. All this must be done while I count thirty. Then the lights will go out, so that you cannot see the object, and I shall call upon you to describe it. In the dark you will tell me everything that your visual memory has retained. I shall check with the lights on, and compare what you have told me with the actual object.
>
> (Stanislavski 1980: 79–80)

The students are shocked to learn through this exercise how little they habitually absorb of their surroundings. As homework, they are asked to go over their day while lying in bed, noticing which objects have drawn their attention and the emotional content they carry. The work is intended to improve their powers of recall and of emotional analysis. Tortsov suggests that the young actors will later be able to transfer an awareness of the emotional associations everyday objects hold for them into their understanding of a fictional character's relationship to an object. The actors reflect on objects to open their emotional awareness. It's notable that Stanislavski places this lesson as coming from the 'movement' teacher, Tortsov, rather than the 'acting' teacher. Tortsov rejects the idea of students forcing every object to have significance by 'endowing' it with qualities or associations it does not have for them: 'It is not necessary to endow every object with an imaginary life, but you should be sensitive to its influence on you' (Stanislavski 1980: 89). Paradoxically, the notion of 'endowing' objects with emotional significance becomes more important to some of Stanislavski's American followers than being 'sensitive' to their intrinsic properties.

Variations of this exercise are still widely used in acting training. In the following account, the focus is not so much on the actor's powers of observation as on what is revealed about the nature of communication. Acting teacher Ian Ricketts describes an object exercise used with students in their first year at the Guildford School of Acting:

> I have a box full of extraordinary things: some are very simple, like old tools, sheep shears, an otter's skull, a Civil War brass buckle, an Elizabethan schoolhouse key;

all of them are things that the students have not seen before. We sit in the circle and I pair off people and ask them to close their eyes. I open the box and put one of these objects into the hands of one member of each pair. The one who has the object describes it to his partner. They can name it if they choose, but they don't have to.

(Mekler 1989: 146–7)

Just as in Stanislavski's exercise, one student gives a verbal description of the object, but in this case, the students jointly reach an understanding by talking to each other. Ricketts' intention is to show students that what they perceive is determined both by the previous experience of the questioner and the describer, and by the relationship between them:

Suppose it were an apple and suppose I knew nothing about apples. I would experience the object in my hand as being smooth-skinned, cool, and just fill-ing my palm. That's it. I wouldn't be able to go further with my description. But supposing you, my partner, had been brought up on an orchard and your father had 106 species of apple trees that you knew. Your questions about the apple would direct me to a sensory perception of it that I would not have thought possible. You could direct me to the stalk and the area around the stalk and ask me to compare that to the rest of the skin [...] So it doesn't matter who has the knowledge, the one who questions always determines in part what is experienced.

(Mekler 1989: 147)

While both Stanislavski and Ricketts aim to develop the actor's intuitive sensory response to objects, Ricketts claims that most acting students already have 'a rich intuition that will feed upon any material that is brought to them' – but that they need to go beyond intuition to understand the concept of dialogue. They come to see 'how much their behaviour depends upon what they receive from other people, upon the quality of attention in another, upon that other's listening in their presence' (Mekler 1989: 146). This understanding of communication as a dialogic process is fundamental for live theatre.

For Ricketts, the notion of dialogue also pertains to the exchange between object and person. He notes that although the motor force to move, lift or transform a thing may arise from the human, it can only be efficiently deployed when combined with a perception of the qualities of the inanimate:

In all action there is the ingredient of submitting as well as that of doing. You can only lift something if you receive from it information about its weight and texture and form, just as you can only relate to a person by receiving whatever it is that he or she brings to you. This feeds directly into the listening part of acting.

(Mekler 1989: 144)

From observation, Stanislavski's students moved on to recreating lifelike actions – a search for a lost brooch, for example, or the building of a fire. This involved the miming of everyday actions.[9]

> 'Please give me some prop money,' I said to a stagehand standing in the wings.
> 'You don't need it. Play with "nothing",' ordered Tortsov.
> I started counting non-existent money.
> 'I don't believe you!' said Tortsov stopping me as soon as I stretched out to take the imaginary packet.
> 'What don't you believe?'
> 'You didn't even look at what you were touching.'
>
> (Stanislavski 2008: 617)

Tortsov coaches the student by reminding him of small physical details such as how packets of banknotes are typically tied up with string. The students then repeat the exercise with prop money. Tortsov asks the performers and spectators which sequence made the most vivid impression on them. He reminds the students that actions that seem natural in real life feel 'strange, distant, complex' on stage. By analysing a sequence of actions 'from the outside in', the actor rediscovers 'familiar motor sensations' and thus evokes the audience's belief in the truthfulness of the actions (618). In contrast, when using real objects, there are inevitable lapses of concentration and gaps in the analysis because of the automatic, habitual nature of the actions. Tortsov tells his students that even as an experienced actor, he works on 'actions without objects' for 15–20 minutes a day (621). The aim is to generate more precise and compelling work with props. In this context, Tortsov recalls Eleonora Duse performing in *La Dame aux Camélias* 40 years previously:

> There was a long pause in which she wrote a letter to Armand. I can remember that famous improvisation not 'in general' but in all its constituent moments. They have stuck in the memory with unusual clarity, brilliance, in all their perfection: I loved that improvisation as a whole and in its parts, as one loves a magnificent example of the goldsmith's art.
>
> (622)

The image of the goldsmith evokes both the precision of craft skills suited to work on the most minute scale, and a broader artistic understanding of how elements can be combined into a whole.

A list of 50 improvisations recorded by Stanislavski is a time capsule not so much of particular objects as of the physical gestures associated with them: alongside actions such as playing musical instruments and drinking tea, there are activities that as unfamiliar today as swiping a touchscreen or balancing on a skateboard would have been to Stanislavski's students.[10]

> 5. I am on sentry duty.
> 9. I take water from the ice-hole.

10. I train the goat.
15. I reap rye.
21. I guard a melon patch, kindle a fire, cook a meal.
22. I catch birds in the woods.
27. I stoke the oven.
39. I draw water from the well.
43. I set the samovar, wash dishes.
46. I sharpen and clean knives.

(Stanislavski 2008: 653–4)

While an antique prop like a samovar or scythe can today be located or recreated more easily than ever before, the practices and ways of using old technology are not self-evident.

IN AMERICA: LEE STRASBERG, UTA HAGEN AND THE DISAPPEARANCE OF THE OBJECT

In the popular understanding of acting in the United States, Stanislavski's work is inextricably associated with Lee Strasberg and 'The Method', with its huge impact on acting in American theatre and film.[11] Strasberg gave objects a central place in his method of actor training, but there is a significant shift in emphasis from material objects to imaginary objects, something that is also found in the exercises described by other American acting teachers, particularly Uta Hagen, potentially leading to solipsism.

The Method teachers' search for a 'reliable' stimulus to produce a predictable emotion culminates in the concept of the 'trigger object'. Stanislavski's delicate suggestion of 'influence', 'interest' and 'interaction' between object and human is replaced by references to 'trigger' objects which reliably – mechanically, as it were – produce a response. Hagen suggests that an actor can use a 'tiny remembered object' only indirectly connected to the remembered emotional event – 'a polka-dot tie, an ivy leaf on a stucco wall, a smell or sound of sizzling bacon, a grease spot on the upholstery' – to produce the required feeling at the right moment (Mekler 1987: 48).[12]

Paradoxically, in these acting methods based on Stanislavski, the concrete object disappears, even as it is given increasing significance in the actor's 'tool kit' as a skeleton key to the emotions. The real object, which might, in its full recalcitrant presence, be a less reliable trigger of the required emotion than an actor would wish, is replaced by a simulacrum. These versions of Stanislavski's exercises, originally intended to sharpen actors' awareness of their surroundings, can instead have the effect of isolating the individual in a solipsistic world. The actor and teacher John Lehne, who worked with Strasberg and taught at the Actors Studio for three years, comments that after about ten years of teaching Strasberg's sensory exercises, he

began to notice that things were often missing in the work when it was used professionally. The actor's experience, if used to the exclusion of other things, isolates him, makes him more concerned with creating his own world in terms of his personal experience and less concerned with how that world is related to the situation and character of the play.

(Mekler 1987: 235)

Strasberg's sequence of 'sensory exercises' was intended to develop the performer's kinetic recall of simple experiences and to stimulate the recall of private memories:

The purpose of these acting exercises is to train the actor's sensitivity to respond as fully and as vividly to imaginary objects on stage as he is already capable of doing to real objects in life. He will, therefore, have the belief, faith, and imagination to create on stage the 'living through' that is demanded of the performer.

(quoted in Malague 2012: 37)

The 1935 course in acting that Strasberg developed with Elia Kazan and Joe Bromberg begins with simple observation of an object using as many senses as possible: 'For example, a book – its form and color, cover texture, weight, smell, sound of turning leaves etc.' (Kazan 1984: 35). In the following class, the students' powers of observation are checked by the performance of a 'suitable action'. If the object is a watch, 'Let one student be a watchmaker to whom another student describes his watch so that the watchmaker can build another of the same kind' (ibid.). As in Stanislavski's exercise quoted above, the emphasis here is on verbal communication between actors, but in later work at the Studio this element seems to have been lost, with an increasing focus on the actor's inner experience.

From observation, the student actor moves on to imaginative recreation of sensory responses to a series of objects. Strasberg gives the following examples: drinking a cup of coffee; putting on make-up, or shaving, in front of a mirror; putting on shoes or socks; putting on underclothes in front of a full-length mirror; touching three different fabrics; feeling sunshine on the face and body. The objects are chosen to involve all the senses.

While Stanislavski suggested that 'imaginary objects demand an even far more disciplined power of concentration than material objects' (Stanislavski 1980: 87), some Method teachers have taken this as justification for banning real objects from the rehearsal room. Ed Kovens, for example, says, 'I don't want a student to work on the real thing, but the sensory object' (Mekler 1987: 134). He claims that real objects provide dangerous short-cuts for the imagination: 'the student already knows what emotion is going to be elicited' by an object of personal significance, and therefore quickly exhausts it. Because an imaginary object has to be actively constructed, an actor may invest more energy in this work, and pay more attention to material qualities than when handling an apparently familiar object. But by removing the real object from the classroom, the Method teachers remove an unreliable, complex 'other', and narrow the range of possible responses to the material world. Since real objects vary according to the actual conditions of the environment, they provide constantly changing stimuli.

This shift from material to imaginary object is also found in Uta Hagen's training. In *Respect for Acting*, Uta Hagen gives a vivid picture of the conditions pertaining in commercial theatre. She prepares actors for working with more-or-less suitable props, generic objects that may not have been given the full attention of a designer or props department. In a chapter which deals mainly with how actors can produce the required dramatic action by mentally substituting a more personally significant object from their own experience, Hagen ends with a discussion of her concept of 'particularization', by considering a prop ashtray. The ashtray provided might be completely fitting for the play. For example, if the play is set in a Greenwich Village garret, then a cheap, mass-produced ashtray would be exactly right: 'it *is* tin sprayed to look like copper, probably came from the dime store, has two grooves to hold cigarettes, is shiny with a few cigarette stains in the bottom, is lightweight'. As a result, the actor 'can deal with it correctly under the given circumstances'. If, however, this same object is supposed to belong in a 'Park Avenue penthouse', the actor has to 'make it particular' by 'endowing it with qualities it does not possess'. She draws on her 'previous knowledge of elegant ashtrays': 'I turn it into real copper, assume it comes from Tiffany, and is heavier than it looks'. The actor can also endow it with psychological characteristics:

> My husband gave it to me last week for a sentimental occasion. I had wanted it for a long time, and now it sits proudly on my coffee table. Obviously, the simple act of flipping ash into this ashtray will be influenced by the way in which I have made it particular to me in my character in the play.
>
> (Hagen 1973: 45)

While recognising the work that actors can do to invest objects with properties they don't possess, both muscularly (the miming of weight that isn't there) and in gesture (the attitude behind the flipping of ash into the ashtray), Hagen does indicate that the audience is not easily fooled. From the audience, the ashtray 'may even pass for elegant' – but probably won't. An audience picks up a great deal of visual information about physical properties, and even if these perceptions do not rise to consciousness, they contribute either to a successful image or to a nagging sense that something 'doesn't ring true'. There is a conflict between Hagen as an observant spectator, alert to the meaning of materials and design, and Hagen as an actor confident that she can endow an object with any material or emotional properties she desires. Hagen insisted that 'truth in life as it is, is not truth on stage' (Hagen 1973: 75); the problem lies rather with the notion that 'life as it is' is an unproblematic, seamless entity, with boundaries and characteristics on which we all agree.

FINDING A SEQUENCE OF PHYSICAL ACTIONS

In Stanislavski's later work, he developed what he called 'the method of physical actions'. This can be related to the discussion in the late nineteenth century by William James of the sequence in which we perceive and respond to events. James counters the common-sense view that the 'perception of some fact' leads to an emotional response and that this in turn leads to a 'bodily expression' such as a gesture or grimace: 'we lose our fortune, are sorry and weep; we meet a bear, are frightened and run; we are insulted by a rival, are angry and strike.' He suggests that on the contrary *'the bodily changes follow directly the* PERCEPTION *of the exciting fact, and that our feeling of the same changes as they occur* IS *the emotion'*. Thus, 'we feel sorry because we cry, angry because we strike, afraid because we tremble' (James 1884: 190–1).

Following this logic, Stanislavski suggests that instead of inner work, the actor might identify a sequence of physical actions that have to be carried out to fulfil the character's purpose in a scene. Stanislavski gives as an example Salieri's intention to murder Mozart in Pushkin's *Mozart and Salieri*. Salieri murders him 'by means of a series of physical actions: first by choosing a wine glass, next by pouring the wine, next by dropping in the poison, and only then by handing the glass to his rival' (Carnicke 2000: 26). The actor 'tests' this sequence by performing it silently. 'If the actors successfully communicate the key elements of the scene in a *silent étude*, they have created useful scores for performance' (27).

Stella Adler studied with Stanislavski during the period in which he was developing the method of physical actions. She brought back to America the emphasis on scoring a sequence of activities that could be linked to a character's overarching action or 'objective'. A list of sample actions includes: 'to argue; to fight; to take care of; to explain; to teach; to reveal; to denounce; to defy; etc.' (quoted in Carnicke 2000: 97). For Strasberg, the action comes from the director; for Adler, it is found by the actor through study of the script. Sharon Carnicke sees a crucial distinction between their approaches. In Adler's work, 'it is through the action that actors are empowered to make political choices. Instead of asking actors to reach into their memories for moments when they felt angry or oppressed, Adler tells them to denounce and defy' (ibid.). Adler places great emphasis on the actor's analysis of the 'given circumstances' of a play, defined as the 'social, cultural, political, historical, and geographical situation' in which the characters exist (Carnicke 2000: 99). Where Hagen would ask students to bring an object from home to rehearsal (an item of clothing, a cup etc.), Adler would require students to learn to sharpen knives or use a samovar. The actor's quite specific, practical research lays the ground for a materialist analysis of the wider circumstances that lead a character to behave in a particular way. In this respect, Stella Adler's work with objects in rehearsal has parallels with that of Bertolt Brecht.

THE OBJECT AS SCORE RECORDING SOCIAL AND MATERIAL HISTORY: BRECHT

Brecht's interest in objects in performance was reflected in poems and critical writing on the work of actors and designers. In a poem that pays tribute to Helene Weigel, he compares the actor to a poet: just as the poet searches for the right words, the actor selects props for her characters. The poem mentions the props Weigel chose for various roles, including Antigone and Mother Courage. The poet concludes that it is Weigel's practical experience that helps her choose the right objects for performance, by considering their age, function and beauty, not only her 'knowing eyes' but her 'bread-baking/Soup-cooking hands' (Brecht 1961: 72).

For Brecht, the manner of handling props was even more important than the choice of object, since it could potentially define a *Gestus* and reveal a social and historical world. Peter Thomson suggests that Brecht's much-discussed term *Gestus* is fundamentally a way of talking about semiotic analysis of behaviour. Carl Weber, who worked with Brecht in Berlin, describes the *Gestus* as 'mainly determined by the social position and history of a character', and discovered by the actors through 'careful attention to all the contradictions to be discovered in the actions and verbal text of the role' (quoted in Thomson 2000: 110). Weber stresses the 'practical, even playful manner' in which a *Gestus* was defined. Props could be crucial tools for expressing a specific social *Gestus*: for example, as Mother Courage, Helene Weigel experimented with different ways of closing her large leather purse, 'making a loud "snap" at the end of a transaction', while as Vlassova in *The Mother*, she handled a pot of lard in a way that showed 'the reverential attitude towards food of those who live close to starvation' (Eddershaw 1996: 32–3). Objects identified as props could prompt specific kinds of behaviour through their own unique sets of sound and movement potential. The poem, 'Of all the works of man', discussed in the Introduction, refers to the worn places in the wooden handles of old cutlery: for Brecht (as for Stanislavski), these marks of use can be read as a 'score' for movement.

Although Brecht left no specific programme for training actors, a list of 'exercises for acting schools' was found among his papers. It is thought to relate to lessons given by Helene Weigel at a Finnish theatre school. The first six call for observation of daily life:

    a. Conjuring tricks, including attitude of spectators.
    b. For women: folding and putting away linen. Same for men.
    c. For men: varying attitudes of smokers. Same for women.
    d. Cat playing with a hank of thread.
    e. Exercises in observation.
    f. Exercises in imitation.

(Brecht 1987: 129)

Peter Thomson provides an engaging gloss on the wider questions implied by these exercises:

> We ask of the conjuror, how did you do that, but why are some spectators amazed and others dismissive? Do women and men do things differently? Why? Is doing things with linen a female thing? Who determines that? How can an activity as common as smoking betray the social class of the smoker? What do people play with? How do we know, when playing with a cat, that the cat is not playing with us? The observation of society ends with a question mark, too.
>
> (Thomson 2000: 105)

Other exercises on the list make more playful use of objects, such as 'Rhythmical (verse-) speaking with tap dance' and the use of objects of the wrong scale: 'Eating with outsize knife and fork. Very small knife and fork.' These clowning games resemble the training exercises devised by Vakhtangov and Meyerhold that are discussed later in the chapter. Meyerhold, too, was very interested in the rhythmic demands of tap dance and made it part of the daily training routine.

It is, however, the following object exercise that is most revealing of Brecht's dialectical approach to theatre-making and its political purpose: 'Situation: two women calmly folding linen. They feign a wild and jealous quarrel for the benefit of their husbands; the husbands are in the next room' (Brecht 1987: 129). As Thomson suggests, the physical action is deliberately at odds with the emotional quality of the words, allowing the scene to comment on the 'commonplace activities' of both 'folding and quarrelling'. In both activities, there are elements of routine (a familiar physical activity and the clichés of the row) and of collaboration. The juxtaposition makes 'strange what we might otherwise scarcely notice' (Thomson 2000: 106).

Interactions with physical objects in Brecht's plays provide innumerable opportunities to demonstrate that each action is a choice. Brecht gives the example of Helene Weigel's Mother Courage in the last moments of the play, when she has to pay for the burial of her son: 'Even in paying for the burial, Weigel gave one last hint of Courage's character. She fished a few coins out of her leather bag, put one back and gave the peasants the rest' (Thomson 2000: 107). The actor's task is to show that the character has chosen 'not this but that', to show that reality is a construction and therefore changeable. Chapter 5 includes further discussion of the role of the designer in demonstrating 'not this but that'.

Like Stanislavski, Brecht is interested in the history and associations of the object, but he sees it as a nexus of social and cultural interactions that relate to the history of its making and subsequent use. Careful research and reflection on the object can give actor and spectator access to other realities, a way of understanding not just the facts but the felt experience of the past or unfamiliar social worlds. In the present day, this approach chimes with calls to look at the 'cradle to cradle' environmental impact of objects and materials we use. And just as there are no objects without history, every new material has the potential to enable new human relationships. In an article from 1929, Brecht suggests that the 'proper way to explore humanity's new mutual relationships is via the exploration of the new subject-matter':

> The first thing therefore is to comprehend the new subject-matter; the second to shape the new relations. The reason: art follows reality. An example: the extraction and refinement of petroleum spirit represents a new complex of subjects, and when one studies these carefully one becomes struck by quite new forms of human relationship. A particular mode of behaviour can be observed both in the individual and in the mass, and it is clearly peculiar to the petroleum complex. [...] Petroleum resists the five-act form; today's catastrophes do not progress in a straight line but cyclical crises. [...] Even to dramatise a simple newspaper report one needs something much more than the dramatic technique of a Hebbel or an Ibsen. This is no boast but a sad statement of fact.
>
> (Brecht 1987: 29–30)

Brecht's identification of the 'petroleum complex' as giving rise to new human relations seems prescient today. Playwrights taking up Brecht's gauntlet include John McGrath with *The Cheviot, the Stag and the Black, Black Oil* (1973), structured by the ceilidh tradition, and the site-specific opera *And While London Burns* (2010) by Isa Suarez, John Jordan and James Marriott. Further examples of matter shaping new relations might include pesticides such as DDT, and plastic waste – both particles of degraded plastic from larger objects and the microbeads used in cleaning products and cosmetics. Studies of the circulation of plastic particles within the sea and of the traces of DDT in the bodies of humans and animals show that these new materials have created new relations between the most distant parts of the globe.

OBJECT AS CONSTRAINT

Other actors and acting teachers who had worked with Stanislavski developed the practice of the *silent étude*, a sequence of actions that demonstrates a character's intention and produces emotion. Yevgeny Vakhtangov, a virtuoso comedian, infused the *étude* with lightness; 'tricks' that had an important place in training and in rehearsal. For Vsevolod Meyerhold, the *étude* became the central plank of actor training, a way of embodying dramaturgy in miniature as well as a method of training the body. Michael Chekhov's notion of the Psychological Gesture owes an obvious debt to Stanislavski, but aimed at escaping from naturalism. In the exercises described by Meyerhold and Chekhov that employ simple objects such as balls, sticks and scarves, these objects are not intended to have significant personal associations for the actors; the materiality of the object is a stimulus for physical action, rather than memory. Here, the physical object is primarily a constraint – something the actor must listen and respond to – yet it has the potential to generate characterisation and ways of interacting that will be used in performance.

Yevgeny Vakhtangov

The actor and director Yevgeny Vakhtangov was a student of Stanislavski, Nemirovich-Danchenko and Meyerhold, and a friend and colleague of Michael Chekhov.[13] Despite his untimely death at 39, he had an enormous influence on the theatre, his experiments anticipating some aspects of the work of Artaud, Brecht and Grotowski (Malaev-Babel 2013: 3). In Chekhov's memoir *The Path of the Actor*, Vakhtangov is a memorable presence with the anecdotes told about him presenting a more playful – if equally obsessive – aspect to the actor's work with objects than that found in Stanislavski's writing. Chekhov describes his friend playing a drunk man:

> It was not only he, Vakhtangov portraying the drunk, who was funny, but the very objects he was acting with – the match, the cigarette, the galoshes, the coat – they were all very funny, they came to life in his hands and took on something approaching individuality. Even many days afterwards, the objects he had brought to life in this way were still suffused with his humour, you had to laugh when you saw them.
>
> (Chekhov 2005: 199)

Another colleague comments that Vakhtangov 'treated stage props with amazing dexterity – they lived in his hands' (Malaev-Babel 2013: 30). Such humorous interactions with objects took a great deal of physical preparation to appear effortless. Off-stage, particularly on tour, Chekhov recalls, Vakhtangov liked to invent small sequences of 'business' with props which he and the other actors would then spend hours elaborating and practising:

> For example, we had to portray someone who wants to drop a match into an empty bottle but misses the neck; he doesn't notice this and is amazed when he sees the match on the table and believes that the match has miraculously passed through the bottom of the bottle. We repeated this and similar tricks dozens of times, until we had reached a virtuoso level of execution.
>
> (Chekhov 2005: 53–4)

Such tricks could not be 'laboured', Chekhov emphasised, they required 'lightness' (ibid.).

Having begun by playing, Vakhtangov would nonetheless become increasingly involved with the characters generated through these 'tricks'. He suggested that this kind of game should be included as part of actor training.

For Vakhtangov, the hands were the most expressive part of the actor's body: 'Hands are the eyes of the body' (Malaev-Babel 2013: 254).[14] This is reflected in his tactile engagement with the world, and in the gestural language of the actors in productions such as *The Dybbuk*.[15] His rehearsal notes capture the attention he paid to hand props. He writes to an actor, 'Evdokia Andreevna, where are your spoon and pince-nez? Why are you doing away with such details?' and to stage management, 'An unforgivably careless oversight: the green tablecloth is so rumpled, it looks as if someone sat on it especially for this purpose. Will the head prop-man please take the trouble always to check this' (Vendrovskaya and Kaptereva 1982: 73–4). In his 1922 production *Princess Turandot*, Vakhtangov brought his own ability with props to the work of the ensemble. The actors 'dashed' onto the set and 'picked up fabrics and objects lying on the deck. Light, colorful fabrics and improvised props soared in the air' (Malaev-Babel 2013: 224). The actors threw and caught the objects in time with the music, as well as contributing to the orchestra by playing improvised instruments such as combs wrapped in tissue paper. Demystifying the act of transformation, the actors then dressed themselves in full view of the audience in impromptu costumes, using the same fabrics and props. These costumes had been improvised in rehearsals by the actors, in collaboration with the designer Nivinsky.

> These costumes were constructed out of everyday objects and fabrics found in the studio storage. Wiseman headgear could be built out of woven bread baskets, soup spoons, photography trays, linen napkins, etc.
>
> (Malaev-Babel 2013: 231)

A headdress was made out of a lampshade, a ball and tennis racket became orb and sceptre.

The work of the company with Vakhtangov and Nivinsky here anticipates the improvisational approach of Improbable and Complicite described in the following chapter. In similar ways, they use play with objects in rehearsal to discover design elements which are then re-presented live to the audience – as if invented for the first time – to convey a sense of improvisation, lightness and the freedom to transform the objects of the world and put them to new uses.

Vsevolod Meyerhold

Alongside his directing work, the actor and director Vsevolod Meyerhold developed the actor training system known as biomechanics, in which simple objects play an important part. The success of biomechanics was, according to Edward Braun, 'largely responsible for the introduction of some form of systematised physical training into the curriculum of every Soviet drama school' (Braun 1995: 176).[16] Jonathan Pitches explains that while the biomechanical exercises were not visible as such in Meyerhold's productions, there was a 'symbiotic relationship' between workshop and theatre that meant biomechanics always 'informed' the productions.

A programme for the Meyerhold Workshop for the academic year 1922–3 indicates the importance of object training. It includes

> sporting activities with objects ('throwing of the disc, the spear, the shot put'), biomechanical aspects of object work ('coordination with the stage space, one's partner and the stage properties') and gymnastic or circus-inspired exercises ('balancing a ball', 'juggling wands', 'balancing...a wand with the foot')
>
> (quoted in Pitches 2007: 98–9)

Pitches notes that from Meyerhold's earliest experiments he had made use of sticks or batons – translated as 'wands' in the quotation above. For Pitches, the latter term, with its associations of magic, is the appropriate one. The stick is a crucial object in biomechanics, firstly

> because it brings together a number of Meyerhold's training sources – sport (the javelin, the foil), circus (the baton, the juggling club), *commedia* (the slapstick), silent comedy (Chaplin's cane); and secondly because the stick constitutes a kind of *ur-prop* in biomechanics. It is an object that carries all the associations of those disciplines but none of the baggage, an object that speaks to the performer as much as it does to the audience, an object which, in terms of the development of biomechanics, increasingly speaks for all other objects: the prop of props, if you will.
>
> (ibid.)

Alexei Levinski, a contemporary Russian teacher of biomechanics, explains that it was Meyerhold's habit to hold an hour-long training session before daily rehearsals.[17] In the first half of the session, students practised circus skills – juggling, acrobatics, balancing on a beam – and different ways of falling, as well as exercises with sticks. In the second half of the session, they worked on the biomechanical *études*. This daily sequence demonstrates Meyerhold's view of the relationship between training and performance: a progression from abstract physical training, through the miniature movement dramas of the *études*, to a dramatic script.

In a video documenting Levinski's teaching of Meyerhold's work, the students work with sticks about the weight and length of a broom handle. At first, they stand in a circle, working individually but in time with each other. The sticks are tossed from hand to hand, spun before being caught, balanced laterally on the shoulders and allowed to slide down the arm before being caught, to be balanced vertically on the palm of the hand, the shoulder, the knee and the foot. The work develops hand-eye coordination and balance. Coordination is a fundamental term in the biomechanical system: both with external objects and with other actors. Levinski comments that this work 'teaches you to work closely and carefully with an object – and that's fundamental'. Working with sticks is 'a very simple, initial kind of coordination, and it's very simple to show the criteria'. Although the stick work is demanding, it makes very straightforward use of objects. However, even at this level, the human relation with objects is not merely instrumental. Levinski describes three kinds of human-object relation, saying that the actor needs to 'master', 'tame' and 'make friends with' the stick. He introduces the idea of a dialogue between human and object:

> It is very important that you don't try to impose yourself on [the stick], to control it, but that you're having a kind of dialogue. The stick has its own qualities and the person has his or her own qualities and you need to coordinate these. It's very important to feel its weight, size, and to know its possibilities for dynamic movement – to turn – and its possibilities to be static, immobile.
>
> (Levinski 1996)

Sticks or batons are also used in Michael Chekhov's teaching and in contemporary training for puppetry.[18]

As Pitches points out, Meyerhold moves from work with concrete objects (sticks, balls) to imagined objects in his five *études*: 'Throwing the Stone', 'Shooting the Bow', 'The Slap', 'The Stab with the Dagger' and 'The Leap to the Chest'. Unlike the imaginary objects used by Uta Hagen or teachers of 'The Method', these objects are conceived as part of a reality jointly created by the actors working in a group. 'Throwing the Stone' and 'Shooting the Bow' are solo – for an audience. Each *étude* has a three-part structure of 'preparation', 'action' and 'completion'; Meyerhold suggests that by providing a physical understanding of this structure, the *étude* can help performers to analyse larger dramatic units of action such as scenes and plays.

Michael Chekhov

Michael Chekhov (1891–1955) was a member of the Moscow Art Theatre's First Studio from 1912, where he studied with Stanislavski and Vakhtangov. In the 1920s he moved to Germany and set up his own studio. Between 1936 and 1939 he was based at Dartington College of Arts. He then moved to Connecticut in the United States where he wrote *To the Actor* (1953), a manifesto and record of exercises and improvisations.

While Chekhov's exercises are rooted in the body and its movement in space, and his examples for improvisations are full of business with props, he attacks the 'materialistic world outlook' which he sees as having dominated art, science and everyday life from the end of the nineteenth century: 'only those things which are tangible, only that which is palpable and only that which has the outer appearance of life phenomena seem valid enough to attract the artist's attention'. This leads, he suggests, to an overestimation of the physical, neglecting the psychological. As the actor 'sinks deeper and deeper into this inartistic milieu, his body becomes less and less animated, more and more shallow, dense, puppet-like, and in extreme cases even resembles some kind of automaton of his mechanistic age' (Chekhov

2002: 2–3). Thus many of his exercises begin with observations of the physical world, but go on to suggest how actors might move 'beyond' surfaces,
beyond reproducing everyday gestures. Chekhov disparages the 'hypnotic
power of modern materialism' under the influence of which actors are

> inclined to neglect the boundary which must separate everyday life from that of
> the stage. They strive instead to bring life-as-it-is onto the stage, and by doing
> so become ordinary photographers rather than artists. They are perilously prone
> to forget that the real task of the creative artist is not merely to copy the outer
> appearance of life but to *interpret* life in all its facets and profoundness, to show
> what is behind the phenomena of life, to let the spectator look beyond life's
> surfaces and meanings.
>
> (Chekhov 2002: 2–3)

It is perhaps this emphasis that has given his methodology a particular
appeal for actors working in 'physical' or 'visual' theatre.

Chekhov's work as an acting teacher takes as its starting point
Stanislavski's later work on a 'method of physical actions', travelling in
the opposite direction to Lee Strasberg and the Method teachers. Rejecting
the concept of emotional memory which Strasberg made his cornerstone,
Chekhov appealed 'not to memories of everyday life, but to the subcon-
scious and to the whole of human nature' (Senelick 1992: 149). His concept
of the Psychological Gesture was a way for the actor to work physically
to find the essence of the character 'in *condensed* form', making the actor
'possessor and master of its *unchangeable core*' (Chekhov 2002: 68, italics in
original).

> There are two kinds of gestures. One we use both while acting on the stage and
> in everyday life – the natural and usual gesture. The other kind is what might be
> called the *archetypal* gesture, one which serves as an original model for all possi-
> ble gestures of the same kind. The [Psychological Gesture] belongs to the second
> type. Everyday gestures are unable to stir our will because they are too limited,
> too weak and particularized. They do not occupy our whole body, psychology
> and soul, whereas the [Psychological Gesture], as an archetype, takes posses-
> sion of them *entirely*.
>
> (Chekhov 2002: 70)

Chekhov's concept of the 'Psychological Gesture' has been defined by Felicity
Mason, who studied with Chekhov at Dartington College and in New York,
as 'a physical movement which makes you feel something' (Mason 1993). In
a workshop she led in 1993, Mason demonstrated Chekhov's introductory
exercises on characterisation using three contrasting objects: a scarf, a ball
and a stick. The actor handles each one in turn, exploring its texture, weight
and potential for movement. Mason suggests that the actor should first of
all 'take in the *quality* of the object'. Moving about the room while holding
the object, the actor tries to reflect its physical qualities in movement: 'Now

you're a *ball-type* person, bouncy and rubbery [...] Now you're *stick-like*, a rather strong person, but rigid...' These three objects provide sensory experience of three contrasting sets of material properties: lightness and fluidity (the scarf); resistance and springiness (the ball); rigidity and brittleness (the stick). After exploring these qualities through touch, the students recreate the qualities in their own bodies without touching the original objects.

Chekhov outlines four 'movement qualities' or types of interaction with the material world: *moulding, floating, flying* and *radiating*. These are described in terms of interaction with archetypal substances, rather than specific objects. For each quality, there are three stages of movement – wide, broad movements with the whole body; movement through isolated parts of the body; everyday gestures. Each material quality is explored at different tempos, and using isolated parts of the body such as shoulders, knees, forehead and so on. But these are not abstract gestures. The first exercises in *To the Actor* are based on recreating familiar physical interactions:

> Do a movement that resembles a blacksmith *beating* his hammer upon the anvil. Do different, wide, well-shaped, full movements – as though you were in turn *throwing* something in different directions, *lifting* some object from the ground, *holding* it high above your head, or *dragging*, *pushing* and *tossing* it.
>
> (Chekhov 2002: 6).

Chekhov makes analogies with the work of visual artists, advising actors to say to themselves, for example, when working on the quality of moulding: 'Like a sculptor, I *mold* the space surrounding me. In the air around me I leave forms which appear to be chiselled by the movements of my body.' Advising the students to practise the same action many times, he says this resembles 'the work of a designer who, again and again, draws the same line, striving for a better, clearer and more expressive form'. Like Vakhtangov, Chekhov believes that the hands are particularly expressive and suggests that actors should train their hands and fingers separately, working through the four movement qualities on a small scale: 'take, move, lift up, put down, touch and transpose different objects, large and small. See to it that your hands and fingers are filled with the same molding power and that they, too create forms with each movement' (Chekhov 2002: 5). The relatively abstract training is seen as having direct benefits for work with props in performance: 'When coming in contact with different objects, try to pour your strength into them, to fill them with your power. This will develop your ability to handle the objects (hand props on the stage) with utmost skill and ease.'[19]

Jacques Lecoq

Like Michael Chekhov, Jacques Lecoq (1921–1999) was interested in the movement analyses carried out by Delsarte and Dalcroze; for Lecoq, the introduction to their work was made through the work of Copeau and Decroux. A trained gymnastics teacher, Lecoq also drew eclectically on techniques from clowning, sports training and martial arts. The school he established in 1956 continues to operate, with a curriculum that includes diverse areas of study, from *commedia dell'arte* and mask-work to improvisation and the exploration of performance with 'portable architecture'.

Lecoq described himself as bringing together two theatrical routes: movement analysis and improvisation. The former is demonstrated in movement analysis classes which take as their subject activities such as 'cutting wood, throwing a disc, mixing a complicated cocktail in 181 steps, or climbing a wall in fifty-three steps'. As in other traditions described in this chapter, students learn to break down their interactions with familiar objects into sequences of discrete actions. Like Chekhov, Lecoq invites students to imagine familiar substances such as the four elements – air, water, fire, earth – as a way of analysing, characterising and producing specific sensations and bodily configurations.

For Lecoq, any object can be considered a structure of spatial and kinetic relations that suggest certain kinds of movement. This is particularly clear with objects worn on the body such as shoes or masks. A mask produces certain kinds of posture and vocal qualities as well as visually signifying a particular character. It has, in Veltruský's terms, an 'action force' as well as a sign function. As Lecoq writes:

> A theatre mask contains a more or less expressive character that refers to the human face, which it hides behind another which is larval, stylised, or even symbolic. But the mask is also a form, which acts in space like a vehicle, which moves according to the directions which it itself suggests. It turns, it corners, like a real tool, following its own planes, lines, points and masses.
>
> (Lecoq 1987: 121)

Lecoq's understanding of objects as offering both 'scores' and 'constraints' for movement can be seen not just in the work of Complicite (discussed in the following chapter) but also as an influence on puppeteers or object theatre practitioners such as Agnes Limbos, who trained with Lecoq (discussed in Chapter 9).

John Wright

Director and teacher John Wright, the co-founder of Trestle Theatre and Told By an Idiot, makes frequent use of objects in training actors. He encourages actors to explore diverse ways of moving – to use rhythms and gaits other than their own habitual ones – by asking actors to wear masks, to handle unusual objects or try on strange shoes. He argues that an individual's rhythm is as characteristic as a face: 'We can generally recognise who is coming into the house by the rhythm of their movements. If you know the person well you can recognise what mood they are in or even what they are wearing' (Wright 1998). Because rhythm is made audible and visible in the interaction between the body and objects, Wright asks actors to explore rhythm by responding to particular objects. The following exercise, using shoes, was observed in a workshop for about 20 performers.[20]

Participants remove one of their shoes, placing them in the centre of the room. Each chooses a new shoe that more or less fits, and walks around the room. They explore the kind of movement suggested by the shoe, according to whether it is narrow or wide, flat or high-heeled, hard or soft-soled and so on. Wright now suggests that the new shoe has 'a life of its own': while the actor attempts to walk normally, the shoe will shoot off in another direction, stay stuck to the floor, or move in its own tempo or rhythm, dragging the actor's body behind it. By attributing all the energy and will to the strange shoe, the actors are able to explore movement that they would normally disown or suppress. The shoe is treated almost as a magical object, which acts on humans (rather than the other way around), like the seven-league boots of fairy-tales, or the red shoes of Powell and Pressburger's 1948 film. The action is not realistically mimetic – the performer deliberately amplifies the impulses received from the shoes – but it is not otherwise distinct from the ways in which different types of shoe 'produce' specific posture and gait in everyday life.

In a variation on this exercise, two or three actors are seated facing the rest of the group. While their eyes are shut, their shoes are removed and replaced with a different pair. One by one they stand up (still with eyes closed). Wright asks them to think about the difference that the shoes make: '"Is your weight further forward or further back?" I might ask. "Do you feel taller or smaller? Are you more athletic or more frail or just clumsy in those shoes?"' (Wright 2006: 60). They move around the chair, and across the space. Wright asks further questions: 'How old are you? Do you have a boyfriend or a girlfriend?' Posture, tempo and vocal qualities are all affected as the actors respond to the sensations provided by the shoes, and it is striking how powerful an imaginative stimulus the shoes appear to be. The strange shoes act on the body of the actor directly, by shifting the centre of gravity, the alignment of the bone structure, the use of muscles, the points of pressure, and indirectly, through the cultural associations of the design and material properties of the shoes, such as their hardness, springiness, tension, warmth and so on. Because the performer's eyes are closed, the information all comes from the kinaesthetic sensations rather than visual impressions.

Clearly, however, the same objective properties may have different meanings for different people. In this exercise, a woman whose own shoes were tightly fitted, with sculptured heels, was presented with a pair of large puffy trainers. Her voice became soft and sleepy, and in response to Wright's questioning she drawled that she couldn't be bothered to walk around the room or perform any of the other actions he suggested. For her, the feel of the shoes suggested laziness and comfort. The owner of these trainers, however, was an energetic, sporty person, for whom the softness of the shoes meant 'cushioning' and protection to enable activity. 'You might well be wearing a flash new pair of trainers, but with your eyes closed you might feel clumsy and awkward in them and if you follow that logic you might think that you're an old lady in her nineties, or that you're somebody in hospital recovering from an operation' (Wright 2006: 61). The exercise shows that tactility (the feel of the object) is more than a fingertip sensation – it engages the whole body–mind complex. Wright quotes the comic actor Beryl Reid: 'I don't know who I am until I've found the shoes.'

In these exercises, the object serves a purpose that might equally be fulfilled by a written text; like a piece of writing, the object embodies a group of physical qualities and socially constructed meanings which the performer can inhabit. To speak a text means not only understanding 'sense' but literally 'getting your tongue round it' – adapting your breathing to the length of the sense units, your usual speech rhythms to the rhythm of the text, and responding to the patterning of sound textures as well as to the development of thought. This parallel is brought out clearly in John Kane's comments on rehearsals for Peter Brook's 1970 production of *A Midsummer Night's Dream*. The actors rehearsed with batons, passing them from hand to hand as they walked or danced about the space. John Kane compares the batons to the words of the play: 'As we passed the sticks from hand to hand, to the rhythm of the drums ... so we were to learn to handle words and speeches, sharing and experiencing them as a united group' (Mitter 1992: 35).

In the work with simple objects described by Lecoq or Wright there is no firm boundary between the phases of training, playing together to build a company, improvising, devising, rehearsing or warming up for a performance. By drawing the performers' attention to objects, materials and physical elements they raise awareness of the ways people use them in everyday life, the various kinds of interaction that are possible. The performer becomes an anthropologist of the everyday and a playful designer, reinventing the everyday. The following chapter describes how this kind of practice develops into performance.

Chapter

3   Improvising with Stuff

When objects and raw materials are taken as starting points for improvisation, props enter the rehearsal room on an equal basis with other elements such as text, music and lighting. At the same time – and not by coincidence – all the artists with responsibility for those particular elements are treated as co-creators of the theatrical work. This means that makers and designers often find that they have a much larger role to play in the devising process than in conventional theatre structures.

This chapter will focus on some rehearsal exercises and methods of devising that are used by theatre-makers associated with the British companies Improbable and Complicite. These practitioners trace their approach to objects back to pioneers such as Delsarte, Decroux, Laban and Lecoq. The companies are also notable for the way that the choice of props and materials is highlighted in performance. Shows by Improbable, for example, have given newspaper and Sellotape starring roles. Their work often – though not always – highlights human interaction with objects, choosing to make visible and explore the relationship between living beings and inanimate matter. In improvisatory play, the object can serve as both text and constraint. The performance draws our attention to the spectrum of animation, as objects and performers are shown changing their positions on the spectrum. These changes often become key moments, linked to the play's themes and illuminating them. The chapter ends by looking at some examples of the use and transformation of an everyday kitchen table.

As with the complex story of influence and transmission between Stanislavski and his colleagues, students and followers briefly sketched in the previous chapter, there is a network of collaboration and exchange between practitioners in the field of improvisation and physical or visual theatre. These terms in themselves are contested and subject to changes in fashion.[21] Although there are a number of full-time courses with these titles, transmission is more often via workshops or short courses at any point in a performer's career. There is therefore a more fluid relationship between training and creation of performance.

Improvisation can be thought of as free play within constraints, a dialogue between imagination and the physical possibilities of the material world. In this sense, it can be compared with *bricolage*, as in Lévi-Strauss's deployment of the term. *Bricolage* is used in French to describe an approach to household construction and repair which emphasises inventiveness and 'making do'. The *bricoleur* turns

> to an already existent set made up of tools and materials, to consider or recon-
> sider what it contains and, finally and above all, to engage in a sort of dialogue
> with it and, before choosing between them, to index the possible answers which
> the whole set can offer to his problem.
>
> (Lévi-Strauss 1966: 18)

This description chimes with what is found in improvisation with materials – a dialogue with the props and materials and a lengthy exploration of
their properties ('possible answers') before settling on one. For the *bricoleur*,
'necessity is the mother of invention': many artists have explored the ways
in which constraints give rise to more inventive solutions and also force the
audience to do imaginative work, to 'fill in the gaps'. See, for example, the
notion of 'adhocism' developed by Jencks and Silver (1973). In an interview
with Elizabeth Wright, designer Alison Chitty discusses how this can apply
particularly to theatre in the round. The audience's attention is focused
on people and props, rather than background scenery, and the objects are
viewed from all angles. Chitty describes how expressive the 'economical'
use of props and furniture can be. To suggest a prison, for example, you
might place a man and a Bible in a pool of light. Similarly,

> if you were going to express a very lavish drawing room in *The Rivals* you might
> only need three very elegant pieces of furniture and one flown light fitting or some-
> thing and the right floor ... I began to see how with very little you could express a
> lot, and also how that meant it was possible to change from one scene to another
> in a very fluid way.
>
> (quoted in Wright 2009: 260)

Wright notes that the 'communication of precise meaning is complicated by
the multiplicity of perspectives in any one audience'. Chitty agrees, but suggests that the alternative – 'thousands of eighteenth-century objects telling
them they're in the eighteenth century' – leaves 'less space for the audience
to take part' (261).

The notion of leaving space for the audience's imagination has a corollary in the performer giving up the desire to control objects and materials.
By asking actors to work with 'large and abstract' objects or materials,
like cardboard or a large piece of fabric, Enrique Pardo deliberately gives
them something 'too large to control cleverly'. Actors have to discover a
way of handling the object without manipulating it in order to 'bring out
its autonomous movements and sensual qualities, its 'will' and 'caprice'
(Pardo 1988: 170). Through this process of receptive interaction, they 'establish a dialogue with the object-world, beyond personal psychology and its
expressivity'. This approach is particularly suggestive when considering

human relations to substances, forces and phenomena that seem beyond human control. In a similar spirit, Miranda Tufnell and Chris Crickmay provide a series of prompts for performers working with simple objects, such as sticks: 'let the objects be your equal/acting on them and being acted upon by them' (Tufnell and Crickmay 1990: 119). When the artists responsible for different spheres of the performance are treated as equal partners in the creation, the relationship between designer and performers as they devise new work will be a fluid, subtle interaction. Roles can change – an actor might suggest a new prop, a designer might improvise with a prop in front of an audience.

John Wright describes an improvisation game with objects as having two possible modes: closed and open. This is the 'object game' in its closed form:

> Choose an object, anything will do as long as it isn't too fragile. In how many different ways can you use this object that it wasn't designed for? In other words, if you're playing with a chair, it can be anything other than a chair. So we might see a chair becoming a television, a horse, an open book or a window.
>
> (Wright 2006: 83)

Versions of this game are often used outside theatre to generate new ideas or even to 'test creativity'. Wright suggests that while this can stimulate people to generate lots of new material, the weakness of the 'closed' version is that the ideas are unrelated and can be forced, rather than flowing:

> To turn this into an open game you have to remove the imperative of having to think of a new idea every time and just play with the object, move it about and look at it. Ask yourself how the object wants to move, what can the object do? Then the ideas start to come to you more naturally.
>
> (ibid.: 84)

This 'open' version of the game involves playful complicity with the object and can produce narrative sequences of daring and epic sweep.

IMPROBABLE THEATRE: WORKING WITH THE MATERIAL IMAGINATION

Phelim McDermott of Improbable Theatre has adopted some of Michael Chekhov's exercises for use in his own teaching, suggesting that awareness of the four movement qualities (moulding, floating, flying, radiating) offers an imaginative route to mastering the physical skills involved in visual theatre or puppetry.[22] For example, performers may have to create the impression of weight where there is none (an empty suitcase is made to look heavy), give the illusion of a puppet moving independently, or establish a believable relationship to gravity for an object as it performs an action that is impossible in nature, such as a book flying through the air independently.

In McDermott's account of these exercises in a workshop on Michael Chekhov for the International Workshop Festival, he emphasised the sensory experience of touching, moving through the four elements – earth, water, air and fire – as ways of imaginatively finding Chekhov's four movement qualities. He expanded on how these 'primary colours' can be contrasted or combined in rehearsal or performance, to define character or direct choral movement. For example, giving an actor a note to 'mould' or 'float' might cause small adjustments to posture or gaze, or transform the tempo and energy of a gesture; or a director might unify a group of actors each performing an activity to represent 'village life' – churning, scything, milking, ploughing – by asking them all to find a 'moulding' quality in their disparate actions.[23]

Participants in the workshop followed a series of exercises based on the movement qualities: exploring one quality at a time while walking, sitting or performing other simple activities; varying the 'volume' of the quality; switching abruptly or gradually from one quality to another. They combined two or more qualities over time to create dramatic development or combined different qualities across the body to generate characters – for example, head and shoulders 'flying' while legs were 'moulding'. The four movement qualities were also transmitted to everyday objects such as cups, books and chairs – making a clear connection to Improbable's work with object animation.

In performance, Improbable often focus attention on props and objects in a way that highlights their material qualities of weight, texture, grain and so on, as much as their connotative meaning. The process of exploring material possibilities is often brought before the audience as performers construct props and puppets live on stage. In the improvised shows *Animo* and *Lifegame*, performers draw freely from a stock of raw materials piled at the side of the stage. The materials typically include lengths of cloth, sticks, rolls of paper, sheets of foam and corrugated cardboard and rolls of sticky tape. The performers may talk together in front of the audience about what they are doing as they decide what to use and how to construct a figure or landscape.

While *Animo* is typically a series of sketches of varying length and mood, *Lifegame* is structured through an interview with a different guest on stage each night. It begins with the interviewer leading an informal conversation about the guest's life, perhaps touching on memories of growing up, first love, school, travel or work. At some point, the interviewer might ask, 'Would you like to see that moment?' Company members then improvise the scene, perhaps creating instant puppets from the stock of raw materials or using tables and chairs to represent mountains. In a family dinner scene, the guest's mother might be played by a bearded, middle-aged man or represented by a head made of crumpled newspaper: the disjunction is part of the comic effect, but also allows both the guest and the audience members to project their own ideas and memories onto the scene.

In such quick work, characterisation partly depends on stereotypical gestures and signs. The actor playing 'the mother', for example, might tuck a length of cloth into the waist of his trousers to serve as an apron, 1950s housewife style. Yet the deliberately open and unfinished nature of the image allows audience members to complete it themselves, and thus the stereotype has the potential to act as an archetype, or to be transformed into something more personal. The performers aim to capture the rhythm of interactions and underlying emotion, taking their cues from the guest's original account. After showing a scene, they might check with the guest: 'Is that how it was?' If the guest is doubtful, or can't recognise their own experience in this version, the scene might be re-run, feeding in new details ('What would your mother say?' 'Where did you usually sit?'). If the scene works, despite the incongruities of the staging, there is often a nod of surprised recognition from the guest – 'That's exactly how it was'. The performers in *Animo* take suggestions from the audience in the same way as verbal improvisers, but are able to draw on the stock of materials and their skills in construction as well as their verbal playfulness. In both these improvised shows, lighting and sound designers might be physically distant from the stage, perhaps sitting in a technical box or in the wings, but they participate in the improvisation by responding to what's happening on the stage, supporting or transforming the scene just as the onstage improvisers do.

What is happening when an audience sees a scene constructed before their eyes from a store of old props and raw materials? Dan Rebellato has proposed that a useful way to think about theatrical representation without getting entangled in a discourse of 'illusion' is to revisit the concept of metaphor. He notes that a metaphor does not state the connection between its two elements: it is up to the listener to decide in what ways 'Juliet is the sun' for Romeo. Similarly in theatre, 'Old can play young, women can play men, black can play white, wood can play stone, large rooms can play small rooms, a wooden O can play the fields of France…' (Rebellato 2009: 25). Metaphors demand imaginative participation, and the two elements thus brought together shed new light on each other. In watching improvisation with objects, the audience is invited to imagine the resemblance between incongruous things. How does a blue polyethylene tarpaulin held outstretched by a number of performers become the sea? Depending on the way it is manipulated and the spectator's own associations, the connection may be visual (the colour, the sense of a substance filling the whole visual field, the wavelike motion), aural (a low rustling or a rhythmic snap and thwack), or associative (a similar kind of tarpaulin commonly being used on fishing boats) – or a combination of more than one of these. As well as establishing the sea for the purposes of the performance, the metaphor-making inevitably draws our attention back to the tarpaulin too – to the sound and movement qualities of a material that's not usually celebrated.

One of Improbable's first shows, *70 Hill Lane*, although carefully rehearsed and plotted, gives the impression that it is improvised storytelling, making do without set or props and using a kitchen table and rolls of Sellotape instead. It opens with Phelim McDermott standing on a bare stage and addressing the audience directly as he tells a story about the poltergeist that haunted his childhood home. As he talks, he creates the outline of the house by stretching Sellotape between metal uprights. The tape makes its characteristic ripping sound as it is pulled across the stage, emphasising the distances and the process of construction. Once in place, the taut lengths of shiny, translucent tape catch the stage lights. They appear like lines drawn in the air, evoking a sketch drawing and at the same time outlining a room at full scale to provide a set for a performer to move around in. Later, Phelim tears the tape from the supports and bundles it together to create an ectoplasmic figure trailing shimmering strands, a puppet of the poltergeist. It's a powerful material image: the poltergeist is made from the substance of the house and tears it apart in the process of becoming visible.[24]

DEVISING WITH THEATRE DE COMPLICITE

The approach to the material world found in the work of Complicite (established as Theatre de Complicité in 1983) has been shaped both by the training experienced by many of its performers and by a profound engagement with texts by writers including Bruno Schulz, Daniel Kharms and John Berger. As Murray and Keefe (2007) point out, the company has moved freely between purely devised work, adaptations of novels and short stories, and productions based on play texts from Shakespeare to Ionesco: 'Across all these different points of departure, however, Complicite has brought the ethos and the creative pragmatics of devising to the task of making theatre' (Murray and Keefe 2007: 97). Simon McBurney, artistic director of Complicite, trained initially with Jacques Lecoq, as did fellow founders of the company Annabel Arden and Marcello Magni. Other teachers important to members of the company have included Philippe Gaulier and the Feldenkrais teacher Monika Pagneux. Annabel Arden describes Pagneux's ethos of 'play':

> Monika is able to find a way of releasing full expression of the creative self through the body. She enables the body to become a rich source of different landscapes: your body sings, one moment you are a rock, or a heathland, or a nomad in the desert. The central idea is transformation. No actor needs the perfect body; they need their body to be fully available to them, working at the maximum potential with the minimum of effort.
>
> (quoted in Murray and Keefe 2007: 106)

The company now works with an 'increasingly loose alliance of collaborators' (Williams 2005: 248) so the creation of these conditions in rehearsal is key.

The transformations Arden describes above find an echo in the Bruno Schulz stories that were the source for *The Street of Crocodiles* (1992).

At dinner, Father insists that 'the migration of forms is the essence of life' and 'Matter can change in an instant'. His view is embodied by the other members of the household who get to their feet:

> The Father puts an arm around his son Joseph as they watch the others begin their clucking, crowing and tweeting transformation into birds. The Father moves around the table delighting in this 'migration of forms' as the characters thrust and jerk their heads, necks and elbows: 'here we have a peacock and here [standing behind his wife] we have a broody hen.'
>
> (ibid.)

There is no sense that the actors are trying to sell us the illusion of *becoming* birds; they are, rather, inviting the audience's imagination to engage in the task. In this scene, as in many other instances across Complicite's repertoire, we see both the actor *and* the characters evidently enjoying the play of trans-formation.

In preparation for *The Three Lives of Lucie Cabrol*, designer Tim Hatley 'scoured the country' to 'buy, scavenge and scrounge' antique tools from flea markets and farms. Although a scythe or a zinc bucket might have been purchased with a sense of the moment in the scenario in which it could be used, Hatley brought his discoveries into the rehearsal room and left them for the performers to discover for themselves:

> I would just leave all the things I'd found in a pile in the corner. Some of them were used, some of them weren't. Some of them you really loved, and you'd think: 'Oh please pick this up and use it', but the minute you said 'use it', no one would. So I would deliberately not [say anything], I would deliberately put the things I loved at the bottom of the pile.
>
> (Hatley 2001)

The working method of the company demands that performers define and create the stage world for themselves. Designers (including sound and light-ing designers) are present at Complicite rehearsals whenever possible and create the stage world with the company:

> If they're doing an improvisation with tables, I'm there, and I can say: 'But wouldn't it be great if the table legs were the sort that could collapse, so then it could become...' It's a two-way process – it's never a question of me versus the actors. They come up with ideas and I come up with ideas. It's as simple as that.
>
> (ibid.)

Tim Hatley describes Complicite's way of working as 'incredibly tough', because every decision has to be discussed, rather than being divided into separate areas of responsibility: 'You have to fight for your corner...make your voice heard' (Hatley 2001).

IMPROVISING WITH TABLES

Tables have an emblematic significance in improvisation work, as well as in object theatre. A table is a little stage, as well as a piece of moveable furniture on a stage. In performance, the boundaries of the table define a 'world', just as for Gaston Bachelard, 'the lamp-lighted table is a little world in itself' (Bachelard 1994: 1970–1). Thus the table is often used to play with scale, moving from a realist use in which it might represent 'a kitchen table' to its use as a platform for puppets in which it might represent a whole world.

Improbable

In *70 Hill Lane* by Improbable Theatre, a table becomes a small stage for a newspaper puppet. Light brightens on a wooden table as two men approach it. A sheet of newspaper lies flat on the table, an invisible layer on the surface. Placing his hands flat on the paper, the first man seems to feel the paper rising under his hands, gently waking, rumpling and gathering itself. One hand lifts off the table, bringing up a knot of crumpled paper while the other hand roots the rest of the sheet of paper to the table. The knot turns from left to right – for the audience, it becomes a head that looks from side to side. The second performer joins the first, placing his hands on the paper on the table and beginning to animate the lower half of this newly born figure. The 'legs' begin to move. The figure walks about on the table, discovers its edges, peers over the side to discover a vertiginous drop. The table is a whole landscape for this character.

The directors of Improbable Theatre describe newspaper improvisation as having vast potential scope:

> In watching performers improvise with newspapers we see that each perfor-
> mance, from beginning to end, is a miniature act of creation. How this improvisa-
> tion is birthed and brought to conclusion is a whole journey. The puppetry table
> becomes the whole world and the stories that happen can be epic in their themes.
> (McDermott and Crouch 2000: 13)

An awareness of the 'real' or 'human' scale of the kitchen table is maintained by the presence of the manipulating performers. This 'double vision' is one of the crucial features of the improvisation work – materials and objects used can at one moment serve a fiction and the next be brought back to their literal human function. A newspaper puppet might climb the sheer Alpine cliff of a table leg, and then be tidied away into the table's drawer. This rapid shifting between different realities is described in puppet theory as oscillation or opalisation (see Tillis 1992), and has the potential to be used for commentary by the performers, in Brechtian style, on the characters or dramatic situations. (Commentary may be simply implied, through a look to the audience or between the performers.)

Theatre de Complicite

A table can also stand for a landscape in a drama with purely human performers. In *The Three Lives of Lucie Cabrol* (Theatre de Complicite 1994), Lucie shouts to her brother Émile across the whole width of the stage (she is in the mountains; he is living in Paris). She asks whether he has seen the Eiffel Tower. He answers, 'You see it everywhere. It's more than three hundred metres high.' Émile later returns home and sits at the kitchen table to eat. On the table, he places a model of the Eiffel Tower. It's not more than 30 centimetres high – a tourist souvenir. He brings his experience of the big city back to the village with him – but it appears shrunken when placed on the table, set in the context of the family and the demands of subsistence farming. Hoping to impress the family with another figure, he tells them there are two million horses in Paris. In a verbal deflation of the capital city to match its miniaturisation in the model, his father retorts derisively, 'Two million horses! That's lot of shit!' as he heads back to work. In *Mnemonic*, the table is a frame for shifts not in space, but in time: performers roll repeatedly over a table as the play moves from the present day back into prehistory.

Guy Dartnell

Guy Dartnell, a long-time collaborator with Improbable Theatre as well as a solo artist, explores objects and materials with a sculptural interest in their properties. For example, in his solo *Something or Nothing* (2011) Dartnell draws on a large blackboard, then scribbles thickly over the marks. The chalk dust produced falls into a box beneath the board. Later, Dartnell sprinkles powdered chalk from the box onto the black theatre floor, and uses his body to draw shapes through the powder, suggesting that even a 'raw' or neutral material has a history, in this case as the residue of earlier attempts at communication. An earlier solo show, *Would Say Something* (1998), makes metaphysical play with scale, working only with his own body and a set of simple objects – a table, a blackboard, a lectern. Perching on the edge of the table, Dartnell says, 'I had this table specially made to be the right size so I could sit on it, like this.' He luxuriates in swinging his legs like a child – that is, like someone who enjoys discovering new ways of using objects that are precisely *not* made to his scale. In the theatre space, and through his play with it, the table draws the spectator's attention in a new way. As Baudrillard writes, this 'space' exists through a transcendence of function:

> Space exists only when it is opened up, animated, invested with rhythm and expanded by a correlation between objects and a transcendence of their functions in this new structure. In a way space is the object's true freedom, whereas its function is merely its formal freedom.
>
> (Baudrillard 1996: 18)

Through his performance, Dartnell gradually shifts objects away from their explicit function, for example by wrapping himself around a lectern and lowering it very slowly to the ground.

The objects Dartnell uses in *Would Say Something* are abstracted versions of the lectern, table and blackboard. In their everyday function, as props for didactic speech, they serve the play's exploration of rhetoric and 'ways of speaking'. But the furniture on stage is idealised – the pieces are beautifully made, with no visible screws or nails, so that they can be lit as sculptural abstractions. The blackboard, covered with diagrams illustrating a theory of existence, becomes an abstract backdrop (reminiscent of the blackboards which Joseph Beuys used during his lectures, now preserved in museums). The board is a vertical 'table' for organising ideas – the connection with 'table' being closer in other languages (*Tafel* in German or *tableau noir* in French). Later, talking about a friend's explanation of the 'twelve steps to enlightenment', Dartnell climbs onto the table. Prowling about the tabletop, he wonders aloud: if the twelfth step takes you into the totality of everything, in which direction should you step? And do you need to take the eleven preceding steps, or can you just go straight to the twelfth? These metaphorical steps are presented in the performance as literal steps across the table. When he talks about the step which will take him into another state of being, we see him standing on the edge of a world. The relationship with the table provides a 'symbolic model of a philosophy [...] but then it becomes a symbolic model of the world' (Dartnell 2001). The table is a small stage, a small patch of reality lifted out of the larger reality of the performance space. Throughout the piece Dartnell explores the effect of gravity on the body and on objects. Like a giant puppet, whose relationship to gravity is an illusion created by the puppeteer, Dartnell stands on a small world which represents the 'real world', the world people live in, subject to gravity. When he steps off the table, he is 'like a god' looking at a microcosmos. Such metaphysical play, natural to puppets, is rarely seen using human performers.

FURTHER READING

Derek Bailey, *Improvisation: Its Nature and Practice in Music* (1980); Keith Johnstone, *Impro: Improvisation and the Theatre* (1981); John Wright, *Why Is That So Funny?* (2006); and *Body Space Image: Notes towards improvisation and performance* by Miranda Tufnell and Chris Crickmay (1990).

Chapter

4 An Abundance of Little Objects

This chapter looks at the heyday of the prop in the late nineteenth and twentieth centuries, examining how playwrights and directors used everyday objects to give insight into character and social worlds, and ends by discussing two recent productions of canonical realist plays that staged materiality in unexpected ways.

Discussions of the dramatic movements of realism and naturalism often mention the innovative use of everyday objects as props, beginning with T. W. Robertson's introduction of 'real bread and real tea to the London stage of the 1860s', while in Paris at the Théâtre Libre André Antoine 'provided authentic settings with real objects – most famously a side of beef' (Banham 1995: 907). Antoine explained how these props lend 'an authentic character' to the scene:

> In our interior sets, we must not be afraid of an abundance of little objects, of a wide variety of small props. Nothing makes an interior look more lived in. These are the imponderables which give a sense of intimacy and lend authentic character to the environment the director seeks to recreate.
>
> (quoted in Innes 2000: 53)

As the following chapter describes, it is far from the case that real objects, food and drink appeared for the first time on the stage in the nineteenth century – Aristophanes even wrote a play in which he mocks Euripedes for relying too heavily on props. Rather, it was the idea of presenting everyday reality on stage, in meticulous detail, that was new. For the 'naturalists', influenced by contemporary scientific and sociological theory, the aim of creating such a realistic stage picture was to show how environments influenced human behaviour.

Writers and directors continued to worry at the question of how 'real' a staged reality could be. How could actors repeat everyday actions and words night after night and give the impression that they were impelled to do so by real and present motives? Stanislavski's approach to acting emerged out of the problems of staging realist drama, and has had a continuing influence, partly because realism – loosely defined – remains the dominant mode in cinema and television, as well as in much mainstream theatre. This chapter looks at some of the fault-lines in the theory of staging realism, characterised by the assertion by acting teacher Uta Hagen that 'truth in life as it is, is not truth on stage'. The chapter concludes with a discussion of the notion of historical accuracy in performance from a designer's point of view.

One way to look at nineteenth-century realism would be to see it as an expression of the recurring impulse to introduce 'reality' (or, sometimes, 'contemporary life') into art. As novelist David Shields puts it: 'Every artistic movement from the beginning of time is an attempt to figure out a way to smuggle more of what the artist thinks is reality into the work of art' (Shields 2010: 3). He describes his collage-essay *Reality Hunger* as a manifesto for

> a burgeoning group of interrelated but unconnected artists in a multitude of forms and media – lyric essay, prose poem, collage novel, visual art, film, television, radio, performance art, rap, stand-up comedy, graffiti – who are breaking larger and larger chunks of 'reality' into their work. (*Reality,* as Nabokov never got tired of reminding us, is the one word that is meaningless without quotation marks.)
>
> (ibid.)

Shields reminds us that 'reality' is subjective and constructed – it is only 'what the artist thinks is reality'. But the absence of 'theatre' from his generous list of forms and media is striking. Theatre's medium is cut from the same stuff as the world outside the work of art – bodies, chairs, cups and saucers. So bringing chunks of 'reality' into the theatre ought to be easy. Yet among those who aim to bring chunks of reality into the theatre, there seems to be a fluctuation, sometimes within the same paragraph, between the lure of the real (identified with a new object, some example of excessive matter, or a 'more truthful' interaction) and caution, even anxiety, about the disruptive power of the real.

Take an ordinary upright chair, for example. The heroes of classical drama might have had little reason to sit down, except in scenes that called for a throne, but chairs became essential props for dramas set in drawing rooms and salons. As Bert States puts it, the chair made dramatic 'conversation' possible for the first time: 'casual or exploratory talk leading to tension and crisis; the carving of the true subject out of the seemingly phatic encounter ("Well, let's have that nice little chat, Mrs. Tesman")' (States 1985: 45). As well as enabling this prosaic talk, the chairs, tables, teacups, and views from the window all contributed to the definition of status – 'the great subject of the modern drama' (ibid.: 45–6). Bert States describes Ibsen's characters as sitting on the edge of their chairs, 'bursting with news or curiosity' because only from chairs can the intricacies of motive be unraveled' (ibid.: 73). Yet the introduction of naturalistic seating reputedly caused actors great problems, creating 'a temporary frenzy among the actors, since the art of acting – or grand acting, at least – had never required skill in moving around household obstacles' (ibid.: 41). The actors' problems with chairs relate to the phenomenological reappearance of the body – a reappearance that is often embarrassing, potentially comic, as Bergson explains in *Laughter*:

> No sooner does anxiety about the body manifest itself than the intrusion of a comic element is to be feared. On this account, the hero in a tragedy does not eat or drink or warm himself. He does not even sit down any more than can be helped.
>
> (ibid.: 44)

As Bergson suggests, drawing attention to the reality of the actor's body in any way can be problematic, opening up a potential gap between actor and character, as discussed further in Chapter 7.

Theatre is perhaps absent from Shields' list of the artistic forms that aim to incorporate 'chunks of reality' because of the paradoxical situation that while theatre is made out of the same stuff as commonplace reality – bodies, furniture, cups and saucers – 'theatre' and 'reality' are opposed almost as often as 'fiction' and 'reality'. As States puts it, in the theatre 'we are, technically, within the museum: all that is on stage is art' (States 1985: 39). Yet in theatre, it seems, this framing has the effect of emptying out some part of the reality of the object. Props tend to be regarded as possessing 'less reality' than their counterparts outside the theatre, with the papier mâché prop an emblem of 'theatricality', as in this exchange from Noel Coward's *Present Laughter*:

> **Joanna**: You're being conventionally odious but somehow it doesn't quite ring true. But then you never do quite ring true, do you? I expect it's because you're an actor, they're always inclined to be a bit papier mâché.
>
> **Garry**: Puppets, Joanna dear, just creatures of tinsel and sawdust; how clever of you to have noticed it.
>
> (Coward 1943: 45)

Like papier mâché, the actor is defined as an infinitely malleable material without any intrinsic qualities, fated to be nothing but imitative. However, writers and directors in the movements of realism and naturalism shared the ambition David Shields describes among contemporary artists: to bring 'real things' such as everyday objects and idioms into the artwork.

In his 1881 essay *Naturalism in the Theatre*, Emile Zola notes a change in the public's taste. Twenty years previously, he suggests, *L'Ami Fritz*, a play 'in which people eat all the time and the lover talks in such homely language', would not have been applauded at the Comédie-Française. Similarly, he finds that the public is attracted by lifelike paintings, which used to repel them: 'a secret fermentation has been at work' (quoted in Innes 2000: 47–52). Zola is, however, still searching for the playwright who will be able to produce the 'simple formula of naturalism' by 'sifting' it out of the confusion of life, who will 'do great things' with subjects and characters we think of as 'small': 'it will be proved that there is more poetry in the little apartment of a bourgeois than in all the empty, worm-eaten palaces of history' (ibid.).

Zola sketches out an idea for a realist play that recalls the setting of his Rougon-Macquart novels and was eventually to be effectively realised in film – a crowd scene that reproduces the variety of life by including various classes and trades. For example, he suggests, one act could be set in the market of les Halles in Paris:

> The setting would be superb, with its bustling life and bold possibilities. In this immense setting we could have a very picturesque ensemble by displaying the porters wearing their large hats, the saleswomen with their white aprons and vividly-coloured scarves, the customers dressed in silk or wool or cotton prints, from the ladies accompanied by their maids to the female beggars on the prowl for anything they can pick off the street.
>
> (ibid.)

He goes on to list half a dozen other suggestions for scenes that offer a variety of human activities: a factory, a mine, a gingerbread market, a railway station, flower stall, racetrack and so on. Most importantly, the scenes ought to be 'reproductions', rather than vague or partial representations, in order to provide material for scientific research and satisfy 'the need for exact studies'. In this respect, detail was essential but ornamentation for its own sake was not: 'What we need is detailed reproduction: costume supplied by tradespeople, not sumptuous but adequate for the purposes of truth and for the interest of the scenes' (ibid.).

The definition of the quantity of reality that was 'adequate for the purposes of truth' was to prove problematic. In Stanislavski's production of *The Cherry Orchard*, the first act ended with a chorus of rustic sound: 'A shepherd plays on his pipe, the neighing of horses, the mooing of cows, the bleating of sheep and the lowing of cattle are heard' (Carnicke 2000: 29). Sharon Marie Carnicke suggests that Stanislavski included these sounds mainly for the benefit of the actors:

> He assumed that the more the actors could believe in the reality of the play's environment, the better they would act. Therefore, all production details, and most especially sound, served to stimulate the actors' imaginations by creating distinct 'atmospheres'. In the same spirit, Stanislavsky allowed his actors to use make-up and costumes as early as two months before a play opened.
>
> (ibid.)

The playwright, however, found the density of sound effects excessive and teetering on absurdity. Chekhov threatened to write as the opening line of his next play: 'How wonderful, how quiet! Not a bird, a dog, a cuckoo, an owl, a nightingale, or clocks, or jingling bells, not even one cricket to be heard' (35). The question of what quantity and quality of material reality might be 'adequate for the purposes of truth' would continue to trouble directors and stage managers into the present day.

CUP AND SAUCER DRAMA

The stage directions in the plays of T. W. Robertson are so detailed that they resemble a prompt copy or audio description script more than a modern playscript, with the smallest actions carefully set out, including notes on the emotional tone in which speeches should be delivered. Henry James later recalled the Robertson's comedies among others he had seen staged at the Prince of Wales's Theatre: 'The pieces produced there dealt mainly with little things – presupposing a great many chairs and tables, carpets, curtains, and knick-knacks, and an audience placed close to the stage' (Booth 1980: xii). An emblematic scene occurs in the final act of Robertson's play *Caste* (1867). As Polly Eccles sets out tea things, she tells Major Hawtree, 'I won't ask you to take tea with us, Major – you're too grand'. Nevertheless, Hawtree decides to stay. Her fiancé, the newly independent plumber, glazier and gasfitter Sam Gerridge, is disgruntled, as his actions show:

> SAM cuts enormous slice of bread, and hands it on point of knife to HAWTREE. Cuts small lump of butter, and hands it on point of knife to HAWTREE, who looks at it through eye-glass, then takes it. SAM then helps himself. POLLY meantime has poured out tea in two cups, and one saucer for SAM, sugars them, and then hands cup and saucer to HAWTREE, who has both hands full. He takes it awkwardly, and places it on table. POLLY, having only one spoon, tastes SAM's tea, then stirs HAWTREE's attracting his attention by doing so. He looks into his tea cup. POLLY stirs her own tea, and drops spoon into HAWTREE's cup, causing it to spurt in his eye. He drops eye-glass and wipes his eyes.
>
> (Robertson 1980: 163)

Michael Booth points out that it was not the detailed furnishing of the stage (the 'real doors, real locks, the snow blowing into the hut') that was Robertson's innovation, since 'impeccable stage furnishing and realistic stage effects went back in the former case to the management of Madame Vestris at the Olympic in the 1830s and in the latter at least to the well-mounted melodramas of several managements in the fifties and early sixties' (Booth 1980: xiii). What was revolutionary was the combination of these design elements with restrained ensemble performances and writing and acting that displayed 'domestic realism'.

Nevertheless, the domesticity in Robertson's plays sometimes has a comic effect. One play, *Ours*, set in the Crimean War, 'includes a mass of detailed kitchen business including the making of a real roly-poly pudding on stage

a few yards from the battlefield' (ibid.). One of the characters exclaims:
'A roly-poly pudding in the Crimea! It's a fairy-tale!' as he dismantles a
stool to use its leg as a rolling pin (Robertson 1980: 107). Nevertheless,
Christopher Innes describes Robertson's own productions of his plays as
laying the 'groundwork for naturalism'. They provided

> meticulously detailed reproductions of Victorian social habits, which won them
> the label of 'cup-and-saucer drama'. The most significant of these were *Society*
> in 1865 and *Caste* in 1867 – titles that embody his characteristic subject, the class
> system, as well as indicating a proto-naturalistic emphasis on the social group
> rather than a single protagonist.
>
> (Innes 2000: 9)

Robertson had served a long apprenticeship as an actor and stage manager.
His stage directions suggest an imagination rooted in physical actions, but
also a strong sense of the sort of 'business' that will communicate to the very
back of a large theatre, such as the comic contrast between the slab of bread
and the small lump of butter, exaggerated by their both being presented on
the point of a knife (rather than being offered on a side plate, say). Changes
in production techniques at this period such as improved lighting also enabled small details to be more visible, making them more rewarding to write
and perform.

IBSEN'S TIMED EXPLOSIONS

It seems appropriate that Ibsen's *A Doll's House* is full of things, and people
talking about things. The play itself might be considered a small world
that the dramatist plays with, moving toys as well as characters around the
Helmers' apartment: a Christmas tree, a toy sword for the children, a packet
of forbidden sweets, a piece of knitting, a fancy dress costume, a letter in a
locked letterbox.[25] But as Andrew Sofer argues, the objects in Ibsen's plays
are more than realist set dressing, and more charged than the objects that
serve as plot devices in earlier well-made plays:

> Like other playwrights who limited the action to a single room and a discrete,
> successive time period, Ibsen needed to find a way to dramatize the past while
> avoiding lengthy exposition. Objects were his solution [...] Ibsen's props embody
> the decisive influence of the past on the present...
>
> (Sofer 2003: 173)

For Ibsen, Sofer continues, 'no prop is innocent' – almost every item is a
'depth-charge primed to explode into revelation at its allotted point in the
action' (ibid.). The signature that Nora forged is a very clear example of an
object that records the past (precisely because it is a dated legal document),

but her tarantella costume also records the past – it's a travel souvenir, with rips and tears from its previous use. When Nora wears the dress, in combination with the music on the gramophone player (also, in a different medium, a record of a past moment), it transports her into an earlier physicality. With the help of these souvenirs, Nora remembers, and re-enacts the steps of the dance. In a similar way, the signature does not stand alone: it can only affect the present if it is 'read' (and interpreted – by more than one reader) as a forgery.

While the theory of theatrical naturalism rooted in the presentation of everyday detail can imply that lives are determined by environment, the concrete decisions made in every performance complicate this picture. Toril Moi points to the role of metatheatrical scenes in Ibsen's plays, such as Nora's tarantella in *A Doll's House* (Moi 2006: 26); more recently Kim Solga discusses the choices made in Carrie Cracknell's Young Vic production of the same play to explore how Hattie Morahan was able to 'convey a historicized, socially and economically informed "truth" about Nora's "being"'(Solga 2015: 51). In portraying Nora's anxiety and exhaustion in the private gaps between her 'performances' as wife and mother, Morahan unpicked the conventions of emotional realism that (in Elin Diamond's memorable phrase) 'laminate' body to character (42). Varun Begley also argues for a more nuanced understanding of 'realism' as 'inherently multivalent' (Begley 2012: 338).

REVISITING REALISM IN CONTEMPORARY PRODUCTIONS

What implications might this have for contemporary productions of classic realist plays? For Christopher Innes the plays of Ibsen, Chekhov and Shaw have a peculiar status in relation to history: they are associated with the past in their concerns, conventions and fashions and 'yet, unlike plays from most other eras, they are hardly ever performed in modern-dress productions'. The language that characters speak is close to modern usage, and the way the dramatic action is structured is still used today. They are 'simultaneously anachronistic and contemporary' (Innes 2000: 16–17). Writing in 1989, Frederick J. Marker and Lise-Lone Marker note that

> a more or less lightly stylized but still substantially 'museological' Victorian parlor set has remained the rule for revivals of *A Doll's House* [...] The tangible specificity of the 'tastefully but not expensively furnished living room' described in the stage directions has been moderated at times, but rarely abandoned altogether.
>
> (Marker and Marker 1989: 75)

They argue that this 'allegiance to material reality' ends up by reducing the scope of a work that goes beyond the realistic plane. This approach, that of treating these plays as 'period pieces', was once particularly prevalent in British theatre, while in the theatres of mainland Europe there was a much greater readiness to relocate the modern classics in time and place. Marker and Marker describe landmark productions by Peter Zadek and Ingmar Bergman that swept aside teacups and wallpaper. At the Bremer Kammerspiele in 1967, Zadek and designer Guy Sheppard created a stage space for *A Doll's House* 'that was hardly a room or even a "setting" at all – a door on either side, a veranda window as background, an old-fashioned sofa at the diagonal mid-point of the stage, and virtually nothing more' (Marker and Marker 1989: 76). Ingmar Bergman's production of *A Doll's House*, under the title *Nora*, at the Residenztheater in Munich in 1981, was designed by Gunilla Palmstierna-Weiss:

> The entire stage space was a limbo cut off from any contact with the world of reality – a void encompassed by an immense, non-representational box that was uniformly lined with a dark red, velvet-like fabric. Within this vast, confined space, a smaller structure was created by high dark walls that suggested the panelled interior or a court-room.
>
> (Marker and Marker 1989: 81)

On a platform in the centre, objects created a succession of fragmentary settings: a heavy upholstered sofa, an elaborately trimmed Christmas tree with mountains of presents heaped beneath it:

> Scattered across the front of the small stage-platform were more wrapped and unwrapped presents and toys: a helmet, a sword, a decorative brass doll's bed, and, most striking of all, two large dolls with pale and oddly human porcelain faces. Together, these objects made a silent but eloquent comment on the Helmer world as a playpen, a doll's house of eternal childhood.
>
> (ibid.)

In the final scene of the play, the focus was not, as in Ibsen, the dining table, but a large brass bed, an enlarged version of the child's toy seen at the beginning. A naked Helmer wakes to find Nora sitting on the end of the bed dressed for travel, an overnight bag in her hand. The production lifted the play out of the distracting clutter of 'period' design while still working materially with the play's significant objects.

The previously 'museological' tendency in British theatre has shifted in recent years. A number of high-profile productions of Ibsen and Chekhov in London have been performed in modern dress and settings, or in a style that is historically informed but not aiming for a complete reproduction. I will discuss two productions staged at the Young Vic, London: a 2012 production of Chekhov's *Three Sisters* directed by Benedict Andrews, with design by Johannes Schütz and costumes by Victoria Behr; and a 2014 production of Arthur Miller's *A View from the Bridge*, which was directed by Ivo van Hove and designed by Jan Versweyveld, both long associated with the Toneelgroep, Amsterdam.

Three Sisters

With a script full of contemporary echoes and a soundtrack that included Nirvana's 'Smells Like Teen Spirit', several eras collided in the props and costumes of the 2012 *Three Sisters*: candlesticks, a flouncy frock and samovar from Chekhov's world; tracksuits, buggies and baby monitors from our own. Anfisa inhabits a scene from 1970s Russia: she sits at a small table covered with a lace cloth, with a thermos, a transistor radio, an ashtray, a desk lamp and a small bunch of wild flowers in a vase. The sisters seem almost to have chosen their own costumes from an archive of historical styles – Olga in a severe drop-waisted dress with a pleated skirt, Masha in an Amy Winehouse-inspired look of tousled glamour, and Irina in an ivory silk party dress with puffed sleeves.

The production gave plenty of room to the characters' attachment to objects, retaining moments like Chebutykin smashing a porcelain clock and Fedotik spinning a toy top that holds everyone mesmerised as it gradually slows. The language in Andrews' version of Chekhov is contemporary as the music. In this scene Fedotik makes a birthday gift to Irina:

> FEDOTIK: (*To IRINA*) I got you a pressie today – from Pyzhikov's on Moscovskaya Street. These really cute colouring-in pencils, and look – this awesome pocket knife.
>
> IRINA: You still treat me like a child but I'm a grown woman.
>
> *She takes the pencils and penknife.*
>
> Wow, cool.
>
> (Chekhov 2012: 53)

While the language was updated, the sequence of events was the same. Paul Taylor, writing in *The Independent*, found the deliberately jarring anachronism problematic: 'it updates the language and the cultural references but it does not revealingly revise the life-expectations of Chekhov's pre-revolutionary characters or the intimations of impending seismic change' (Taylor 2012). Andrew Haydon, in contrast, felt that the devices were almost too much 'in the service of the play' in a production without a clear political purpose (Haydon 2012). I'd like to suggest that the way the performers worked with the set established a new layer of commentary on relationships to the material world which reflects Chekhov's ecological concerns while giving them a contemporary resonance.[26]

The audience sits around three sides of a rectangular grey platform, the surface apparently scored into metre squares. At the very back, there is a mound of earth. The company uses the platform as the main playing area – a dining table and chairs are set upon it – but it gradually becomes apparent that the platform is made up of 150 small, square tables. Throughout the second half of the play, performers break up the platform by pulling out individual tables, carrying some away and overturning others. The second act begins with the ringing of a fire bell, and Anfisa speaking of the Kolotilin children who have escaped from a fire 'huddled under the stairs, crying their little eyes out' (Chekhov 2012: 63). The sisters are left marooned, their beds set on separate islands in a grey sea. The mound of earth, a distant landscape in the first half, its lower edge concealed by the platform, is now part of the same space as the performers and audience. The image evoked – for this spectator at least – coastal inundations caused by rising sea levels, as a contemporary parallel to Chekhov's depiction of a crumbling society. In this production, it would make no sense to consider the props separately from the scenography as a whole, nor from the work of the company in developing the action.

A View from the Bridge

Many of the props that might once have been disruptive presences on stage are now so commonplace that it is their absence – as in the 2014 production of Arthur Miller's *A View from the Bridge* – that proves surprising and enlivening. Although Miller's description of the set specifically eschews a 'complete' stage picture, suggesting that the 'skeletal' frontage of a tenement building can be juxtaposed with a law office, without fully furnishing either, he does stipulate furniture and a significant number of props in the stage directions and dialogue (Miller 1988: 378). Food and coffee are brought and consumed; records played; Beatrice talks of buying a new tablecloth when guests are due. Eddie Carbone's relationship to fabrics is particularly interesting: on seeing the new tablecloth, he is described as 'silent, staring down at the tablecloth, fingering the pattern', and his niece Catherine engages him in a discussion about a new purchase that assumes he takes an interest in clothes:

> Catherine: Guess how much we paid for the skirt.
>
> Eddie: I think it's too short, ain't it?
>
> Catherine, *Standing*: No! not when I stand up.
>
> Eddie: Yeah, but you gotta sit down sometimes.
>
> Catherine: Eddie, it's the style now.
>
> (Miller 1988: 380)

These words and stage directions mean that a spectator's attention will be drawn to the actual tablecloth and skirt in any particular production – to

think about their specific materiality, rather than remain at the level of a gen-
eralised impression. Later in the play, Catherine lays out a paper pattern on a
length of cloth on the dining room table; as earlier with the tablecloth, Eddie
'sees the pattern and cloth, goes over to it and touches it' (421). However,
Eddie expresses great suspicion of the young Italian immigrant Rodolpho
who sings, cooks and sews. In Eddie's world, there are distinct activities for
men and women, recalling Peter Thomson's gloss of Brecht – 'Do women
and men do things differently? Why? Is doing things with linen a female
thing? Who determines that?' (Thomson 2000: 105). Clearly, Miller is deeply
interested in materiality and how it affects people.

Miller's 1958 introduction to the play describes the London production,
directed by Peter Brook, as having a 'more realistically detailed' set than the
New York production which had a 'rather bare, if beautiful' background:
'Overhead and at the sides and across the back were stairways, fire escapes,
passages, quite like a whole neighborhood constructed vertically' (Miller
1988: 51). Miller praised Brook's production for giving a stronger sense of the
context of the action, partly through this compressed image of a neighbour-
hood and partly by including many more extras. In his introduction, Miller
describes 'realism' as 'neither more nor less an artifice […] than any other
form. It is merely more familiar in this age' (53). He acknowledges that realism might be used 'as a covering of safety against the evaluation of life', while
warning against a flight from realism into another set of conventions, such
as clichés of post-Brechtian staging and the verse dramas of Fry and Eliot:

> neither poetry nor liberation can come merely from a rearrangement of the lights
> or from leaving the skeletons of the flats exposed instead of covered by painted
> cloths; nor can it come merely from the masking of the human face or the transfor-
> mation of speech into rhythmic verse, or from the expunging of common details
> of life's apparencies.
>
> (ibid.)

Ivo van Hove's 2014 production did indeed expunge the 'common details',
doing away with dining table, rocking chair, desk, gramophone, cups, plates
and tablecloth, thereby increasing the focus on the physicality of the actors'
bodies. The lawyer, Alfieri, who introduces the characters in a chorus role,
prowled around the edge of a stage enclosed by low glass walls – rather like
a scientist observing the interactions in a petri dish. The audience sat around
the stage on three sides, as in an operating theatre. This aspect of the design
was perhaps a gesture to the scientific ambitions of naturalism, while the
characters' interaction with water and blood was staged as a primal encounter with the elements. In the opening scene, the two dockers, Eddie and Louis,
their muscular chests bare, a visible reminder of their daily physical labour,
washed under a stream of water from a high showerhead. In the final scene,
blood poured from the showerhead, soaking all the characters as they pressed
together in a struggling mass like players locked in a deadly game or animals

in a slaughterhouse, unable to escape their fate. The technology to bring the water and blood onto the stage – a system of pipes and drains – would not have been unknown to Ancient Greek theatre, yet this production reinvigorated the play by using them. By eschewing hand props, the production opened up the possibility of a more corporeal engagement with materiality.

As these two examples show, an inventive treatment of materiality, even in productions of plays from the broadly realist tradition, offers the possibility of exploring contemporary concerns. In 1898, Arthur Wing Pinero wrote in a note to the stage manager that preceded the script of *Trelawny of the 'Wells'*, that

> the costumes and scenic decoration of this little play should follow, to the closest detail, the mode of the early 'sixties – the period, in dress, of crinoline and the peg-top trouser; in furniture, of horsehair and mahogany, and the abominable 'walnut-and-rep'. No attempt should be made to modify such fashions in illustration, to render them less strange, even less grotesque, to the modern eye.
>
> (Pinero 1936: 5)

A playwright today might hesitate to give such strict instructions on the historical accuracy of costume and set, while few directors would feel constrained by them. Even at Shakespeare's Globe, staff acknowledge 'that they cannot produce a fully authentic early modern theatre … [nor] a "fully authentic" early modern prop or audience to rightly interpret that prop' (Karim-Cooper 2012: 97). Nevertheless, the notion of 'period drama' still appears in critical writing on theatre, film and television. In the following discussion, the designer Tobias Hoheisel argues that the very notion of a 'period production' is an outdated Anglophone concept that serves neither theatre-makers nor audiences.

'PERIOD. QUESTION MARK?'

Tobias Hoheisel

This is an extract from the 2012 Edward Gordon Craig lecture, presented by Tobias Hoheisel in the form of a discussion with Judith Flanders.

Judith Flanders is a social historian who has focused on the texture and detail of daily life in nineteenth-century Britain.

Tobias Hoheisel is a stage designer and director, the set and costume designer for more than 70 theatre and opera productions worldwide. He studied theatre design at the Hochschule der Künste in Berlin, studying with Achim Freyer (set design) and Martin Rupprecht (costume design).

TH: Living and studying in Berlin in the 1980s opened up the possibilities of what theatre design can achieve. Achim Freyer considered himself a fine artist, and his imaginary world was a mix of expressionism and abstraction. Meanwhile, the most influential German theatre at the time was the Schaubühne, run by director Peter Stein and dramaturg Dieter Sturm. They held research in high esteem, and productions ranged from Robert Wilson's slow motion minimalism to Stein's hyper naturalistic, 'Stanislavskian' productions of Chekhov. The contrast between these two men showed that many different answers were valid.

There was also an abundance of visiting theatre companies, such as Ariane Mnouchkine's Theatre du Soleil, Peter Brook's company and Giorgio Strehler's productions for theatre and opera, not to mention all the important German-speaking theatre companies which came to the annual 'Theatertreffen' festival.

This background allows me to approach every production with an open mind. Although you don't necessarily think of them as a list when you're working, the three possibilities for the setting of any production are:

1) The period the play or opera was originally set in by the author
2) The period when the piece was written
3) A period chosen for interpretative reasons (including modern dress)

JF: So the decision is not simply whether the production will be 'period' or not?

TH: Certainly not. The choice of period and style is to give the audience cues to the ideas in the play and how we interpret it. I like the way Giuseppe Verdi expressed his idea of the process: it's a question of finding the right *tinta* for a piece, that is, each piece has a 'colour', and it is the designer and the director's job to find what they feel that colour is.

Anglo-Saxon theatre has traditionally focused on realism. The question, 'What period are you setting it in?' – which is so standard in English-language theatre – came as a surprise to me when I first worked here. I remember when I designed Janáček *Katia Kabanova* for Glyndebourne in the late 80s I was criticized for not giving any period or class context, just shapes and colours! I've always expected to find the *tinta*, which consists of many 'ingredients', not to do 'Edwardian', 'Restoration' or 'Modern Dress'.

JF: So to take as an example Handel's *Xerxes*: you could look at Persia in the fifth century BC; Handel's own period (1685–1759); or perhaps, in addition, Handel's view of the fifth century BC – which is certainly not ours.

TH: Exactly. So you very often end up with something of a 'composite'. What we're doing in the theatre is not, and cannot be, historical reconstruction. Think of Joseph Mankiewicz's film *Cleopatra* or Josef von Sternberg's film *The Scarlet Empress*. Even in Luchino Visconti's far subtler film *Senso*, set in mid-nineteenth century Italy, the make-up, hairstyles and even the cut of the costumes betray the fact that the film was made in 1954!

Period design is not archaeology. We produce quasi-historical reconstruction, or an image of nature, or an abstraction – all as metaphors informed by our points of reference and those of the audience. It goes without saying that there's no such thing as a production 'as the author would have imagined it'. How far you stray from Verdi, Ibsen or Handel is up to your conscience, level of knowledge and – may I say – taste.

Let me illustrate that with two of my current projects, both of which have presented quite distinct historical questions.

First, there is *Arabella,* the last collaboration between Richard Strauss and Hugo von Hofmannsthal: written in the late 1920s, premiered in 1933, but set in the Vienna of the 1860s. When I began work with Tim Albery, who is directing the production for Canadian Opera Company and Santa Fe Opera, my opening questions were: Why did Strauss and Hofmannsthal choose the 1860s? And would their reasons be clear to contemporary audiences?

After the mythological and fairy-tale excursions of Strauss and Hofmannsthal's previous collaborations, culminating in the highly complex *Die Frau ohne Schatten,* they wanted to hook on to their greatest early hit, the comedy *Der Rosenkavalier* which had been set in mid-eighteenth-century Vienna. They wanted to write something like an operetta, so they chose the period when this art form blossomed – around 1860. For various reasons this time coincides with the beginning of the end of the Austro-Hungarian Empire. From their traumatized post-World War I perspective, this was synonymous with the collapse of European civilisation.

For us at the beginning of the twenty-first century, this choice has slightly different connotations. We were looking for a period that would resonate with contemporary audiences in a similar way but still be imaginable when you listen to Strauss's music & Hofmannsthal's language. The management of the company, the Santa Fe Opera Festival, which commissioned this production, was keen to have a 'period' production – which shows that there are many factors involved in the choice of a period – so anything like modern dress was more or less out of the question.

In the end we decided that the time just before the First World War would probably serve all those purposes. Apart from a personal antipathy on my side towards the wedding cake-like costumes worn in Vienna in the period Strauss and Hofmannsthal intended (yes, personal taste also plays a role!) and the experience of alienation which can happen when you watch singers or actors in very elaborate costume, the 1860s in America would not necessarily be associated with operetta – and certainly not with a world beginning to fall apart – but rather with Scarlett O'Hara.

The second production I'm working on at the moment, *Anna Bolena*, has even stronger 'period' demands. In this case I was determined not to do 'a Holbein'. This opera is not a biopic – something it is important to point out when every second film today is 'based on a real story'. It puts the audience on the wrong track to pretend that this is about historical personalities.

The fact that the production for Oper Köln will not be performed in a conventional proscenium arch theatre but in an old cable factory, made it even easier to rethink the Tudor trappings of the piece. Like the 1860s costumes of *Arabella*, Tudor costumes are incredibly 'costume-ish': heavy in both the literal and figurative senses, restrictive. They lock actors and singers into a static acting style which in the case of the already highly stylized 'bel canto' opera can easily lead to a more or less beautifully costumed concert, and they lock the audience into history, rather than allowing them to inhabit emotionally the events that are occurring on stage.

So, returning to that original list I gave you, I then looked at the period in which the piece was written. I thought long and hard about why the Tudor period was so interesting to Donizetti. He wrote two further operas about Elizabeth I – *Roberto Devereaux* and *Maria Stuarda* – while Rossini and others also contributed to the 'Tudor mania' of the day. Apart from the fashion for all things northern in the wake of emerging Romanticism, I guess that the hopes that he and his fellow artists held for Italian national identity made the English national creation myth very attractive. The country we now know as Italy was under Austrian, Spanish, French and papal rule. They were sending a clandestine message to their pre-revolutionary audience – a good example of the idea that a period can be chosen for political reasons.

JF: The date of *Anna Bolena* is 1830, so you end up with a cliché costume problem again. In British history the late 1820s and 30s are Regency, slightly post-Jane Austen. You could easily end up looking like Sunday teatime viewing on the BBC, all bosoms and bonnets.

TH: Certainly that would be the wrong *tinta* for this piece, giving the wrong signal in relation to the political dimension. Probably for a German audience there wouldn't really be any cues: even if people know about Italian history at that period, they wouldn't necessarily pick up on it. Rather, they might wonder why we had set the piece in a sort of 'Biedermeier' period [approximately 1815–1848] almost as far removed from our times as Tudor England. As designers, we are very quick to say – that's early 1820s, that's late 1870s – and have a sense of what that might mean historically, but one has to take into account that audiences have a much hazier historical knowledge.

So we decided to shift the focus to the conflict between the two leading ladies. I began to search for contemporary sources where artists were inspired by period shapes and connotations to create something modern but historically informed. I wanted to allow the audience to engage directly by giving the show the feel and look of a 1930s movie with two strong female protagonists fighting for love and power. For the costumes, this led me to the twentieth-century fashion designer Cristobal Balenciaga, whose garments have exactly the quality I was looking for: they look contemporary but also somehow timeless.

Considering the set, the stately homes one can see here in England came to mind: some Elizabethan timber here, a Georgian doorway there, Edwardian furnishings with some vaguely modern family portraits of often rather dubious artistic merit on the walls... The result is immediately recognisable as being English and of a certain class without exactly saying 1500 or 1830.

It's important to remember that historical purity, or fidelity, is not real. Exact period design looks often somehow fake, despite all the effort lavished on research and detail. A 'mix' is much more life-like. After all, architecture doesn't vanish at the end of a historical period, or decade. People live in Victorian houses with modern additions without ever thinking about it.

JF: This brings us to a core question. Is historical period onstage anything more than a convention? As a historian, I know that the periods of time are conventional: we talk of the 'long nineteenth century' – from French Revolution to the First World War – precisely because things didn't change just because an old man died and a young woman came to the throne in 1837.

TH: On stage – film is different – we use period detail to create the metaphor, the *tinta* that the production is trying to clarify, that the author wants to convey. A good theatre costume is an expression of character or intention, not period.

This brings me to another important point, which is the difference between fashion and reality. Our sources, especially pre-photography, are mainly of high society and royalty – the 'ideal' not only in attire but also in what was considered to be beautiful. One should not forget that the majority of artists had to flatter their patrons.

If I wanted to do *Anna Bolena* in Tudor period costume, it would be quite easy to research – paintings of Tudor royalty show me what they looked like, and we know exactly what their houses and furnishings were like. But if I were doing a piece set in the same period among the peasantry, it would be much harder to research, and even harder for audiences to understand what I was doing: we have far fewer records of ordinary people, and these are not the images most people in the audience would know. It sounds obvious, but it's easy to forget – these images are the ones we have, but they don't describe a whole world.

JF: This is what in history is known as the 'great man' syndrome. Until the last half-century or so, history mostly focused on rulers, on wars, on great economic trends. Now we are much more receptive to women's history, or the stories of small communities who might not have been literate. But of course, what can be explained on the page can't necessarily be onstage. So if you were going to do a production of *Der Freischütz*, which is set amongst peasants and minor gentry, you would run into exactly these problems.

TH: I think there have been hardly any productions of *Der Freischütz* recently, as far as I know, that have been designed in the period in which this piece is set, right after the Thirty Years' War. Even when you look at the costume designs for the first ever production in Berlin in 1821 you notice a strong Biedermeier accent in the supposedly seventeenth-century clothes. The period question in this case is about the exact moment in history: a piece set in a post-war period, and written in Germany after the Napoleonic wars. I'd say that the atmosphere of insecurity and fear in an uprooted society is the key. An explicitly seventeenth-century look would almost certainly not get your audience on the right track. What's more – the clothes of peasants and the working classes look astonishingly similar through the ages!

JF: And that's in Germany, where there is some expectation the audience will even have heard of the Thirty Years' War.

TH: There's probably a fine line between the audience's preconceptions and creating a sense of historical reality. It really takes us back to the beginning: the creative team has to take the audience's knowledge into account. So I don't expect German audiences to know about early nineteenth-century Italian history; and an *Arabella* I design for Santa Fe will be very different from one I would do for a German theatre.

I think period is a construct, just as 'Tudor clothes' are – there is of course no absolute reality. You can arrive at something which gives a genuine impression of the right period for the piece, for example, looking absolutely eighteenth-century without a powdered wig or a red heel in sight! As we said: it's a construct, not a reconstruction.

I believe good design should tell you more about the play you are watching, and enable the audience to understand it better; bad design tells you only about the designer which is not only wrong but also tedious. Similarly, there is no such thing as 'good period', or even 'accurate period'. Theatre design should help to take you to the heart of the author's intention. Bad design gives you space to worry whether Queen Victoria would have worn underwear like that.

Chapter

5   Other Realities

A 'realist' approach to props is dominant today in film, TV and much theatre. But there are – and always have been – other ways of relating to the material world. These contrasting approaches to reality can exist in the same moment: street ballads, religious ritual and naturalistic drama could all be identified as examples of performance in Germany in the early twentieth century; television soap opera, musical theatre and site-specific monologues in our own era. Many theatre-makers have been inspired by ideas about historical performance techniques, whether looking to the use of masks as resonators in the ancient world, or to the possibilities of a bare stage furnished largely by the audience's 'imaginary forces'. Even when ideas about the past turn out be historically inaccurate – in *Staged Properties in Early Modern English Drama* (2002) Jonathan Gil Harris and Natasha Korda begin their call for a materialist reading of early modern theatre by countering the received idea of Shakespeare's bare stage – they may have a significant impact on theatre practice, by offering an alternative to dominant modes of representation. This chapter offers snapshots of other approaches within a Western, and mainly British, tradition, as an inspiration for further reading.

It is almost impossible to state exactly what costumes or props were employed by a past performance, or how they were used on a specific occasion. What is documented or survives may be the exception rather than the rule. Even today, with access to rehearsal scripts, reviews, written and video documentation, it can be very difficult to reconstruct a specific detail of performance. For example, the stage directions for Martin McDonagh's play *The Beauty Queen of Leenane* give precise instructions for heating a bottle of oil: Maureen 'walks to the kitchen, dazed, puts a chip-pan on the stove, turns it on high and pours a half-bottle of cooking oil into it, takes down the rubber gloves that are hanging on the back wall and puts them on' (McDonagh 1996: 46). In an introduction to a volume on theatre and violence from nearly 20 years later, actor Catherine Cusack writes:

> One of the most horrifying moments of violence I ever saw onstage (it's subjective, of course) was in *The Beauty Queen of Leenane*. You believed you had seen a pan of water come to the boil on a stove. And this boiling water was then thrown over

someone. It was very much how the actor (Jane Brennan) chose to do it. Not in a sudden violent way, but matter-of-factly.

(quoted in Nevitt 2013: xi)

This recollection shows that memory is fallible when it comes to concrete details – the liquid thrown has changed from oil to water. Nevertheless, what might interest a future theatre-maker most is Cusack's memory of the *attitude* towards the boiling liquid, the gesture made by the actor. Exploring historical performance practices – by following up the leads suggested by material culture studies, through playscripts and other literature, visual imagery and even into the archives of purchases, legacies and contracts – offers new possibilities for present-day work with props.

This chapter offers brief samples of some current thinking about props in Ancient Greek comedy and tragedy, medieval drama and Elizabethan and Jacobean theatre, with suggestions for further reading. In the twentieth century, the reaction against naturalism focused a spotlight on objects. Brecht's productions and his discussion of props offer an appreciation of the work of actors, designers, makers and spectators that shows the complex ways in which material acquires meaning.

ANCIENT GREEK PERFORMANCE

A recent essay on props in the ancient world notes that while there are surveys of the function of props in the work of individual playwrights, there is no systematic treatment of their wider material and symbolic dimensions: students of props in Greek or Roman theatre have 'nothing comparable' to the studies by Jonathan Gil Harris and Natasha Korda of props in early modern English drama (Harrison 2013: 32). Evidence about props in dramatic performances in the ancient world can be gathered from various sources: direct references in the surviving playtexts, along with other written material, such as contemporary accounts of performances; intertextual references, such as one playwright quoting or making an allusion to the work of another; and images on vases, murals and other visual works (see Easterling 2005). There are debates about the status of each of these categories as evidence to assemble a props list, let alone the deductions about how props were actually used. Some props probably functioned straightforwardly as character 'labels': an old man carries a stick, for example. In other cases, plots turn on a prop: in *The Libation Bearers* by Aeschylus, Electra recognises her brother by a lock of his hair and the garment she had made him years earlier. A sense of how quickly such conventions change is indicated by Euripides' version of the Electra story – written 40 years later – in which the heroine herself questions the validity of such 'recognition tokens'. Although recognition tokens and other significant objects turn up in both comedies and tragedies, there are important differences between the ways props are used in the two modes.

Props are central to comedy, often used in their everyday function. Sarah Powers points out that Aristophanes' comedies, for example, make great use of props, set and costume:

> We could think of the giant dung beetle that the hero rides up to heaven in *Peace* (though some might classify that as stage machinery), Dionysus's lion skin and club in *Frogs*, and the baskets of goodies to which Paphlagon and the Sausage-Seller treat Demos as they fight for his support in *Knights*.
>
> (Powers 2010: 23)

There are many props shown in vase paintings depicting scenes from other Old Comedies (i.e. those written in fifth century Athens), the texts of which have not survived; and the plots of the plays known as New Comedies (written between late fourth century and the second century, most notably by Menander) often revolve around significant objects such as keys, swords and garlands. In addition, they call for everyday objects such as food and crockery, clothes and accessories, tools and documents. *Knights*, an early drama by Aristophanes, requires some 40 items, including 'numerous items of professional sausage-making equipment' such as a ladle, meat hooks, knives, oil and garlic (Tordoff 2013: 101). Tordoff notes that such objects have been neglected in scholarship because they lack an obvious symbolic importance (compared to, for example, Philoctetes' bow). He enumerates the objects used in various plays (both those mentioned directly and those that can be inferred, such as a walking stick to indicate the infirmity of an old man), in order to calculate the 'relative materiality' of each play.

The objects in tragedy tend to be fewer in number but more heavily weighted, acquiring their particular significance through language. Sarah Powers describes these as heightened or 'rhetoricised' props, citing the purple fabric that Clytemnestra spreads before Agamemnon in Aeschylus's *Agamemnon* as a prime example:

> Its significance to the scene suggests that it must have been a real object on the stage, but that object is so laden with symbolic value through the play's language that it takes on a much deeper and more complex meaning than an ordinary garment or carpet, even a sumptuous one. In his objection to it, Agamemnon even uses imagery of speech or crying out to describe the inappropriate nature of walking on such ornate fabric.
>
> (Powers 2010: 24)

Clytemnestra and Agamemnon discuss the cloth at length. Powers concludes that, 'Language is thus central to the shaping of this object, and one might even go so far as to suggest that the idea of the object becomes more important than the object itself' (ibid.). In Ted Hughes' translation, Agamemnon is reluctant 'to trample such richness', the 'heaped-up, spilled-out wealth of my own house'. The colour perhaps evokes the blood of Agamemnon's 'own house' spilled when he sacrificed his daughter Iphigenia.

The sense of transgression that walking on this precious material represents in Aeschylus was given a powerful realisation in the design by Vicki Mortimer for Katie Mitchell's 1999 production at the National Theatre: the carpet was made up of dozens of small dresses, sewn together, in different shades of red, as if stained with blood. This object performed many things at once: it brought women and women's work onto the stage, by recalling childrearing, just as the original audience might have recognised the purple woven or embroidered cloth as women's handiwork; it referred to Agamemnon's killing of his daughter; and it connected to contemporary life – as the production did more broadly. The Chorus in this production was a group of veteran soldiers, using wheelchairs, wearing poppies and 'equipped with a range of personal props [...] which seemed to include little urns, perhaps containing the ashes of sons who had gone to war and returned in a jar'. Remembering this detail, J. Michael Walton speculates about his memory and interpretation of the production: 'Was this my invention? It was a touch so poignant it ought to have been intentional' (Walton 2005: 204). Lorna Hardwick suggests that the production 'created an analogue between the fifth-century BC audience's ability to relate the myth/cultural memory of Troy and its aftermath to their recent experiences (against Persia perhaps), and the invocation of the modern audience's collective memory (two world wars set against the 1990s Balkan resonances of Agamemnon's dress and the music)' (Hardwick 2005: 219). The programme for the production played a part in directing the interpretation of the design, reinforcing 'the network of associations communicated by the carpet of dresses' with 'photographs showing children's clothes, shoes and toys, half buried in the sand, pock-marked with bullet holes and numbered as though presented as pieces of evidence in a criminal trial' (Hardwick 2005: 219).

Some ancient tragedians were criticised for relying too heavily on props; in his play the *Archarnians*, Aristophanes lampoons Euripides for this very fault. In the play, Dikaiopolis decides he needs a costume to help him make a persuasive speech, and visits the playwright Euripides, who just happens to have a stock of suitably ragged costumes. Dikaiopolis borrows one, but this is just the first in a series of requests. He comes up with various props he'd like to complete his look, including a 'beggar's cane', a 'little basket burned through by a lamp', a 'little goblet with a broken lip', a 'little bottle plugged with a sponge', and 'some withered greenery for my little basket'. As Sarah Powers puts it, Dikaiopolis gets so caught up in the excitement of the props that he begins to ask for things that he doesn't need for his role but simply desires:

EURIPIDES: And what need, o wretched one, do you have of this braided basket?

DIKAIOPOLIS: No need, but I want to have it all the same.

(Powers 2010: 30)

The repetition of 'little' as the attribute of many of these props reinforces the sense that Dikaiopolis has a rather childish desire to collect small and picturesque objects around him. For Powers, 'There seems to be something unusual and a little bit untragic' about this props list. It's possible that Aristophanes was observing and mocking the way actors behave as much as he was mocking his fellow playwright. Contemporary prop-maker Eric Hart expresses a similar view of actors who request props such as canes or fans that aren't specified in the script: 'Some actors are notorious for picking a prop or two at the very first rehearsal to play with' (Hart 2011a).

Images painted on terracotta vases have been an important source for evidence about the material culture of the ancient world. However, Oliver Taplin was surprised to discover that of the tens of thousands of vase paintings now discovered, surprisingly few have 'any clear or open theatrical association' (Taplin 1993: 6). Looking beyond Athens, Taplin discusses South Italian and Sicilian vase painting as a source of evidence for comedy and tragedy; from about 400 BC onward, the vase-painters of Taras (now Taranto) in southern Italy 'unlike those of Athens, overtly reflected the theatre in their painting' (11). While vases depicting scenes from tragedy tend not to represent the theatre architecture, or even specific moments from the plays – the 'painters draw on the tragedy but do not adhere to it' (27) – depictions of scenes from the comedies are much more theatrical. The characters are often framed by stage platforms, most commonly with a short flight of stairs up to them. As well as large prop elements such as altars, trees and chairs, there are religious or mythological props such as a herm (a stone post bearing a sculpted head, usually of Hermes, used as a boundary marker) or the egg from which Helen of Troy (daughter of Zeus and the swan, Leda) hatched. In addition,

> there are portable objects in profusion: containers of every material, musical instruments, food, ladders, writing tablets, baggage, etc. Indeed the clutter and variety and entertaining unpredictability of all these props is highly characteristic of comedy, at least of Aristophanic comedy.
>
> (Taplin 1993: 36)

Taplin discusses two vases (now in separate museums in New York and Boston) that depict scenes from the same drama. The picture is defined as set in a theatre by the comic mask hanging above, and the ornate stage-doors to the right. On stage, there are three figures: one 'wears the mask of an old woman, the other two have male masks and are unclothed except for a body-stocking, with conspicuous body-padding and an outsize pendant phallus'. The props are a dead goose and a basket containing one or two young goats. Taplin describes the gestural language:

> The old woman stretches out her hand; the younger, unbearded man has a hand nonchalantly on his hip and holds his rod in a way that looks threatening. And,

strangest, the central old man stands on tip-toe with his hands above his head. The scene sets puzzles which the uninformed viewer cannot unscramble.

(Taplin 1993: 30–31)

Words issue from the characters' mouths, like speech bubbles. The old woman says, 'I shall hand…over'; the old man says something that appears to mean 'he [or she] has bound my hands above me'. No rope is shown – so perhaps the old woman has cast a spell on him. Taplin concludes that the words of dialogue make this image 'as scene-specific as it could possibly be – it is something close to a snapshot of a moment in the theatre' (31).

He then turns to a vase painted about 30 years later that shows the same two male figures, along with the same props:

> The same old man, the same ugly young man with the rod, and above all the baskets with the two kids and the goose, all put it beyond doubt that this is another scene from the same play. The differences are that there is a herm with a cloak (the old man's tunic?) and an aryballos [a flask for oil or perfume] on it, and that the old man far from being tied up is pouring some oil on his palm.

There are no speech bubbles, but since the goose is shown as alive in this scene, it probably comes before the scene with the old woman: 'the demise of the goose may have been a significant event in the plot' (32). From such small fragments of material culture, the knowledge of props and how they were used in the ancient world is built up.

A number of projects have explored how knowledge about stage properties might influence contemporary performances of the classics and ideas about their meaning. A fascinating exchange between material culture, text and performance can be found in the 'Masks for Menander' project. Speculating that a set of miniature terracotta masks held at the Kelvingrove Museum in Glasgow might have been made as a way of recording the design, proportions and features of performance masks so that new sets could be made in situ by theatres on the periphery of the empire, Chris Vervain and Richard Williams commissioned full-size masks from the models and explored their performance potential (see Williams and Vervain 1999).

MEDIEVAL MYSTERY PLAYS IN ENGLAND

The first records of the York Mystery Play date from 1376, and there are similar plays recorded in Chester, Towneley, Coventry, Newcastle and Norwich. The mystery plays tell the story of mankind from Creation to the Last Judgement and are divided into 'pageants' each performed by a different craft guild. They were performed on wagons, either moving around the city and stopping at various 'stations', or arranged around the perimeter of a playing area, to be animated in sequence. Extant guild records provide astonishing detail of the routes, rehearsals, props and costumes and the costs of purchase, the actors' names and the wages they were paid. They also suggest an important relationship between commerce and performance in this period.

Sybil Rosenfeld characterises the medieval staging of the miracle plays and moralities as resembling the pictorial art of the time, the illustrated manuscripts and church carvings. The resemblance lies not just in the use of iconographical symbols, but in the simultaneity of presentation, in which several episodes can appear in a single composition. Later, in the Elizabethan theatre, Rosenfeld notes, scenes were played on an open stage with 'only a few properties, brought in or discovered as needed and then removed or concealed. Simultaneity had been replaced by succession' (Rosenfeld 1973: xvi–xvii).

In the medieval period, there was an obvious continuity between the everyday material world of the spectators and of the drama. The playing space might be a square used for the weekly market. The performers were artisans in daily life and the episodes they were assigned to perform typically had a relationship to their ordinary labour. Jonathan Gil Harris describes how 'guilds associated with sailing, the sea, or water would commonly be assigned the story of Noah, Goldsmiths the episode of the Magi, and Bakers the Last Supper pageants' (Harris 2002: 42). Props might belong to the town and be lent to the guilds to glorify the town, or demonstrate the craftsmen's skills:

> Any prop in the Corpus Christi cycle plays potentially had the status of a visual pun, functioning as a multivalent metonymy for a cluster of distinct but interrelated corporate structures. The bread of the Bakers' Last Supper pageants, for example, was at one and the same time the contemporary product of skilled labor by English artisans, the historical food shared by Christ with his disciples, and the eternal sacrament of the Eucharist; it thus materialized the Bakers' triple property in their mystery of baking, in sacred history, and in the body of Christ. When the Bakers of Chester flung their loaves into the audience at the end of their play, these three properties were supplemented by a fourth that was already implicit in the other Last Supper episodes: with what amounted to a secular recoding of the Eucharist – sharing their bread in communal solidarity with their fellow townspeople – the Chester Bakers asserted their guild's property of membership within the corporate body of their town.
>
> (Harris 2002: 43–4)

The promenade model still provides a flexible structure for performances that bring together carefully wrought performance and an everyday, commercial setting. The scenographer Pamela Howard describes how in the development of *Border Warfare* (1989), an epic history play depicting the warfare between England and Scotland from 1200 to the present day, the writing and design evolved simultaneously. Both Howard and the writer and director John McGrath responded to the possibilities of a cavernous abandoned tramshed in Glasgow, drawing on contemporary popular culture – the football match – as well as the pageant wagon tradition:

John had written the last act as an allegorical football match with Scotland at one end and England at the other. The two ends of the stadium would be united by a carpet of artificial grass with a single white line painted across the middle as on a football pitch.

(Howard 2009: 46)

Each scene shaped the space differently, with the audience being moved between theatre-in-the-round, traverse and end-on configurations with the help of four moving stages pushed by stage management. Characters journeyed between Scotland and England on 'sawhorses mounted on wheels with realistic papier mâché horses' heads'. In the final act, the full length of the theatre was open and the audience was moved to the sides, 'revealing for the first time the metaphor of the football pitch'. Howard comments that the large space of the Tramway 'became the signal for the text's invention. The need to keep the story moving through time meant that the text had to present events' (ibid.).

The contemporary revival of the mystery plays in York is discussed from various points of view in the collection edited by Margaret Rogerson (2011), and there are also festivals drawing on the mystery tradition in Coventry and Chester. Many other examples of performance with a similar relationship to locality and commerce can be found in community performance. In *Catford Tales* (2015), a promenade performance devised by Lewisham Youth Theatre and based on oral history interviews with local residents, scenes took place in half a dozen locations around the town centre. Temporary platforms were set up in a nearby shopping centre. In a small Vietnamese restaurant, audience members were invited to eat small portions of food while 'eavesdropping' on other customers. In another scene set in a cafe, props relating to work were used to signal a shift in time: objects such as a manual typewriter prompted recollections of working life in the 1960s. This peripatetic performance, incorporating local businesses and their goods, showed the continuing dynamism of the medieval promenade structure.

EARLY MODERN DRAMA AND SHAKESPEARE

In the meantime I will draw a *bill of properties* such as our play wants.
(*A Midsummer Night's Dream* 1. ii. 94)

The craftsmen-actors in *A Midsummer Night's Dream* are worried that their audience will fail to recognise characters or settings without signifying objects. As Frances Teague puts it, 'The properties fascinate these bad actors [...] Bottom worries about drawing his sword, Snout about the lion's costume, and Quince about the moon and wall' (Teague 1991: 57). The worries of the literal-minded performers are all-too recognisable for contemporary theatre-makers: will the prop function in performance as intended? Will the audience pick up a verbal or visual hint or is a more explicit signpost needed?

For all their naiveté, the players draw on a language of objects that was widely shared, found in proverbs and emblem books as well as in mystery plays and masques. Peter Quince responds to Bottom's suggestion that real moonlight falling through an open window might be used to indicate the moon by referring to the moon's traditional attributes: 'one must come in with a bush of *thorns* and a *lantern*, and say he comes to disfigure, or to present, the person of Moonshine'. A diary account of the 1601 'devices' at Whitehall notes 'the man in the moon with thorns on his back'; and a seal of Edward II shows 'the crescent moon surrounding a man bearing, on a stick over his shoulder, a bundle of thorns; he is accompanied by a dog' (Oxford 1998: 180).

When the play is finally presented to the noble audience, Hippolyta judges it 'the silliest stuff that ever I heard'. Theseus responds with generosity, pointing out the role of imagination in filling out the inevitably incomplete theatrical illusion, 'The best in this kind are but shadows, and the worst are no worse if imagination amend them'. Romantic writers, including Coleridge, who idealised a theatre of the imagination that would not be cluttered by solid material objects, turned to *Henry V* as a model of a theatre of bare boards and words. In the prologue, the Chorus invites the audience members to fill out the 'unworthy scaffold' – the wooden stage – with their imaginations so that they become 'the vasty fields of France'. The Prologue is quoted below in full:

O for a Muse of fire, that would ascend
The brightest heaven of invention,
A kingdom for a stage, princes to act
And monarchs to behold the swelling scene!
Then should the warlike Harry, like himself,
Assume the port of Mars; and at his heels,
Leash'd in like hounds, should famine, sword and fire
Crouch for employment. But pardon, and gentles all,
The flat unraised spirits that have dared
On this unworthy scaffold to bring forth
So great an object: can this cockpit hold
The vasty fields of France? or may we cram
Within this wooden O the very casques
That did affright the air at Agincourt?
O, pardon! since a crooked figure may
Attest in little place a million;
And let us, ciphers to this great accompt,
On your imaginary forces work.
Suppose within the girdle of these walls
Are now confined two mighty monarchies,
Whose high upreared and abutting fronts
The perilous narrow ocean parts asunder:
Piece out our imperfections with your thoughts;
Into a thousand parts divide one man,
And make imaginary puissance;

Think when we talk of horses, that you see them
Printing their proud hoofs i' the receiving earth;
For 'tis your thoughts that now must deck our kings,
Carry them here and there; jumping o'er times,
Turning the accomplishment of many years
Into an hour-glass: for the which supply,
Admit me Chorus to this history;
Who prologue-like your humble patience pray,
Gently to hear, kindly to judge, our play.

The speech has a knowing, self-deprecating quality which is complicit with the audience. It suggests that a spectator might be quite used to recognising a soldier by his accoutrements (a 'casque' or helmet): the task now is to multiply a few 'ciphers' into a vast spectacle (a 'thousand' on 'vasty fields'). Rightly celebrated as an evocation of the power of the audience's imagination, the speech cannot be taken as evidence that the Shakespearean stage was bare of props.

What, then, did a sixteenth-century theatre company have in the props store? Material culture studies draw not only on performance documentation but also on contemporary accounts of an explosion of consumer goods, both imported and domestic. Jonathan Gil Harris and Natasha Korda list some of the evidence available: eyewitness accounts of contemporary theatergoers, play-scripts, inventories of costumes and properties, 'and even the writings of anti-theatricalist Puritan divines' (Harris and Korda 2002: 3). They refer back to *Henry V* and

> a pronounced tendency to valorize the Shakespearean stage as a simple 'wooden O' appealing to its audience's minds rather than their senses, or to their ears rather than their eyes. Many primers on Shakespeare, for example, routinely inform their readers that his contemporaries went to *hear* rather than *see* plays – the implication being that public theatergoers were thoughtful auditors, not mindless spectators.
>
> (ibid.)

To counter this view, they note how often spectators of Shakespeare's plays mention props:

> Samuel Rowlands, for example, was struck by Richard Burbage's constant caress of his stage-dagger in performances of *Richard III*. [...] Simon Forman's attention was captured by numerous stage properties, including a chair in *Macbeth*, the bracelet and chest of *Cymbeline*, and Autolycus's 'pedlers packe' in *The Winter's Tale*.
>
> (ibid.)

As well as performances in dedicated theatres, this period was rich in masques and street performances. The list of properties for a street performance devised by playwrights Ben Jonson and Thomas Dekker for the entry into London of James I in 1604 includes animals made of wire and canvas, human figures cut out of wood and mounted on trolleys to be pulled across the floor, and 'mountains, forests, beasts, serpents and artificial plants and flowers' (Rosenfeld 1973: 6).

Ben Jonson later collaborated with the architect and stage designer Inigo Jones on lavish court entertainments. However, the 25-year collaboration came to an end when Jonson designated himself the primary 'inventor' on the published text of the masque *Love's Triumph Through Callipolis* (1631). As Nicholas Till explains, the designs by Inigo Jones had become increasingly significant in relation to the text of the masques: the printed text is largely given over to descriptions of Jones's scenery and costumes with only 180 lines of speech. Jones felt slighted by Jonson's decision to give the designer second billing. The resulting argument led to Jonson writing a poetic attack on Inigo Jones as a social climber whose clothes and accessories were no more substantial than props and costumes:

> Your Trappings will not change you. Change your mynd
> Noe velvet Sheath you weare, will altor kyndc.
> A wodden Dagger, is a Dagger of Wood
> Though gold or Ivory haftes would make it good.

> (quoted in Till 2010: 154)

If Inigo Jones preferred to shape his masques without a poet ('What need of prose/Or Verses, or Sence t'express Immortall you!') then he would have to rely on the spectators' understanding and their ability to interpret iconography, to rely on 'eyes' that could 'pierce into the Misteryes' of colours and mythological imagery:

> Oh, to make Boardes to speake! There is a taske.
> Painting and Carpentry are the Soule of Masque!
> Pack with your peddling Poetry to the Stage!
> This is the money-gett, Mechanick Age!

As Till points out, Jonson's attack was articulated 'at just the moment in which the English theatre was making its transition from the open poetic stage of Shakespeare and Jonson himself to the pictorial stage of the Italian theatre, which Jones himself had introduced to England after visits to Italy' (155). The taste for rich spectacle and material goods reflected the world of commodities outside the theatre. Stow's *Survey of London* reports on Londoners' extravagant spending in shops that 'made a very gay Shew, by the various foreign Commodities they were furnished with'. In about 1580, the wares included:

> Gloves made in *France* or *Spain*, Kersies of *Flanders* Dye, *French* cloth or Frizado, Owches; Brooches, Agglets made in *Venice* or *Milan*, Daggers, Swords, Knives, Girdles of the *Spanish* Make, Spurs made at *Milan*, *French* or *Milan* caps, Glasses, painted Cruses, Dials, Tables, Cards, Balls, Puppets, Penners, Inkhorns, Toothpicks, Silk-Bottoms and Silver-Bottoms, fine earthen Pots, Pins and Points, Hawks-Bells, Saltcellars, Spoons, Dishes of Tin.

Stow describes passers-by as so attracted by the 'knickknacks' on display that they could not stop themselves from buying them, 'though to no Purpose necessary' (Stow 1598).

Harris and Korda look at contemporary stage directions to argue that – like these consumer items – the objects of the early modern stage were often lavish and dazzling, intended 'not merely to catch, but to overwhelm the eye by means of their real or apparent costliness, motion, and capacity to surprise' (4). The list of props includes a sea-horse to be ridden by Neptune, a Trojan Horse and a flying, flaming bed.

Douglas Bruster draws on a list compiled by Frances Teague of the props mentioned in Shakespeare's plays to suggest that the playwright was more prolific in material culture than is usually remembered:

> How many hand props appeared in Shakespeare's plays? Teague counts the props in the thirty-six Folio plays, and in *Pericles*. She records them on their first appearance only, and omits references to costumes, unless they come to function as a property – such as, for example, Osric's hat, and Troilus's sleeve. Teague's figures suggest an average of thirty-four properties per play. What these numbers show at once is that Shakespeare's plays used more props than actors.
>
> (Bruster 2002: 78)

Bruster argues that Shakespeare's use of hand props changed over his career: 'plays written at the beginning of his career have more props than plays written between 1598 and 1604; plays written after 1604 – most probably under the influence of Jacobean taste for spectacle – resume the pattern established early in his career' (Bruster 2002: 90). He suggests that as Shakespeare draws attention to a particular object (a skull, a handkerchief) in plays such as *Hamlet* or *Othello*, he reduces the total number of props available for contemplation by the audience, and that this trend is found among other playwrights of the seventeenth century. But by the late seventeenth century, there is evidence that not everyone was dazzled by material objects on stage: 'So much ado, so much stress, so much passion and repetition about an Handkerchief! Why was not this call'd the *Tragedy of the Handkerchief*? What can be more absurd…?' Thomas Rymer's scornful comments on *Othello* (quoted in Harris and Korda 2002: 8) recall Aristophanes' mockery of Euripedes, several centuries earlier, for the same sin of relying too heavily on props.

Similarly, in a pamphlet of 1582, the anti-theatrical writer Stephen Gosson questioned the value of contemporary plays that relied on recognition tokens:

> Sometime you shall see nothing but the aduentures of an amorous knight, passing from countrie to countrie for the loue of his lady, encountring many a terrible monster made of broune paper, & at his retorne, is so wonderfully changed, that he can not be knowne but by some posie in his tablet, or by a broken ring, or a handkircher, or a piece of cockle shell, what learne you by that?
>
> (quoted in Kolb 2011: 50)

A catalogue of British Renaissance drama edited by Martin Wiggins lists plays, both lost and extant, alongside more fragmentary scenarios, giving details of the characters and likely doubling, and notes on staging, music and props required. Props may be inferred from stage directions, from references in the dialogue (although caution has to be taken with metaphorical references) or staging necessity ('if a character is directed to stab himself he must have some kind of blade weapon, even if there is no explicit mention of it in the spoken or written text' (Wiggins 2012: xxxiv)). Scenarios provide intriguing clues to drama that can only be imagined today. For example, an episode in the manuscript entitled 'The plotte of the deade mans fortune' (1591) describes how Algerius and Tesephon are brought in for execution. King Egerion and the prisoners enter with the executioner, who brings his sword and block, accompanied by officers of the law carrying halberds. Then, to the accompaniment of music, three 'antic fairies' enter dancing: 'the first takes the sword from the executioner and sends him away, the other carries away the block and the third sends away the officers and unbinds the prisoners.' The play ends when the character Pantaloon causes a trunk or chest to be brought forth. What it contains, we'll never know, but it probably relates to the fortune of the title.

Eye-witness accounts of performance are also used and, as in the medieval period, account books represent a valuable source of information about raw materials, costumes and props used in performance. A 'Mariner's Masque', for example, required full body suits made of wicker, linen cloth and scales of gold, silver, red and green paper, as well as hoods, visors, horsehair and dog chains (Wiggins 2012: 121).

From 1559, all players had to be licensed, according to a proclamation by Elizabeth I. Companies were formed under the patronage of noblemen; one of these was known as the Admiral's Men, after Charles Howard, the Lord High Admiral. The company is particularly linked to performances of plays by Christopher Marlowe, and also staged the first performances of Shakespeare's *Richard III*. From 1594 it was managed by Philip Henslowe. An inventory of the company's playscripts, costumes and props was published in a 1790 edition of Shakespeare's plays edited by Edmund Malone. Malone explains how he came across the list:

> Just as this work was issuing from the press, some curious Manuscripts relative to the stage, were found at Dulwich College, and obligingly transmitted to me from thence. One of these is a large folio volume of accounts kept by Mr. Philip Henslowe, who appears to have been proprietor of the Rose Theatre near the Bankside in Southwark. [...] In a bundle of loose papers has also been found an exact Inventory of the Wardrobe, playbooks, properties &c, belonging to my lord Admiral's servants.
>
> (Malone 1790: 288)

Malone goes on to comment that the 'curious paper furnishes us with more accurate knowledge of the properties, &c. of a theatre in Shakespeare's time, than the researches of the most industrious antiquary could have attained' (300).

The inventory of the properties includes props relating to specific characters and scenes. Some of these are familiar names (such as Faustus); others, while familiar from mythology, cannot be easily identified with extant plays (such as Iris). Some objects fit into familiar categories: weapons, attributes of royalty (a sceptre, a crown) or of gods (Cupid's bow, Neptune's trident, Mercury's wings), while scenic elements such as a 'hell mouth' suggest that the medieval tradition 'lingered on' as Sibyl Rosenfeld has argued. In many cases, the plays for which these props were required have not survived, and we can only speculate what the props looked like and how they were used. Malone suggests that the 'cloth of the Sun and the Moon' was a painted backcloth (commenting, very much from the standpoint of 1790, that this was 'undoubtedly the *ne plus ultra* of those days. To exhibit a sun or moon, the art of perspective was not necessary'), but it's also possible to imagine a wearable or portable cloth (perhaps carried like a standard on a pole) that could be reversed to indicate the change from day to night:

The Enventary tacken of all the properties for my Lord Admeralles men, *the* 10 *of Marche* 1598.
Item, j rocke, j cage, j tombe, j Hell mought. [Hellmouth]
Item, j tome of Guido, j tome of Dido, j bedsteade.
Item, viij lances, j payer of stayers for Fayeton.
Item, ij stepells, & j chyme of belles, & j beacon.
Item, j hecfor for the playe of Faeton, the limes dead.
Item, j globe, & j golden scepter, iij clobes [clubs].
Item, ij marchepanes, & the sittie of Rome.
Item, j gowlden fleece; ij rackets; j baye tree.
Item, j wooden hatchett; j lether hatchete.
Item, j wooden canepie; owld Mahemetes head
Item, j lyone skin; j beares skyne, & Faetones lymes, & Faeton charete; & Argosse [Argus's] heade.
Item, Nepun [Neptune's] forcke & garland.
Item, j crosers stafe; Kentes woden leage [leg].
Item, Ierosses [Iris's] head, & raynbowe; j littell alter.
Item, viij viserdes; Tamberlyne brydell; j wooden matook.
Item, Cupedes bowe, & quiver, the clothe of the Sone & Mone.
Item, j bores heade & Serberosse [Cerberus] iij heades.
Item, j Cadeseus; ij mose [moss] banckes, & j snake.
Item, ik fanes of feather; Belendon stable; j tree of gowlden apelles; Tantelouse tre; jx eyorn [iron] targates.
Item, j copper targate, & xvij foyles.
Item, iiij wooden targates; j greve armer.
Item, j syne [sign] for Mother Readcap; j buckler.
Item, Mercures wings; Tasso picter; j helmet with a dragon; j shelde, with iij lyones; j elme bowle.
Item, j chayne of dragons; j gylte speare.

Item, ij coffenes; j bulles head; and j vylter.
Item, iij tymbrells, j dragon in fostes [Faustus].
Item, j lyone; ij lyon heades; j great horse with his leages [legs]; j sack-bute.
Item, j whell & frame in the Sege of London.
Item, j paire of rowghte gloves.
Item, j poopes miter.
Item, iij Imperial crownes; j playne crowne.
Item, I gostes crown; j crown with a sone.
Item, j frame for the heading in Black Jone.
Item, j black dogge.
Item, j caudern for the Jewe.
        (Malone 1790: 302–3) Interpolations in brackets are in the original source

A version of this inventory in modern spelling might look something like this (with my annotations in square brackets):

-   1 rock, 1 cage, 1 tomb, 1 'Mouth of Hell'.
-   Guido's tomb, Dido's tomb, one bedstead.
-   8 lances; set of steps for Phaeton.
-   2 steeples, a set of bells, a beacon.
-   1 hecfor for the play of Phaeton, the dead limbs [Peter Thomson suggests *hecfor* is perhaps *heifer* (Thomson 1992: 186); presumably the 'dead limbs' represent Phaeton's broken body, to be shown after his fatal fall from the heavens].
-   globe, golden sceptre, clubs.
-   2 highly decorated cakes of moulded marzipan, the city of Rome.
-   1 golden fleece; 2 rackets; 1 bay tree.
-   1 wooden hatchet; 1 leather hatchet.
-   1 wooden canopy; head of Mohammed as an old man [or elaborate head-dress].
-   1 lion skin; 1 bearskin; Phaeton's limbs and chariot; Argus's head.
-   Neptune's trident and garland for his head.
-   1 bishop's staff or crozier; Kent's wooden leg [perhaps for the eponymous hero of the play *John a Kent*, or for the leg-pulling episode in Marlowe's *Dr Faustus*].
-   Iris's head and rainbow; a little altar.
-   8 masks; Tamburlaine's bridle; a wooden mattock [In Marlowe's *Tamburlaine the Great*, the hero forces a bridle into the mouth of a conquered king].
-   Cupid's bow and quiver of arrows; the cloth of the Sun and Moon.
-   a boar's head and Cerberus's 3 heads.
-   a Caduceus [the staff carried by Hermes – a winged staff with two snakes wound around it]; 2 moss banks, 1 snake.
-   feather fans; Belendon stable [possibly relating to a play of that title, now lost]; a tree of golden apples; Tantalus's tree [as an eternal punishment, Tantalus was made to stand under a tree with fruit hanging from it, just out of reach]; 9 iron targets.

- 1 copper target, and 17 foils [for fencing].
- 4 wooden shields; 1 greave armour [greaves originally covered just the shins; later also the upper part of the leg].
- 1 sign for Mother Redcap [*Mother Redcap* is possibly another lost play, but it is also a traditional pub name, so this item could be a tavern sign]; 1 buckler [a small shield gripped in the fist].
- Mercury's wings; 1 picture of Tasso; 1 helmet with a dragon; 1 shield showing 3 lions; 1 elmwood bowl.
- 1 chain for a dragon; 1 gilt spear.
- 2 coffins; 1 bull's head; and 1 vylter [Peter Thomson suggests *vylter* is a *vulture* or *philtre*, a love potion (Thomson 1992: 175)].
- 3 tumbrils [two-wheeled carts], 1 dragon for *Dr Faustus*.
- 1 lion; 2 lion's heads; 1 large horse with his legs [perhaps the Greeks' wooden horse for the play *Troy*]; 1 sackbut [Renaissance trombone].
- 1 wheel and frame for use in the Siege of London.
- 1 pair of embroidered gloves.
- 1 pope's mitre.
- 3 Imperial crowns; 1 plain crown.
- 1 ghost's crown; 1 crown with a sun.
- 1 frame for the heading in *Black Joan* [another lost play; the scenery possibly for a beheading or a set of stocks or pillory, or a title board].
- 1 black dog.
- 1 cauldron for the Jew [in Marlowe's *The Jew of Malta*, probably written 1589 or 1590, Barabas dies in a cauldron he had prepared for another].

GEORGIAN SPECTACLES

Sibyl Rosenfeld gives a vivid picture of the elaborate effects of the period in her account of the first performance of Handel's opera *Rinaldo* (1711):

Among the scenic effects were a chariot drawn by dragons emitting fire and smoke; a grove with flying birds; a black cloud descending filled with spitfire monsters; a calm sea with mermaids dancing in the water and a boat sailing out of sight; steep mountains rising from the front of the stage to the utmost height of the most backward part with rocks, caves and waterfalls, and the blazing battlements of an enchanted palace.

(Rosenfeld 1973: 65–6)

A contemporary reviewer writing in *The Spectator* [6 March 1711] was disparaging about the design. Allowing that an opera could be 'extravagantly lavish in its Decorations', the author warns against anything 'which may appear Childish and Absurd' as a result of mixing painted scenery and real things – such as a real waterfalls in painted landscapes or real boat 'upon a

Sea of Pasteboard': 'Shadows and Realities ought not to be mix'd together in the same Piece' (quoted in Rosenfeld, ibid.).

The actor, director and theatre manager John Rich (1692–1761) produced John Gay's *The Beggar's Opera* in 1728. Its runaway success allowed him to open the Theatre Royal, Covent Garden (on the site of what is today the Royal Opera House). Rich specialised in spectacle; Alexander Pope satirised him as surrounded by stage effects in the *Dunciad:*

> Immortal Rich! how calm he sits at ease
> Mid snows of paper, and fierce hail of pease;
> And proud his mistress' orders to perform,
> Rides in the whirlwind, and directs the storm.

(III l. 257–60)

In 1744 an inventory was taken of the costumes, scenery and props at the Theatre Royal in order to secure a loan. Ana Martínez describes the document:

> The Covent Garden inventory is long and chaotic, and its only internal logic is the grouping of items by the location where they were stored or found when the inventory was made. The cataloguer simply recorded the items as he encountered them in the different backstage and stage locations.

(Martínez 2011: 225)

By taking a walk – in her imagination – through the Theatre Royal with this inventory in hand, Ana Martínez gives a vivid sense of production realities of the time. She divides the items into four categories: those that clearly belong to particular plays ('the cauldron in Macbeth'); those that are not assignable to specific productions but have a character name or similar; stock items such as 'town'; and technical devices, such as a ra-ree-show (a portable box with a puppet show) (226). In the yard, there is a copper for laundry, and large scenic pieces such as 'the falling rock in Handel's Alcina four pieces' and 'the great traveling machine made for Orpheus', as well as 'miscellany such as music stands, steps for the stage, carpenters' benches, and lamppost' (227). Under the roof, she finds the flying equipment, including wires, ropes, wheels and rollers. The carpenter's shop contains furniture, tools and 'a large model of the stage not finished', suggesting an unfinished conversation between the artisans involved in building, painting and lighting the set.

There were at least four trap doors in the stage floor, one identified as 'the grave trap'. Given that stage conventions took a long time to change, Martínez brings in 'evidence from bills for properties at Drury Lane in 1714 and 1716, which show that fresh earth ("Garden Mould") was used for Ophelia's grave in *Hamlet*' (233). Another trap was used to produce the character 'Hob' from a well in a comic opera. A contemporary image shows 'the well in the background and drenched Hob and his parents in the foreground'. One of the trap doors was described as 'the egg trap'. John Rich had a famous act as part of *The Birth and Adventures of Harlequin* in which he emerged from a large egg. It was, says Martínez, regarded by his contemporaries as 'one of his most captivating specialties' (233). The manager of the Theatre Royal, Edinburgh describes Rich's performance thus:

> From the first chipping of the egg, his receiving motion, his feeling the ground, his standing upright, to his quick *Harlequin* trip round the empty shell, through the whole progression, every limb had its tongue, and every motion a voice, which spoke with most miraculous organ, to the understandings and sensations of the observers.
>
> (Martínez 2011: 234)

In a Hogarth print of Rich's triumphant entry to Covent Garden, she identifies a wagon carrying Rich's theatrical properties, including 'A Box of Thunder and Lightning': 'From the analysis of the inventory, we now know that it used eighty-six thunder balls to create the storm and thunder effects that mid-eighteenth-century audiences once experienced at Covent Garden' (236). Martínez's work suggests the sheer variety of sources – visual, textual, even legal – that can be used to piece together the history of props in performance.

FUTURIST PLAYGROUNDS

In pantomime and farce, collapsing furniture, buckets of 'slop' and custard pies reveal the performer's vulnerable body in the way that Bergson described in *Laughter*: anxiety about the body leads to the intrusion of a comic element. It is the performers' elastic recovery, unharmed, that allows spectators to laugh. As we have seen in Chapter 2, Meyerhold and Vakhtangov were fascinated by circus tricks, and acts of dexterity and skill. In the 1920s, Meyerhold, together with the painters Liubov Popova and Varvara Stepanova, made theatrical use of these comic traditions.

Stepanova's design for *The Death of Tarelkin*, directed by Meyerhold (1922) was made up of abstract 'machines' in the form of everyday objects such as a table, chair and stool. However, these objects came to life and transformed themselves in unexpected ways: 'one table rolled around loudly on its legs, another turned into a bed or a coffin, chair backs collapsed at strategic moments, stools turned – one even shooting blanks at the same time' (Kolesnikov 1991: 92–3). The aesthetics of the piece recalled Russian outdoor theatre traditions, such as the puppet show and folk performance. Coloured balls floated through the theatre – a feature of *Slava's Snow Show*, a contemporary clown show directed by the Russian clown Slava Polunin which has toured internationally. During the intervals, gigantic fake apples were thrown from the balcony, for the audience to try to catch.

Meyerhold's production of *The Magnaminous Cuckold* (1922) was designed by Liubov Popova, with a set that was like a playground with beams, rotating wheels to signify machinery and a windmill. Jindřich Honzl wrote of Popova's design, 'We cannot tell what a contraption on stage is supposed to signify until it is used by an actor'. The structures were indeterminate in shape and colour, and became signs 'only when used for the actor's actions' (Honzl 1976: 78–9).

As for the hand props, some objects were enlarged and others were mimed. According to Jonathan Pitches:

> As part of Futurism's assault on Naturalism, objects needed to be liberated from their role as quotidian adornment of the stage and set in conscious, dynamic interplay with their surroundings. At the same time, their denotative, first level meanings were to be destabilized and allowed instead to embrace a wide range of readings.
>
> (Pitches 2007: 98)

Pitches suggests that it was not so much the design as the manner in which the objects were manipulated that liberated them from everyday use, tracing this back to the biomechanical training methods Meyerhold's actors had pursued. Nevertheless, the combination of indeterminate setting and transformed objects in these designs was to prove very influential on later designers.

BRECHT AND DESIGNERS

In Brecht's search for alternatives to the dominance of realism, he drew eclectically on older forms such as medieval theatre, Shakespeare and street performance. A medieval influence can be seen in *Mother Courage*, set during the Thirty Years' War (1618–1648), both in the episodic structure of the play, and in Theo Otto's design, which puts a wagon – hung with all kinds of objects that might be needed – at the centre of the bare stage.

The introduction quoted Bert States' view that the frame of the stage makes any object into a work of art, an adaptation of Veltruský's assertion that 'all that is on stage is a sign': 'In the theater we are, technically, within the museum: all that is on stage is art' (States 1985: 39). This is an important insight, but not a complete account of the process of making an object 'work' as an art work. For the 'frame' of the proscenium arch or the television screen can equally enclose objects that inertly represent reality and so are themselves 'invisible' as part of a total effect – part of what Barthes calls the 'reality effect' (Barthes 1984). Moreover, it is not enough to seek out 'authentic' props, for a real object is not always 'large' or 'clear' enough to be distinguished from its background. To communicate the meanings embedded in material culture, to show history and social interactions through everyday objects, requires further work from designer and performer.

The prop-maker works, like an artist, with the material properties of objects, sometimes 'distressing' or adding decoration, so that even a newly made object can 'work' on the audience like an authentic object. Brecht praises the designer Caspar Neher for this skill:

> there is no building of his, no yard or workshop or garden, that does not also bear the fingerprints, as it were, of the people who built it or who lived there. He makes visible the manual skills and knowledge of the builders and the ways of living of the inhabitants.
>
> (Willett 1984: 139)

Thus what distinguishes the maker from the user who accidentally shapes an object, is the responsibility to 'make visible' the imagined use, so that it can work on the spectator. The actor has a parallel responsibility, not only to 'choose' the right things but to 'make visible' the object's meaning, the history embedded in it.

The responsibility of actor, designer and director to make meaning 'visible' seems to close the loop – the audience's phenomenological experience of the object is manipulated through crafting of the surrounding signs (including other elements of the set, the actor's gesture etc.). However, the objects chosen may not be fixed as signs with a conventional meaning. For example, the large leather pouch – suggestive of a money belt, ammunition holder and marsupial pouch all at once – that Weigel wore as Mother Courage seems to have no known historical source, and yet it is eloquent about Courage's attitude to money and motherhood.

In 1956, the Berliner Ensemble visited London with three plays by Brecht: *The Caucasian Chalk Circle*, *Trumpets and Drums* and *Mother Courage* (Eddershaw 1996: 50). The critic Kenneth Tynan wrote: 'I defy anyone to forget Brecht's stage pictures....The beauty of Brechtian settings is not the dazzling kind that begs for applause. It is the more durable beauty of *use*' (quoted in Eddershaw 1996: 51). Later that same year, the British premiere of *The Good Woman of Setzuan* was directed by George Devine at the Royal Court Theatre, London, which was also the venue for the first production of John Osborne's play *Look Back in Anger*.

While Brecht's episodic drama might seem an unlikely companion for the detailed realism of the 'kitchen sink drama', the designs for plays from both traditions showed the influence of the Berliner Ensemble's approach. Designer Jocelyn Herbert (1917–2003) had studied with Sophie Harris, Margaret Harris and Elizabeth Montgomery – known collectively as 'Motley' (see *Theatre Props* (1975)). She was engaged by George Devine in 1956 when the English Stage Company took over the Royal Court. She designed the first performances of plays by John Arden, Arnold Wesker, John Osborne and David Storey, as well as working closely with Samuel Beckett. Her work highlighted the intrinsic properties of objects and materials, displayed to the audience's view without illusionistic scenery and furniture. For example, her design for Arnold Wesker's play *The Kitchen* exposed the brick wall at the back of the Royal Court stage and the lighting rig. Pamela Howard has described the impact of seeing Herbert's designs for Arnold Wesker's *Chicken Soup with Barley* at the Belgrade Theatre, Coventry, in 1958. At the time, Howard was an assistant designer at the Birmingham Repertory Theatre. She was bowled over by Herbert's minimal evocation of the family home: 'she'd just put a washing line and three chairs on the stage, and we simply couldn't believe it...' (Wright 2009: 386).

In his book *1956 And All That* Dan Rebellato unpicks the received view that *Look Back in Anger* exploded into a moribund West End that offered little more than drawing room comedies: 'The metaphors which tend to describe this previous era are of the stage being "cluttered" or "swamped" by "unnecessary clobber"'(Rebellato 1999: 94). The account given by Herbert below does indeed reflect this metaphor, but suggests that this approach gave those objects that remained on stage greater significance. Rebellato is critical of the assumption that Royal Court designers were 'decisively influenced' by the work of Brecht, claiming that 'they did not share Brecht's own objective of showing the origin of objects in the social world of human activity' (ibid.. 98). Herbert gives a vivid sense of how this new approach would – at the very least – allow directors and spectators to read props critically:

> George Devine wanted to get away from swamping the stage with decorative and naturalistic scenery; to let in light and air; to take the stage away from the director and designer and restore it to the actor and the text. This meant leaving space around the actors, and that meant the minimum of scenery and props, i.e. only those that served the actors and the play: nothing that was for decorative purposes only, unless the text, or the style of the play, demanded it. So everything on the stage had to be even more carefully designed and made, as they would be so exposed on a comparatively bare stage, not supported by the trappings of the naturalistic set. This in turn made it imperative for designers to examine the materials they used. No longer would painted scenery (however brilliantly executed) stand such close-up scrutiny and such clear light. Props suddenly became very significant: every book, lamp, chair or table – possibly the only visual elements in a scene. What they looked like, what they were made of, where they were placed on the stage, all these became very important. Perhaps it was the beginning of what I call 'considering the actors as part of the design'; considering where the actors will be on the stage and what they will need as the basis of the design; not creating an elaborate picture and then sticking the actors in it.

Herbert recalls observing in the 1950s 'how little influence contemporary painting and sculpture had so far had on theatre design'. The influence of abstraction was not a matter of copying a fashionable style but 'an attitude of mind':

> the belief that photographic naturalism was not the only or the most evocative way of communicating a place or a time. There was also the growing conviction that the bare stage was a very beautiful space and, as with a bare canvas, the moment you put one subject on it – even just a chair – all sorts of things

happened. The actor could immediately use the space in so many different ways. It created distance, division of space, movement around, and so on; and the chair, of course, could become so many different things, according to how the actors used it.

(Herbert 1981: 83–5)

In 1956, when Herbert began to work at the Royal Court, there were no workshops: 'props and small items of scenery were made under the stage – or, when fine, out in the yard'. The theatre bought a workshop about a year later – 'a marvellous, rambling old place where we made and painted our own scenery and props, and where there was room for the costumes to be made as well'. Herbert notes that the workshops were given up by the end of the 1960s as it was felt that 'few new plays were done which demanded much in the way of scenery and costumes' and so the workshops were 'no longer financially viable'. While the shift in attitudes across this period gave props and materials increased attention, the plays performed at the Royal Court typically called for objects of the contemporary world: sourcing props became more important than making. Many city centre theatres have little or no workshop space; where a production calls for more elaborate set construction and prop-making, it is commissioned from independent construction companies. More research is needed on how the lack of in-house workshops might affect the decisions made by producers and designers about the scope of a production. Puppet companies, where construction of puppets and sets is central to the development of the performance, provide some exceptions to this trend. Horse and Bamboo, a company that formerly toured by horse-drawn cart, chose a rural setting when they established their permanent base, in order to have room for construction workshops and rehearsal rooms, and to offer residencies to companies that might want to build puppets as they develop a new performance. At the Little Angel Theatre in London, visitors to the theatre can peer into the workshop through a window onto the street. The National Theatre's recent extension also offers members of the public the opportunity to look into the construction workshop. The following chapter takes up the invitation to look into the prop workshop.

FURTHER READING

On props in Greek and Roman performance:

For a discussion of the complex role of props in Greek and Roman comedy and tragedy, see the very useful collection of essays edited by George W. M. Harrison and Vayos Liapis, *Performance in Greek and Roman Theatre* (2013). For a discussion of masks, and how modern theatre practitioners' experiments with masks can inform readings of classical texts, see Wiles (2004, 2007). *Agamemnon in Performance 458 BC to AD 2004* (2005), edited by Fiona Macintosh, Pantelis Michelakis, Edith Hall and Oliver Taplin includes essays on the performance of the play from the time of its writing to the twentieth century, in many different historical and geographical contexts, including the United States in the twentieth century, the Moscow Arts Theatre in the 1920s and Ariane Mnouchkine's 1990 production *Les Atrides*.

On early modern drama and Shakespeare:

The collection *Staged Properties in Early Modern English Drama* (Harris and Korda 2002) offers – among other things – an important introduction to materialist readings of properties, and essays on clothes, the bed in Shakespearean tragedy, and Othello's handkerchief. Clothes, which can serve as costume or as prop, and can move back and forth between the two functions in the course of a performance, are the focus of the essays in *Renaissance Clothing and the Materials of Memory* (Jones and Stallybrass 2001). See also *Subject and Object in Renaissance Culture* (1996). Andrew Sofer's *The Stage Life of Props* (2003) has chapters on the Renaissance handkerchief and the skull. Literary studies that consider props include Felix Bossonet, *The Function of Stage Properties in Christopher Marlowe's Plays* (1978), Alan C. Dessen, *Recovering Shakespeare's Theatrical Vocabulary* (1995) and Frances Teague, *Shakespeare's Speaking Properties* (1991). These tend to deal with the images that cluster around the object rather than the materiality of specific performances. *British Drama 1533–1642: A Catalogue*, edited by Martin Wiggins with Catherine Richardson, is an invaluable resource for information about the staging of plays in this period.

On baroque and Georgian drama:

For props in the baroque drama of the sixteenth and seventeenth centuries, see Walter Benjamin, *The Origins of German Tragic Drama* (1985). For the inventory of the Theatre Royal, see Philip H. Highfill, Jr., 'Rich's 1744 Inventory of Covent Garden Properties' *Restoration and Eighteenth Century Theatre Research* 5/1 (1966) 7–17.

On Brecht and Caspar Neher:

Christopher Baugh, 'Brecht and Stage Design: The *Bühnebildner and the Bühnenbauer'*, (2010); John Willett, *Caspar Neher: Brecht's Designer* (1986).

Chapter

6 Inside the Prop Workshop

The work of the stage management, design or props team may involve both finding and making objects for performance.[27] This chapter is mainly concerned with making, but the discussion of materials in the props workshop is preceded by a brief excursion to a nineteenth-century prop shop. Purchasing genuine items may be expensive but generally requires a smaller investment of time than making, particularly now that the internet provides a shortcut to some of the knowledge of sources that previously took years to acquire, the little black book of 'shops that specialize in brass beds, vintage firearms, juke boxes, stuffed animals, needlepoint, musical instruments' as Thurston James puts it (James 1987: xiii). Sourcing props may involve sponsorship in kind and loans from friendly businesses as well as hires from other theatre companies and specialist props suppliers.[28] Reproduction, in contrast, requires both time and technical expertise: the maker 'must be a seamstress, welder, carpenter, upholsterer, electrician, taxidermist, and chemist'. Weighing up the virtues of the two approaches, James concludes: 'It takes longer to build a gramophone than to buy one, but if labor is not a consideration, and if in the bargain you can pass along to someone the techniques of property construction, then the time is not so outrageously expensive' (ibid.). As the author of a technical handbook, Thurston James is naturally an advocate of making but there have always been those who were disposed 'to limit the labours of the property-maker, to dispense with his simulacra' and use 'the real thing' instead (Cook 1878).

Prop-making deploys techniques that make cheap materials look expensive and new materials look old – and so the craft has always been associated with illusion, reproduction and imitation. At times, cultural uneasiness about the dissimulation involved in acting has been echoed in a suspicion of prop-making and props. The second half of this chapter discusses how the notion of 'plasticity' has been expressed in two materials that have been very important in the props workshop – papier mâché and polymer plastics.

WHO DOES WHAT?

The way that props are gathered for performance varies enormously, depending on the size of venue, timescale, working methods and structure of the company. At one extreme, a stage manager might be entirely responsible for obtaining the items on a list garnered from the script before rehearsals begin; at the other extreme, actors and designers might be equally responsible for bringing objects into the rehearsal room, with no idea which ones will end up in the final performance.[29] An account of the process in a medium to large theatre company is given by Peter Maccoy:

> The designer is the main point of reference for the way props should look: stage management should work closely with the designer, consulting them regularly and involving them in all decisions. They should aim to build up a relationship of trust by putting forward suggestions regarding props that fit in with the designer's vision. This is where background research pays dividends; an engaged and informed stage manager can make a considerable creative contribution to the process of props finding, and [a] designer who trusts the stage manager's understanding of the design concept may give them a lot of leeway in making decisions about props.
>
> (Maccoy 2004: 209)

This extract reveals the interweaving of different types of knowledge – of human interactions, creativity and aesthetic awareness – involved in the work of supplying props, reminiscent of Hunt and Melrose's discussion of the 'mastercraftsperson'. Handbooks aimed at stage managers and props professionals tend to describe a context in which design, making and acting are separate activities. Eric Hart, for example, suggests that 'the director, stage manager, designer, and props master will develop the props list, with notes on the functions of every prop', though he goes on to acknowledge that this list 'will change as the production progresses, and even more so once rehearsals begin' (Hart 2013: 13). In this model of theatre practice, props are supplied for rehearsals as they are ready, perhaps as late in the process as the technical rehearsal.[30] It's not surprising that performers' opinions about the material reality on stage can be less than welcomed in this hierarchical and fast-paced structure: 'Even actors will start to chime in about what a prop needs to do' (ibid.). This separation of roles is typical of mainstream and commercial theatre but is far less common in devised and other types of performance. The extent to which performers are involved in the process of thinking about props varies; it depends far more upon the nature of the theatre company than on the particularities of the text. Even within one company, the practice can vary, depending on the scale of the production. While Simon McBurney feels that it 'is important that everything you wish to play with in the performance is present during the creative process, otherwise it's impossible to make it live when you get on to the stage', this has not always been possible with Complicite's larger shows: 'In a show with few objects and a simple design you have them in the rehearsal room from day one, but when you have more and larger elements such as in *Out of a House Walked a Man*, the convention is that you get them later in the process and inevitably they don't function as you thought they would' (Giannachi and Luckhurst 1999: 77).

A rigid division between departments of design, making and acting (whether in education or professional practice) can limit the opportunities to explore physical characteristics that exceed 'use value' or the 'mere outline' of the object. Here, Veltruský's concept of the spectrum of animation might serve as a practical tool for discussions between different members of a creative team. If a teapot, say, appears on a props list, members of the creative team might consider what position on the spectrum from inanimate to animate the teapot is to occupy during the performance. If it sits on a shelf throughout the performance, it might remain an inanimate part of the 'setting'. But even without being touched, it could be animated at a distance by verbal references, by longing glances or by a recurring motif in the sound design that evokes the pouring of tea. These choices will affect decisions about the characteristics of the teapot and how visible it needs to be. A teapot in a production of Oscar Wilde's *The Importance of Being Earnest* has the potential to become a performing object, part of a battle for supremacy that is carried on through food and drink. When Gwendolen refuses sugar, declaring that it is no longer fashionable, Cecily 'takes up the tongs' and drops four lumps into her opponent's cup. It is easy to imagine how a performer might use the teapot's weight, design and pouring speed as part of how she characterises Cecily. In a devised production, on the other hand, a metal catering teapot might be brought into rehearsals along with dozens of other objects. Occupying the animate end of the spectrum, it might serve as a percussion instrument, or be turned upside down to become a character, with its flapping lid a mouth – as in the improvised puppetry in the site-specific *Shopworks* by Theatre-Rites. Alternatively, the focus might be on the relationship between performer and object.

Even in a large theatre with separate departments of stage management, set construction, costume and properties, some areas of material reality have to be negotiated between departments. Small 'personal props' – items such as spectacles, walking sticks and fans – are likely to be sourced by the costume department. It is the responsibility of the actors to make sure they have any such items when they go on stage; off stage, they are looked after alongside costumes. However, 'hand props', those that are picked up and manipulated by actors during the performance – such as a coffeepot and cups or Yorick's skull – are looked after by stage management, often using cubbyholes or a table marked into labelled sections to keep track of numerous small items. Items which need to be renewed after every performance, such as food and drink, glasses that are broken in performance, explosives and blood capsules, are described as 'consumables' (see Chapter 7). 'Set props' may include furniture such as chairs and thrones, but depending on the design, these may equally be constructed by set-builders. 'Set dressing' includes moveable items such as books, carpets, ornaments. If it is decided in rehearsal that one of these items is in fact to be handled by an actor, it may need to be replaced or treated (to improve durability or to meet other performance requirements such as lightness – or simply because it is not finished on all sides). Objects used for set dressing can include 'practical props' such as radios, telephones, water taps and lamps that function and can be turned on and off by the actor; 'dummy' props are empty shells, sometimes containing speakers controlled from the sound board. 'Breakaway' props are designed to collapse or break easily into pieces during the performance.

PROP BUYING

The following extract from an article published in the *New York Times* of March 1878 gives a vivid account of a demands made of a theatrical supplier in the late nineteenth century. Eric Hart uncovered this article and other historical discussions of props and has made them available on his 'Prop Agenda' website.

A PLACE TO BUY THUNDER

She has thunder by the sheet, fog by the yard, lightning by the box, snow by the bushel, and the child who cries for the moon can get it there, if he will only wait until it is manufactured. It won't be made out of green cheese, either, but more likely from pale blue silk, for moons have been made out of that before now, and they were eminently satisfactory and couldn't have been told by any one but a connoisseur from the real article; and who is a connoisseur in moons?

And the mistress of all these natural elements is not a Mme. Jove, either, but a nice, ordinary, every day sort of woman, and this queer collection of hers is merely food for herself and her children. Not literally, for even a pretty, pale blue silk moon might be indigestible, but she provides them for 'the profession,' and indirectly they become oatmeal and coffee, roast beef and plum pudding.

It might be thought that the establishment where all these strange things are to be found would resemble those regions supposed to take a low position in the universe, and to be the home of all things unpleasant and flamable [sic], but it doesn't. It is a modest little place, not so far from Thirtieth Street, on the line of the elevated road and the proper business of the proprietor, when it is called by its right name, is that of dealer in theatrical hardware. The visitor would not even guess, in taking a view of the stock, that the word theatrical was appropriate, for nothing but small articles of seemingly ordinary hardware are in sight.

That is not strange, as there is never a demand for the same kind of thunder, lightning, or other theatrical appliances which are supplied on demand of the property man or the stage carpenter, and very little of anything is kept on hand, though they can be had at a moment's notice. The hardware proper is the most prosaic part of the business. That consists of the wheels, bolts, screws—everything that is needed to make the curtains and scenery of a theatre stay where they are wanted, and move when they are not wanted.

THE USES OF 'PROFILE'

Then the carpenter has a great desire for 'profile.' That is a technical term, and does not mean the profile of anything, though it might, but it consists of thin strips of board, four feet wide and ten feet long, not much more than an eighth of an inch in thickness, but tough and strong, so that it will bend and conform itself to all conditions without a break. Keystones and corners of the same serviceable material are things without which the carpenter cannot get along.

Profile is a valuable commodity. There is not much it cannot be used for. An ordinary individual who is not of the profession bought some of it for a cozy corner the other day, and a genuine Japanese *jinrikasha* used in a Japanese play now running, is made of profile. It may be thin, but it is strong, and it supports a young woman of very comfortable proportions for some time.

It is in ways like this that the ingenuity of the theatrical hardware dealer comes in. One word that she does not know is 'can't.' So when they brought her a miniature *jinrikasha* a few inches long and told her that a vehicle to match the sample was needed, she promised it immediately. Then, not she, but a clever son, went to work, and with the profile a nice little carriage that might have come straight from Japan was made, the wheels purchased, but the rest of the little carriage was made for the occasion, even to the upholstering.

[…]

A MUSICAL BROOM

There is no manufacturer for musical brooms, but the dealer in theatrical hardware can furnish one at short notice. It was just an ordinary broom that she furnished for a well known Broadway theatre, but before she had completed it was a regular music box. The entire inside of the broom was cut out, and in the opening left there was inserted a box which contained eighteen bells all carefully tuned. From these bells wires ran up the handle, connecting with push buttons at the top, and then passing up the arm of the sweeper on the stage was connected with a small electric battery that she wore concealed on her back. She played a pretty chime of bells as she swept, and no one knew how it was done.

The elements are not difficult. They belong to a regular stock. The fog is gauze, the lightning is made by magnesium, the snow of scraps of paper, and the thunder of sheet iron of varying weight, according to the depth of the thunder that is to be produced.

'I can furnish everything but rain,' says this mistress of the elements, 'and I guess I could furnish that if it was wanted.'

[…]

The demands of the stage are varied. There was a beef's bladder wanted for Falstaff the other day. None of the blown-up affairs that the peddlers sell would do, and two of the genuine were brought from a slaughterhouse.

'And it was fortunate that we had two,' says the ingenious gatherer of theatrical wares, 'for they burst one the very first night and had to have another.'

Money is one of the commodities that is kept in stock. And the poorest man on the stage never has less than $10 if he has a bill, for stage bills grow in that way. They are regular sized bills, upon which are the words 'stage money' in large letters upon both sides, an 'x' in each corner, and two larger 'x's,' one on either side of the centre. Coins are in gold, silver, and copper—those are the colors they wear—and they may amount to anything according to the supposed wealth of the possessor on the stage, and are coins of any nationality, according to the play, for they are all merely round bits of different kinds of metal that are not marked.

[...]

Something that I am sometimes called upon for, and which I should not have room to keep in stock if I wished to, is the straw that covers champagne bottles. That makes excellent thatched roofs for cottages. It is cut open and laid out in strips, and it is easy to work with.

(Hart 2011c)

A contemporary props team may need to buy furniture or small props from high street shops, look for antiques or broken down items in charity shops, thrift stores and auctions – including online; borrow items from members of the company, other theatres or friends; hire from specialist prop houses. Some of these items will then pass through the props workshop for repair or adaptation, such as dying or painting, wiring up antique lamps with modern fittings so that they can be used practically on stage, or hiding a modern speaker inside the cabinet of a gramophone so that it can be controlled from a distance by the sound operator.

MAKING PROPS: SUBSTITUTION, REPRODUCTION AND IMITATION

Whether purchased or made, props may need to be 'aged' (reproducing the scratches and grubbiness of normal wear and tear) or more heavily 'distressed' (suggesting damage caused by exposure to the weather, fire, water, gunshots etc.). A wooden bench might need to be 'weathered' with bleach and sandpaper, so that it looks as if it has spent seasons outside in rain and sun while remaining strong enough to stand up to use; a cupboard of cheap pine might need to be 'antiqued' with wood-stain and wax to create a patina suggesting years of careful maintenance. The techniques involved in making mass-produced objects look 'lived in' range from 'extreme physical distressing, such as making an upholstered chair look like it has been clawed by cats' to subtle shading that is 'virtually invisible to conscious observation' (Wulf 2000). Antiquing and distressing techniques depend on careful observation of how objects behave in use, looking at the points of wear on clothes or furniture, and at how linings and underlying structures are revealed over time.

The items created from scratch in the props workshop include historical objects that are unobtainable or too fragile to use; luxury items that would blow the budget; documents showing specific dates or characters' names, such as letters and newspapers; and fantastic gadgets for science-fiction. The contemporary prop-maker can draw on a huge range of construction techniques and materials, from carving wood to creating CAD drawings for a 3D printer.[31]

But why don't designers and prop directors simply use 'real' items where they are available? There are a number of considerations: as well as the

Giant props have long been a feature of advertising and shop window displays.
Berry Bros & Rudd, London, 2015. Photo: Eleanor Margolies.

cost of the material (for example, a real gold cigarette case); the labour cost (a table with an elaborate marquetry design); weight; strength and safety. Further, props need to be resilient and reliable. In the planning stage, a prop director will need to anticipate interactions that may not develop until late in the rehearsal process:

> When I am looking at what a static or simple prop needs to do, most of my thought processes focus on how it will be used. Props will be stood on, stepped on, sat on, thrown, dropped, ran into, and generally abused in ways even the director might not foresee. Generally, we find out what the actor is supposed to do with the prop, and extrapolate that to the worst possible scenario. If you are told the actor will stand on a table, assume they will jump on it. If you hear that a vase is supposed to be dropped, you can bet they will be throwing it to the ground with all their might. It is better to overbuild a prop once than to have to rebuild it three times.
>
> (Hart 2013: 13)

Designer Tim Hatley says that in his work with Theatre de Complicite, using the actual objects called for – logs and axe, tin bath and zinc bucket – was often the most obvious and satisfactory solution. However, sometimes the 'real thing' was too heavy for performers to handle, particularly late in a long play, or in conjunction with a particularly demanding speech. 'Sometimes, if it's really heavy, you have to act it. Then you're in the situation of having to make [the object] out of balsa wood, and all that is very boring. The audience shouldn't notice. Unless it's a joke' (Hatley 2001). A performer working with props made of papier mâché or balsa wood has to study movement as carefully as a mime artist, in order to reproduce the muscular effort of working against gravity. This extra 'work', which is not usually needed in the naturalistic theatre, is one of the fundamental processes in object animation. Light materials such as newspapers, fabrics, foils and so on are moved so that they seem to have a weight and muscular effort of their own. Although the spectators perceive the image through sight, it is through corporeal empathy and imagination that the performer creates, and the spectator reads, that image. Objects can be too light, as well as too heavy. In performance, a prop suitcase that will never be opened still needs some contents to weight it, in order to move realistically through space:

> While it is generally a good idea to keep a prop as light as possible, you can find situations where more weight is desired. In outdoor locations, you may need to add weight to props to keep them from blowing away. It may also aid in realism; if a large suitcase is meant to be fully packed, it would look silly if the actor was able to lift it with one finger. We can snidely remark from the sidelines 'why not try acting like it is heavy,' but it is helpful to aid the actors as much as possible with the props so they can focus on their emotions and intentions rather than having to concentrate on simulating an imaginary amount of weight in a suitcase.
> (Hart 2013: 14–15)

On occasion, a 'real' item will not 'read' well in the theatre – it may be too small, or its subtle surface texture may be invisible beyond the first row. Ian Garrett describes working on a production of Naomi Izuka's play *SKIN*, with a design that called for a 'row of living plants between the audience and the stage'. To maintain the plants, the stage management team

> removed the plants from the theatre daily to bring them into the sun. We installed a plastic membrane between the soil and the rest of the set to allow for regular watering. We had to find mature plants, and spares for those that died, to fill a flower bed one foot by 100 feet for two weeks of performances. Finally, we had to figure out where these plants would go when we were finished.
> (Garrett 2014: 65)

Despite all this effort, Garret concludes that 'the plants never looked real':

> In the hyper-designed theatrical realm, their lush leaves looked bland – so much so that they were lit bright green to make them 'pop'. All this effort to include living things, for something that ultimately looked fake. We could have skipped this

life-support system entirely, and plastic plants would have been just as effective, if not more so.

(ibid.)

As Garrett suggests, a substitute can sometimes be more vivid than the real thing – and this may be what is required by the performance's aesthetic. The cross-over between theatrical illusion and interior decoration techniques has always been significant – employing techniques such as marbling, woodgraining and *trompe l'oeil*.[32]

'Real' materials are not always appropriate – real whisky in the decanter, or a real bullet in Hedda Gabler's pistol would have undesirable effects. Making a substitution with something similar in appearance is a familiar tactic – cold tea instead of whisky, a blank in the pistol. In Michael Frayn's backstage farce, *Noises Off*, the stage manager offers to replace a plate of persistently troublesome sardines with mashed bananas. These substitutions are analogous to fight directors replacing a real interaction with a faked one – instead of kicking a prone body the performer learns to kick the floor alongside. Nevertheless, substitution does affect the range of sensual experience available to performers and spectators.

Just as each material makes specific demands on the performer and production team, it also makes available a specific range of gestural or sensory possibilities which a substitute may not. A production of *Arturo Ui* at the National Theatre in 1991 emphasised the play's setting in a Chicago vegetable market. It was decided that in the background of a scene, performers playing stall-holders would strip leaves from elderly cabbages. The propmakers made a plaster mould from a real cabbage leaf, allowing them to turn out infinite numbers of rubber cabbage leaves which were then painted realistically to give appropriate highlights. If the production had only been scheduled to run for a few days, it would have been more cost efficient to use real cabbages, since the initial construction of a mould is labour-intensive. If the performers had needed to tear, cook or eat the leaves, it would of course have been necessary to use real cabbages (Burchill 2001). In contrast, a production of *Ubu Roi* that used vegetables to represent Jarry's characters destroyed these food puppets nightly: the smell and the spectator's visceral reaction to the chopping up of the vegetables was intrinsic to the effect (see Margolies 2014). For the production of *Arturo Ui*, plastics simulated the cabbage beautifully from a visual point of view, but allowed a more restricted range of physical interactions. The 'real' makes other sensory possibilities available which the substitute material does not – the smell of rotting cabbages, the crack of tearing stubborn leaves.

Compromises can be made to retain the desired material properties. In Complicite's *The Three Lives of Lucie Cabrol* real soil was spread on the stage floor, but it was mixed with rubber crumb to make it lighter to handle. The mixture was sprayed with water before every performance to lay the dust, and so the smell of real earth filled the auditorium. The choice between the real and the substitute is a pragmatic decision which takes a number of different factors into account – cost, the likely length of the run, how close-up the object will be seen, how the performers are to work with it and so on.

There are good reasons for opting to build a prop from scratch, and yet the negative associations remain strong: whether it is fake food, reproduction furniture, artificial flowers, counterfeit money or ersatz coffee, the implications are of fraud, illusion, deception and disappointment. In the furniture trade, 'reproduction' denotes items made with similar materials and techniques to the original in order to reproduce as many of the original properties – such as weight, colour and carved detail – as possible. In contrast, an imitation, fake or simulation may employ completely different substances from the original with the aim of obtaining different material properties. In the case of the cabbage leaves, the visual appearance was imitated but the silicon rubber did not feel, sound, smell or decay like vegetable matter. In reproduction, the prop-maker needs to work with the grain of the material just as the maker of the original did. With the materials used for imitation, however, grain is not relevant. What is needed, rather, is 'plasticity' – the ability to flow into any shape, to take on any colour or texture – a material property that has obvious analogies with the shape-shifting work of performance.

PLASTICITY

It is important to distinguish the quality of 'plasticity' from the various substances (distinct in chemical structure), which are loosely called 'plastics'. Before the invention of modern polymer plastics, many other materials realised the ideal of plasticity: plaster, rubber, gutta percha, Bois Durci (wood pulp mixed with albumen, patented in 1856) shellac, celluloid and papier mâché (see Mossman 1997). In *The System of Objects* (1968) Baudrillard describes a 'substantialist myth' which, from the sixteenth century onwards, imagined the possibility of casting the whole world from 'a single ready-made material', such as stucco. He sees both plastic and concrete as partial realisations of this mythological aim (Baudrillard 1996: 38). Early plastic materials were widely used to simulate rare and expensive materials such as tortoiseshell and ivory – polymer plastics too, were typically made to resemble other materials, such as wood or stone, when they were first developed, and right into the 1960s. They were used in prop construction – now supplemented with plastic materials such as alginate, PVA, caulk and acrylic resin.

In the seventeenth century, 'plastic' had an active sense, meaning the power of moulding and of giving life or form: in 1742, a writer refers to the generative, creative powers of 'God, the great plastick artist', and as late as 1877 there is a reference to 'the plastic energy of the imagination' (OED). Although the generative aspect of 'plastic' is obsolete, the double meaning can still be found in the term 'plastic arts', and in references to plasticity in writing on performance. For example, Etienne Decroux refers to corporeal performers as 'plastic artists' – a phrase which combines physical flexibility and control (such performers 'mould' their own bodies) and creative, imaginative powers, as when Decroux envisages 'mobile sculpture' (Decroux 1978: passim). Such references appear whenever the performer is considered as part of the stage design (as in the work of Meyerhold or Kantor) or indeed constitutes the whole materiality of the performance (as in most of Decroux's *études*). Work with the artist's own body as mouldable material is found in performance art: see, for example, Eleanor Antin's dieting-as-sculpture piece 'Carving' (1981), and the body-modifications of Stelarc and Orlan. More recently, work on the 'plasticity' of the brain, and the philosophical implications of this neuroplasticity, has been brought into dialogue with performance studies.[33]

A more familiar sense of plasticity is of 'any material that by its nature or in its process of manufacture is at some stage, either through heat or by the presence of a solvent, sufficiently pliable and flowable […] so that it can be given its final shape by the operation of molding or pressing' (Mossman 1997: 1). An advertisement for Bakelite plastics from 1943 gives a more expansive account:

> They are any shape you choose. They are any colour you want them to be. Sometimes they take simple forms – the door handle, the electric light switch, the bottle cap. Sometimes they assume more complex shapes – the motor cover of a vacuum cleaner, the handle of an electric iron, the modern telephone, the latest type of radio cabinet. Sometimes one may recognise them as beautiful surfaces in pale pastel shades forming the wall finish of a modern interior or the furniture of a cocktail bar. Sometimes they are only seen and known to the technician in the form of some intricate part of a switchboard or the silent gears of an industrial power plant... But in all these forms they have this in common: They speak modernity. They are BAKELITE PLASTICS.
>
> (Fleck 1943: x)

When this advertisement was written, the Oxford English Dictionary had not yet admitted the word 'plastic' as a noun. The adjective 'plastic', deriving from the Ancient Greek meaning 'capable of being moulded' dates back to the seventeenth century. In this passive sense it could be applied to materials such as clay, wax, papier mâché, shellac and rubber. It was only in 1951 that the British Standards Institute formally recognised the term 'plastics' to describe the category of new materials that were being developed from coal and oil. They had previously been known by their chemical description, or under their individual brand names, gloriously futuristic names such as Xylonite, Ivorite and Vulcanite.

The advertisement for Bakelite encapsulates the crucial features of plasticity: 'any shape you choose...any colour you want'. 'Plasticity' means infinite formal possibilities shaped by human desire, unlimited by material constraints. Plastics 'speak modernity'. This association does not just derive from the literal newness of materials from coal and oil in the twentieth century. If plastic materials such as Bakelite 'speak modernity', the notion of plasticity speaks utopia, a fluidity that will never be fixed. As a cultural metaphor, plasticity is incorporated into descriptions of both modernity and postmodernity.

Although prop-makers value 'plasticity', it is closely linked to the notions of imitation and reproduction that, as we have seen, produce such suspicion. Henry Petroski refers to 'the persistence of the names of things deriving from the materials of which they were first made', such as 'tin cans' (now made of steel or aluminium), eye 'glasses' (largely made of plastic) and pencil 'lead' (graphite). This 'suggests the intimate relationship that can exist between ingenious objects and their materials'; they seem to be 'made for each other' (Petroski 1989: 18). Two 'plastic' materials that have been very important in prop-making – polymer plastics and papier mâché – break this deeply felt association between object and material. The rest of this chapter will explore some of the history of these two materials and its relevance to today's prop-makers.

PAPIER MÂCHÉ

Papier mâché has been both celebrated and reviled for its plasticity as a material. In her book on props, Jacquie Govier describes papier mâché as 'the theater's own special material, for it combines the cardinal qualities of strength and lightness' (Govier 1984: 18). In contrast, George Dickinson, writing on the rise and fall of the fashion for moveable papier mâché objects such as tea trays and boxes, defines 'a prejudice against papier mâché' (Dickinson 1925: 130).

Two different kinds of material are commonly described as 'papier mâché': the first is a paper pulp, made by breaking down paper in water (usually with added binders such as glue) so that it forms a thick pulp or clay-like paste which can be moulded or sculpted; the second is made by pasting layers of paper on top of each other – laminated paper, rather than literally 'mâché' or 'chewed'. From the point of view of materials science, the first type of papier mâché is like very thick paper: its strength arises from the matting of longer or shorter fibres. Mixed with glue, it is a composite material, like fibreglass, chipboard or medium-density fibreboard (MDF), in which particles of one substance (e.g. wood) give strength to a more flexible substance (e.g. glue) which in turn binds the particles. The second type of papier mâché is a laminate – a material made of layers glued together, like plywood. The layering of the material (particularly if the grain of each layer runs crossways to the grain of the previous layer) makes the new material much stronger than a solid sheet of equivalent thickness.

Objects were made of pasted and pulped paper in China and Persia, long before paper was discovered in western Europe. The basic technique has remained the same: Egyptian mummy cases were made from pasted layers of papyrus, and in the Second World War, 'fuel tanks and other aircraft parts were made [using methods] in no way different from those employed by the ancient Egyptians except that paper was used instead of papyrus' (Gordon 1976: 178). Both composites and laminates are ubiquitous today in furniture and buildings, as luxury and as cheap materials – from the much-imitated steam-formed plywood chairs designed by Ray and Charles Eames, to the orientated strand board and MDF used extensively in set-building and prop-making.

Papier mâché can easily be moulded to look as if a great deal of craft labour has been invested in carving, and its surface can be finished to resemble other materials, such as stone, wood or metal. As a material, it was once valued primarily for having no obtrusive characteristics of its own, a neutral support for the arts of imitation.

The waxing and waning of the cultural desire to make one material resemble another drove the rise and decline of the short-lived British and American papier mâché industry of the late eighteenth and the nineteenth century. In the early nineteenth century, papier mâché was finished to look like grained wood, marble or tortoiseshell; wood was disguised as bamboo or marble; and slate was disguised as marble or even as papier mâché. One author even includes slate- and marble-topped tables in an account of papier mâché, for on one hand their inlaid decoration was 'obviously inspired by the paintings and inlays with which […] manufacturers were decorating their papier mâché wares', while on the other hand, the secrets of artificial marbling learnt in the slate trade had been brought to the papier mâché industry through industrial espionage by journeymen (Toller 1962: 115, 120).

'Fibrous pulp', made of rag, paper, straw, hay, hemp, nettles or any other available vegetable fibre mixed with plaster, was used to produce architectural ornaments such as ceiling roses, cornices and architraves. Here it was the illusion of a costly investment in labour that was sought. Decoration which would have once been hand-carved in stone or in wood had previously been imitated in plaster, but papier mâché was cheaper and lighter, and much stronger and tougher. Robert Adam commissioned George Jackson to carve moulds for his architectural designs in 1756. The company of Jackson and Sons built up a collection of boxwood moulds of English and French designs from the seventeenth to early nineteenth century, producing mouldings in fibrous pulp and papier mâché for many important buildings in London and elsewhere in Britain, including the Egyptian Hall at Mansion House, the Drapers' Hall and the Clothworkers' Hall. In the 1960s the original moulds were still in use for restorative work (Toller 1962: 35). Theatres and music halls were ideal candidates for embellishments in papier mâché, as it made rich decoration available relatively cheaply. Wilton's Music Hall, off Cable Street in the East End of London, which opened in 1859 and is the earliest music hall building still in existence (now in use again as a venue for music theatre), is decorated with 'sculptures, foliage and scroll-work in the Italian style, relieved in colour and gilding', executed in carton pierre and papier mâché (Honri 1985: 21).

In the rise and decline of papier mâché, a history of the changing balance between the visual and other senses can be traced. Where papier mâché has been used, image has taken precedence over tactile or material properties. For a brief period an extraordinary range of objects and items of furniture were made wholly out of paper: snuffboxes, tea caddies and cabbies' shiny black hats, writing desks, letter racks and match holders, buttons, screens and bellows. Henry Clay made 'several pieces of superb furniture' including tables, chairs and beds out of paper panel for the royal residences, and received a royal patent for making dovetail joints in papier mâché (Dickinson 1925: 27). A whole village of easy-to-assemble houses for export to Australia was pre-fabricated in papier mâché in 1853; the houses survived a flood of two feet of water and were 'not injured'.

More fantastic than these objects themselves is the impression conveyed of a society wild about decoration. Papier mâché's suitability for surface decoration was more important than any other function. Furniture and smaller items served as the ground for flower paintings so beautiful that later historians ask 'Why did the artist choose a tea-tray on which to paint such a picture?' (Dickinson 1925: 76). Tabletops and trays were inlaid with mother of pearl, or used to frame detailed architectural studies. Other pieces were decorated with landscapes, allegorical or romantic scenes, or portraits of royal and famous personages. The houses of the papier mâché village had 'interior decorations so complete as to render it next to impossible to fancy yourself in any other than a brick dwelling. The mantel-pieces in the drawing and dining-room are of papier mâché, have a caryatidal figure on each side, and are of bold design' (DeVoe 1971: 27).

Papier mâché gave nineteenth-century suburban drawing rooms Gothic thrones and copies of Jacobean or Stuart oak chairs. By the 1960s a critic was describing this as a violation of the bond between material and design: Jane Toller describes such pieces as 'a mistake – to take a design meant for a heavy material such as oak, and carry it out in a light material such as papier mâché' (Toller 1962: 75). The reaction against decoration, towards unadorned materials, was a wider trend which became a cornerstone of modernism. In theatre, papier mâché was used to create food, armour, crowns, treasure chests and religious articles. While some makers displayed skills at the same level as colleagues in interior design and manufacturing, there must have been many pieces for theatre that were hastily made and poorly decorated. The ubiquity of papier mâché, its association with cheap imitations, and examples of bad workmanship must have all contributed to giving the material a bad name. While regretting the decline in demand for the technique of painting *trompe l'oeil* backcloths, and the loss of traditional skills, designer Tim Hatley breathes a sigh of relief: 'Thank God everything's not made of cardboard or papier mâché anymore. Thank God sets don't wobble when you walk through doors. Materials are better, technology is better, and design is better' (Hatley 2001).

POLYMER PLASTICS

In the post-war period, many designers believed that if plastic were allowed to express its 'true nature', formed into objects with flowing lines and vibrant colours, rather than imitating traditional materials and forms, it would be seen as beautiful. The plastic utensils and vessels produced in Italy and Germany employed to the full the possibilities offered by the production methods – swirling marbled designs produced by the incomplete mixture of coloured granules, along with shapes that could only be created by flowing material into a mould. These objects express the concept of 'plasticity' in plastic. The streamlined shapes that were brought from military design into the domestic sphere not only saved material and produced objects that were less fragile, having no sharp corners, but also showed off the beauty of glossy plastic, reflecting 'at least one highlight from any angle' (Meikle 1997: 116). Plastic, according to James Meikle, in his cultural history *American Plastic*, became the material of choice for the post-war expansion of consumerism. It was cheap because it derived from the 'inexhaustible' resource of oil, and so lightweight as to be discarded without a second thought: 'Plastic not only offered a perfect medium for this material proliferation. It conceptually embodied it and stimulated it' (ibid.: 176). In the 1960s, popular themes such as 'softness', 'disposability' and 'colourfulness' were expressed through plastic, which in turn made new items such as inflatable furniture and transparent umbrellas possible. Such objects

> raised the specter of a society that in seeking lightness had lost all awareness of gravity – understood both as a sense of rootedness to the past, to nature, to the earth itself, and as a sense of seriousness, of awareness of matters of weight, of consequence.
>
> (ibid.: 230)

Polymer plastics can be formulated to have almost any characteristics desired: varying degrees of conductivity, stiffness, translucency, flexibility and weight can be obtained, and plastics with different qualities can be combined or layered. Unlike many other materials in everyday use, different types of plastic cannot be identified by their material characteristics, but only by chemical testing. This makes recycling a challenge – and is the reason that recyclable plastics like milk bottles are produced with an identification code moulded into the base.[34]

While the visual resemblance between an original and its plastic replica can be exact, a plastic prop lacks qualities such as weight, smell, texture, qualities which are 'grasped with the ear, the hand, the mouth' rather than the eye (Kress and Van Leeuwen 2001: 79). Kress and Van Leeuwen even suggest that plastic might be treated as a 'mode' (i.e. like language, sound, texture or gesture) rather than a medium precisely because 'it does not have its own specific material qualities' (ibid.: 80). This is perhaps a more accurate description of 'plasticity' than of polymer plastics, which do have material qualities of their own, even if they are often disguised.

BAKELITE TILL KINGDOM COME

Although polymer plastics can express the utopian dreams of plasticity, their materiality embodies a contrary principle, that of permanence. In *The Story of Bakelite*, a promotional book from 1924, John Mumford praised the material's 'Protean adaptability to many things', but found more marvellous the chemical reaction by which it set or hardened, after which it would 'continue to be Bakelite till kingdom come' (quoted in Meikle 1990: 42–3). After the initial moment of formation, in which plastics flow into any shape desired, they become rigid and resistant to change. They are 'plastic' only for a few seconds of their life cycle and generally unable to adapt or renew themselves in the way that organic materials can. There is a significant conflict between the desire for plasticity and the reluctance to acknowledge plastic's impact on the environment in terms of consuming raw materials and producing waste. Plastics are practically indestructible: despite the development of biodegradable plastics, most plastic goes into landfill sites or incinerators.[35] Plastic production might be described as a 'time-transcending technology', a term coined by Adam and Sullivan (2000) to describe atomic and genetic modification technologies, because plastics are foreign to the ecosystem, which has no mechanisms for absorbing them.

As David Reeves writes in his history of furniture: 'Unbreakable and unstainable materials, that do not show signs of long and hard use, gradually put us out of sympathy with our furniture. Furniture made from such materials demands no grateful care from us, and we can make no impression on it in using it. It can look after itself; it actually resists our use – as the materials are called, rightly, 'resistant' (Reeves 1959: 30–31). Plastics are in general poorly suited for adaptation and re-use: a glossy surface sheen is easily and permanently damaged by scratches or abrasive cleaning – unlike wood or stone, where a new surface can be revealed by rubbing down the damaged layer; although they can be made in brilliant colours, it is hard to change the colour with a layer of paint – it won't stick; attempts to cut down a plastic object or to drill holes in it can cause fatal cracks. While these are generalisations about the material qualities of plastics, most plastics wear poorly and are hard to adapt.

Most commonly, plastics are used in theatre to simulate other substances which are too messy, dangerous or expensive to use. Most of the plastic that appears on stage is pretending to be something else: plastic food and flowers, paste-jewellery, artificial silks and nylon wigs, rubber hammers and plastic swords, false limbs, fingers and noses. As plastic is light, unbreakable, non-decaying and easily shaped and coloured, it is a frequent substitute for more troublesome materials. If plastic is unlikeable as a material because it is unmarkable, what significance does this have for theatre, where the 'lived-in' face or the worn and battered chair have a special value? In theatrical terms, does the resilience of polymer plastics make them in a sense unlikeable? Can they transmit signs of human use in the way that Brecht's knives and forks, with their worn wooden handles, do?

IMPLICATIONS FOR CONTEMPORARY PROP-MAKING

Is it possible to enjoy 'plasticity' without using polymer plastics? At the Central School of Speech and Drama, Dot Young, Course Leader in Prop-Making, asks students to complete an environmental assessment form for each of their projects. She says that this process in itself raises awareness that they have choices around materials, techniques and the environmental impact of props. She hopes that this awareness will percolate through to theatres and prop-making workshops as students graduate and enter the profession. Designer Tim Hatley expresses a common ambivalence about papier mâché: 'There's a wonderful quality to it, if that's what you want, but it has been completely superseded by technology. Now you can make a mould and vac-form shapes, and that's much, much cheaper. It's just not cost-effective anymore' (Hatley 2001). Yet papier mâché has not disappeared.

Lamination

Although plastic and silicon have in many cases superseded paper pulp for moulding, the layering technique intrinsic to papier mâché is still used in prop-making. Fraser Burchill described how one prop-maker at the National Theatre chose to construct a large sculpture using layers of nylon mesh glued with PVA, due to a personal preference for this method rather than fibreglass moulding. Each technique has its particular strengths and weaknesses: 'Maybe if it had been made with another technique the sculpture wouldn't have broken when a bit of set fell on it, but it couldn't have been mended as easily' (Burchill 2001).[36] This example points to the way in which lamination allows for ongoing repair while plastic produces a faster result that is difficult to interact with subsequently. Writing on the restoration of antiques, Jocasta Innes describes papier mâché as 'the restorer's dream'.

A piece of china skilfully repaired may fool the eye but the only way to reproduce the exact texture and ring of the original is to model and fire a new bit of china to replace the missing one. However, with papier mâché you can build up quite large missing chunks which look, feel and sound – when tapped of course – like the real thing.

(Innes 1976: 115)

Production Title	Environmental Impact, Evaluation. Prop Making	Designer
Venue		Director

Prop item	

Selected 'Main Materials' used in the making of the item:

Material	Nature of Impact on Environment (Chemical waste, landfill, airborn toxin)	Biodegradable: Yes/No	Initial Impact Factor (1-6)	Method of reducing impact (Recycling/Multiple use/Stock)	Resulting Impact factor (1-6)
		Resulting Average Environmental Impact Value Score (Total divided by number of materials)			

Recommendations regarding H&S and the environment when using these materials:

Possible Alternative Materials	Nature of Impact on Environment	Biodegradable: Yes/No	Impact Factor (1-6)	Method of reducing impact (Recycling/Multiple use)	Resulting Impact factor (1-6)

Assessed by		Position		Signed		Date	

Impact	1 Very minor impact	2 Minor impact	3 Moderate impact	4 Major impact	5 High impact	6 Extreme impact

Prop-making students are asked to complete an environmental impact evaluation for every project.

Courtesy Dot Young, Central School of Speech and Drama.

Avoiding harmful materials

As a raw material, paper tends to be far less harmful to work with than solvent-based materials. Papier mâché is enjoying a renaissance among craftspeople, according to puppeteer Ronnie Burkett, who previously suffered many years in fume-filled workshops, covered with fibreglass dust. He notes that 'it is becoming clearly evident that resins, fibreglass, latex rubber and other such artificial substances are harmful to not only the craftsman, but the environment as well' (Burkett 2010).

Karen Wood, a freelance prop-maker, describes the lack of knowledge about health risks in workshops in the early 1980s: 'We used to do fibreglass work with a cigarette in the mouth. [There were West End jobs] where we were grinding fibreglass and most workers were shirtless. No masks' (Karrer 2014: 42). Fraser Burchill recalls, 'When I started, there didn't seem to be many healthy prop-makers walking around at 50' (Burchill 2001). Ronnie Burkett notes that 'many of the old puppeteers I knew when I was growing up have since died of varying lung diseases and cancer'. All three have seen a huge shift to safer working practices in the last 20 to 30 years. There are artistic benefits too. Ronnie Burkett concludes: 'There is a great liberation that comes with not having to create through a ventilation mask.'

Burkett prefers the texture of paper pulp for painting, and finds the resulting puppet heads stronger than fibreglass, plastic wood or automotive plastics. Paper pulp 'is an exciting, versatile medium. When wet, it is like clay. It can be pressed into moulds or modelled over an armature. When dry, it has many of the properties of wood. It can be rasped, sanded and carved' (Burkett 2010). Another example of the rediscovery of traditional materials is given by Chris Vervain and David Wiles, who worked with mask-maker Michael Chase on reproductions of Ancient Greek masks. They found to their surprise that papier mâché masks, and masks of 'antique' materials such as linen, plaster, rabbit's foot glue and shellac, were more resonant than masks made of formasol, a solvent-activated resin (see Vervain and Wiles 2001: 264). Paul Brown, Head of Props at Glyndebourne Opera, describes how he had to make a teacup and teapot for dancers to wear as costume props. He tested and weighed samples of varafoam (a thin cotton fabric impregnated with low temperature thermoplastic) and papier mâché, discovering that the paper was lighter than the varafoam, and able to stand up to the rigours of performance. While Brown might use Foamcoat (a proprietary coating for styrofoam, polystyrene etc.) to cover a sculpture that won't be moved in performance, his first preference when finishing a large polystyrene object would be to scrim it (add a reinforcing layer), often using brown paper and animal glue – this is quicker and cheaper than Foamcoat (Karrer 2014). Carolin Karrer concludes that an experienced prop-maker like Brown, who is familiar with both traditional and new materials, is able to choose the most appropriate one for each job.

Teapot and cup and saucer made of papier mâché by Paul Brown, Head of Props at Glyndebourne Festival Opera, for *L'enfant et les sortileges*, Glyndebourne Festival 2015. © Glyndebourne Productions Ltd. Photo: Richard Hubert Smith.

Recycling and transience

While it is a plastic material that prop-makers can use to serve illusion, papier mâché can also reveal a texture which displays its history. Unlike plastic, but like wood, laminated papier mâché has a directional grain, in which the construction technique and raw materials can be revealed. Artist Andrea Stanley's vessels, such as *Turned Paper Form* (2001), are constructed from newspapers and magazines and turned on a lathe. In the finished pieces, fragments of words can sometimes be seen amidst coloured lines that resemble the swirling patterns of oil and water marbling, or the contour lines of a map. The resemblance of these lines to contour lines is more than visual – they have been made by filing down layers, revealing the colours of paper that was built up like geological strata.

Perhaps papier mâché is disliked because it threatens to provide a glimpse of an object's unglamorous past, revealed in the discoloured newsprint on the reverse of a glossy surface. How much attention is paid by performance to the underside of production – waste? Over its 20 years of operation, theatre company Welfare State International made a point of using local materials – clay, wood, vegetation – wherever possible. John Fox wrote:

we try to cannibalise, to re-use stuff that's around the site, whether it's mud and straw when you're making a sculpture, or computer paper in Bracknell for making papier mâché, or newspapers.

(Fox 1990: 25)

For Welfare State, the metaphorical associations of materials were as important as their construction properties: with 'flimsy' and 'transient' objects, such as lanterns made of bamboo and tissue paper, an audience sees that the objects have been made on site, because they are too fragile to be transported, emphasising the immediacy of the performance; and they may be destroyed in the course of the performance, countering what John Fox calls the 'phoney propaganda which tries to pretend that LIFE is fixed and permanent and that if you are insured death will go away' (Fox 1990: 26).

From an environmental point of view, papier mâché is an attractive material: paper already used as newspapers, letters or packaging can be recycled, and once the new object is discarded, it can in turn be recycled or composted.[37]

Taking time

Making objects with papier mâché is slow. With the layering method, drying time is needed between layers, while moulded paper pulp may take from one to three weeks to dry completely. Ronnie Burkett has simply adapted his sequence of tasks, working on puppet bodies and costumes while he allows paper pulp heads to dry. While the raw material is cheap, and may even be a waste product, making papier mâché is extremely labour-intensive – it is unlikely that papier mâché will be produced industrially in Britain again. It is a material suitable for a theatre in which more labour than cash is invested, such as community theatre. Making papier mâché can be compared to the techniques of 'extra-daily' or 'luxury' balance, which Eugenio Barba found in Oriental performance. The papier mâché object is always a luxury because it is hand-made. When it is destroyed, as in Welfare State's ceremonial burning of large-scale models and puppets, a carnivalesque consumption of beauty and effort is performed. Papier mâché once provided the illusion of a great deal of labour having been invested in an object, but it itself is now regarded as obsolete because it is too labour-intensive. However, as interest in recycling grows, methods of working with paper pulp suitable for mass-production are being adapted for craft production.

As a campaigner who drew attention to the environmental damage caused by plastics, Barry Commoner called in 1971 for a 'voluntary return to labor-intensive traditional materials except in those instances – phonograph records or heart valves – where plastic marked a true innovation' (Meikle 1997: 265). Why would anyone opt for a slower method of construction? In commercial theatre it could only be justified if other materials became proportionately more expensive, but in non-profit groups, labour is available where cash is not; moreover, the time spent making objects together promotes sociability and cooperation.

Baudrillard suggests that attachment to traditional or 'real' materials is sentimental, and that the replacement of organic materials by synthetics and composites – wool, cotton and silk replaced by nylon and polyester; wood, stone and metal by concrete and polystyrene – is an inexorable tendency:

> There can be no question of rejecting this tendency and simply dreaming of the ideal warm and human substance of the objects of former times. The distinction between natural and synthetic substances, just like that between traditional colours and bright colours, is strictly a value judgement. Objectively, substances are simply what they are: there is no such thing as a true or a false, a natural or an artificial substance. How could concrete be somehow less 'authentic' than stone?
> (Baudrillard 1996: 38)

While his critique of the notion of authenticity is important, Baudrillard is too quick to assume that traditional materials will inevitably be replaced by synthetic ones, particularly those dependent on petroleum. It seems more likely that prop-makers and designers will have to continue to balance a great many factors in deciding what materials to use, and that 'old' and 'new' will coexist.

Some argue that even if 'plasticity' was central to the prop-maker's art in the past, it will be eventually replaced by 'additive' construction methods, like 3D printing. But these technologies currently produce a lot of plastic waste, although research is being done into using recycled and biodegradable materials. The problems with polymer plastics as materials for performance point to some of the environmental problems inherent in their wider use. But the example of papier mâché suggests that it is possible to find 'plastic' materials which can be moulded to people's desires and satisfy the desire for luxury and ornamentation without the dire environmental problems caused by polymer plastics.

The following article from 1878 on prop-makers wonders why theatre producers are choosing to use 'actualities' instead of the prop-maker's 'simulacra'. As we have already seen, this is a recurring theme and relates not only to changing techniques but to changing ideas of realism in theatre.

'STAGE PROPERTIES'

Dutton Cook

> The maker of properties, although an important aid to theatrical representations, is never seen by the audience; he is of scarcely less value to the stage than the scene-painter, but he is never called before the curtain to be publicly

congratulated upon his exploits. His manufactory or workshop is usually in some retired part of the theatre. He lives in a world of his own – a world of shams. His duty is to make the worse appear the better article; to obtain acceptance for forgeries, to create, not realities, but semblances. He does not figure among the *dramatis personæ*; but what a significant part he plays! Tragedy and comedy, serious ballet and Christmas pantomime, are alike to him. He appears in none of them, but he pervades them all; his unseen presence is felt as a notable influence on every side. He provides the purse of gold with which the rich man relieves the necessities of his poor interlocutor, the bank notes that are stolen, the will that disinherits, the parchments long lost but found at last, which restore the rightful heir to the family possessions. The assassin's knife, the robber's pistol, the soldier's musket, the sailor's cutlass, the court sword of genteel comedy, the basket-hilted blade that works such havoc in melodrama, all these proceed from his armoury; while from his kitchen, so to speak, issue alike the kingly feasts, consisting usually of wooden apples and Dutch-metal-smeared goblets, and the humbler meals spread in cottage interiors or furnished lodgings, the pseudo legs of mutton, roast fowls or pork chops – to say nothing of those joints of meat, shoals of fish, and pounds of sausages inseparable from what are called the 'spill and pelt' scenes of harlequinade.

Of late years, however, our purveyors of theatrical entertainments, moved by much fondness for reality, have shown a disposition to limit the labours of the property-maker, to dispense with his simulacra as much as possible, and to employ instead the actualities he but seeks to mimic and shadow forth. Costly furniture is now often hired or purchased from fashionable upholsterers. Genuine china appears where once pasteboard fabrications did duty – real oak-carvings banish the old substitutes of painted canvas stretched on deal laths and 'profiled,' to resort to the technical term, with a small sharp saw. The property-maker, with his boards and battens, his wicker-work and gold leaf, his paints and glue and size, his shams of all kinds, is almost banished from the scene. The stage accessories become so substantial that the actors begin to wear a shadowy look – especially when they are required to represent rather unlife-like characters. Real horses, real dogs, real water, real pumps and washing tubs are now supplemented by real *bric-à-brac*, *bijouterie*, and drawing-room knick-knackery.

Faith has been lost, apparently, in the arts of stage illusion; the spectators must be no longer duped, things must be what they seem.

FURTHER READING

On practical prop-making skills:

Gill Davies, *Stage Source Book: Props* (2004); Michael Holt, *Stage Design and Properties* (1994); Andy Wilson, *Making Stage Props: A Practical Guide* (2003) – a guide to making techniques including wood and metalwork, moulds and casting; Jacquie Govier, *Create Your Own Stage Props* (1984) – well illustrated with line drawings and worked projects on different themes, this handbook is particularly suitable for school or community groups; Eric Hart, *The Prop Building Guidebook for Theatre, Film, and TV* (2013) – a comprehensive introduction to standard techniques such as moulding and casting, and materials including wood, metal, plastics and fabric, in a workshop-friendly wire binding. Hart also maintains a website, Prop Agenda, at www.props.eric-hart.com.

On materials and the environment:

Larry Fried and Theresa May, *Greening Up Our Houses* (1995); Philip Howes and Zoe Laughlin, *Material Matters: New Materials in Design* (2012); Mark Miodownik, *Stuff Matters* (2013) – a very readable account of ten materials, discussing both materials science and cultural significance. See also the resources produced by Julie's Bicycle http://www.juliesbicycle.com.

Chapter 7

Consumables and Breakaways

'Consumable' props are those that need to be replenished for each performance, such as food and drink, cigarettes, matches and candles. Many special effects also require consumable materials such as fake blood, 'sugar glass' and pyrotechnical components. 'Breakaway' props are designed to break easily and predictably – like the 'fake chair' in *Mnemonic* – and need to be repaired between performances. These two categories of props provoke a great deal of curiosity from spectators, as well as questions about the relationship of stage reality to reality outside the theatre. As 'Esther', an actor in Tim Crouch's metatheatrical play *The Author* comments, 'The first question everyone would ask is, "What's the blood made out of?"' (Crouch 2011: 178). Our curiosity as spectators about consumables is partly due to the fact that these everyday substances enlist a practical, craft knowledge of the materials and how they look, feel, taste and smell. They can also provoke discomfort and worry: they induce a phenomenological 'reappearance' of the bodies of both performer and spectator, and raise questions about what can be known within the world of the play.

This chapter follows on from the discussion in Chapter 4 of realism, looking in particular at plays that were first performed at the Royal Court Theatre, the historic location for a specific kind of social realism. It considers how stagings of eating and violence can embody contrasting ways of knowing the world.

'AS IF THE POINT WERE TO STRIKE A MATCH!'

Stanislavski's early writing displays a rather paradoxical attitude to material reality – it is a source of inspiration for the writer and actor, but not necessarily safe to bring on stage unmediated. In *An Actor Prepares*, the acting teacher Tortsov instructs his student Kostya to build a fire on stage. Kostya narrates what happened next:

> I did as I was told, laid the wood in the fireplace, but found no matches, either in my pocket or on the mantelpiece. So I came back and told Tortsov of my difficulty.
>
> 'What in the world do you want matches for?' asked he.
>
> 'To light the fire.'

'The fireplace is made of paper. Did you intend to burn down the theatre?'

'I was just going to pretend,' I explained.

He held out an empty hand.

'To pretend to light a fire, pretended matches are sufficient. As if the point were to strike a match! [...] When you play Hamlet – will you need a life-sized sword? You can kill the King without a sword, and you can light the fire without a match. What needs to burn is your imagination.'

(Stanislavski 1980: 43)

Although Tortsov valorises the imagination, this exchange serves as a repressive parable for actors in the realistic theatre, suggesting that they must work within the constraints of existing conventions, as defined by a particular director at any particular moment.

This uneasy attitude to matter is also found in writings by Uta Hagen, some 60 years later, reflecting on the staging of 'kitchen sink dramas'. She states, echoing Stanislavski, that 'truth in life as it is, is not truth on stage':

If I bring real snow into the theater it will melt, even before the curtain goes up. I remember a play in which real milk boiled over on cue on the stage stove. The audience was disillusioned as they audibly speculated on how this had been mechanically achieved.

(Hagen 1973: 75)

Hagen describes an audience that is impressed by a 'chunk' (to use David Shields' term) of reality being brought into the work of art: it is 'real milk'. But when the milk boils, it threatens to upstage the dramatic fiction, to 'disillusion' the audience. The discourse of 'illusion' has already been unpacked in various ways but it is worth noting how persistent this notion is, even as other forms of performance encourage 'speculation' (audible or otherwise) about materials. In contemporary performance art, the body and material world can be the theme rather than a distraction from it. Artist Bobby Baker has used food as a material throughout her career, exploiting its sculptural and painterly characteristics and exploring the political and autobiographical aspects of, for example, care and domesticity through a material closely associated with these themes.[38]

A shift of focus to the material world also occurs when spectators feel anxiety about the actor's body. For Hagen, inevitably, this is seen as a disruption:

In Look Back in Anger, Mary Ure ironed with a real steam iron. Not only did the audience murmur, 'Real steam!' as they missed what she was saying, but at one performance she was scalded, and the curtain was rung down.

(ibid.)

For Hagen, as for Stanislavski, the objects and action on stage must be 'real' only up to a certain boundary – one that is defined by the technical capacities and conventions of the period, and the expectations of actors and spectators.

Stanislavski and Hagen do not admit any doubts about where the boundary between truthful reality and excessive reality lies, but even in the realist theatre it moves all the time as theatre incessantly 'consumes' new aspects of reality (States 1985: 13). Conventions change, and the direction of change is not always towards increasing the amount of material 'reality' that can be put on stage. Early drama, as we have seen, employed many dangerous and difficult to control materials to create astonishing physical spectacles such as fire-breathing dragons and real water fountains. Sophisticated modern technology makes it possible to bring more of 'the real' onto the stage (computer controlled machines generate snowfalls on demand), but safety and cost constraints still lead to the use of substitutes (the snowflakes are foam bubbles). Meanwhile, changing conventions outside the theatre mean that some props previously taken for granted become highlighted. Today in West End or Broadway theatres, audiences may be warned by printed notices that the play they are about to see contains smoking; the recently opened Sam Wanamaker Playhouse is celebrated for being entirely lit by candles.

The objects that fascinate audiences inevitably change over time. Uta Hagen writes as if conventions never change when she excludes snow, boiling water and steam from a theatre otherwise furnished with real objects of everyday life. Yet even if technological changes have made steam irons and electric kettles commonplace, a jet of steam on stage is still troublesome: hard to control and posing a potential danger to the bodies of actors and crew. But the process of evaporation and condensation has an interest of its own. Regardless of changing conventions, some categories of thing 'resist being either signs or images', as Bert States writes, and retain a 'primal strangeness' and compelling interest on stage. The examples States gives include a working clock, fire, running water, child actors and animals (States 1985: 31).[39] Performance art has deliberately employed potentially disruptive elements such as fire, water, knives and guns while ecological theatre has been made with landscapes, animals and living plants. Shifts of attention to the material level of the performance, moments of 'losing the gaze' as Susan Melrose puts it, in props and costumes, in what is not yet a 'sign', are sometimes thought of as moments of 'distraction'. But rather than thinking of a theatrical illusion that is created by real objects but at risk of being destroyed by something 'too real', theatre-makers working with props and materials might instead use the spectrum of animation to think about the work an object does, who interacts with it (and how), and where the spectator's gaze travels, in both attention and distraction.

THE PHENOMENOLOGICAL REAPPEARANCE OF THE BODY

There are phenomenological similarities between violence and eating –
both actions cross the boundaries of the body, and confuse the distinction
between subject and object. But while violence treats a living body as an
object (making the recipient of the blow or wound experience their own
body as 'strange'), eating incorporates foreign objects into the body. Violence
opens the body to the spectator, by literally revealing interiors, or by producing sounds and gestures of pain that reveal something of the internal
world; in contrast, food disappears into regions that are without sensation,
or perceptible only to the individual. One might say that eating incorporates
objects into the animate body (what Husserl calls *Leib*), while violence makes
an object of the body (*Körper*). Because both violence and eating engage the
body in very direct ways, they can make visible the distinction between the
performer's body and the character's body.

The task of staging a fight or a meal therefore always raises many practical, aesthetic and dramaturgical questions. Where food is specified by a
playwright, the question arises in early discussions about design and direction, and again in rehearsal, of whether to prepare the real thing or to use
a substitute. Substitutes may be preferred for a number of reasons: the cost
and practical difficulties of producing hot food on cue, night after night,
may be prohibitive; a full meal may be indicated without there being time
on stage to actually eat it; performers may worry about indigestion, getting
food stuck in their teeth, or choking – because the everyday activity of eating becomes strange and complicated when it has to be performed around a
fixed text. Similarly, any kind of violent interaction between characters poses
staging problems that cross from the practical to the aesthetic realm. How
close will the audience be to the action? Can the point of contact with the
actor's body be masked? Will stage blood be used?

Both eating and violence produce a phenomenological 'reappearance'.
The body is usually in the 'background' of perception, in what Drew Leder
calls a state of phenomenological 'disappearance'. In 'dysfunction' such as
ill-health, conscious awareness of bodily sensations reappears, and the body
becomes a somewhat estranged 'object' of observation. Feminist critiques
of this model have pointed out that women's physical experience may be
slightly different, as the female body also becomes visible as 'matter' in
healthy functioning: in pregnancy, for example, the body becomes strange
to itself, taking on a new shape and weight, and categories of 'inside' and
'outside', 'self' and 'other' become problematised (see Garner 1994: 215–17).
Training for performance and techniques of body awareness such as yoga,
Feldenkrais and Alexander Technique also draw attention to the healthy
body as a material object as well as a body animate with intention.[40]

In both mainstream theatre and in performance art, violent or invasive interactions with matter, including the human body, have been presented as revela-
tory. In contrast, nurturing or creative interactions with matter, and the mode

of 'knowing' they embody, tend to be seen as having less power to reveal the truth. This belief is consistent with the Western system of beliefs about scientific and medical knowledge: the truth of the body is more definitively revealed on the operating table or the dissection table rather than in the palpation and pulse of the living body. Many forms of obtaining knowledge involve violent inter-actions with the object of study – dissection of bodies, crushing or burning of mineral samples, bombardment by subatomic particles. By unwarranted exten-sion, it can be thought that violence is more likely to produce truth than other forms of interaction. For example, it was believed by the Ancient Greeks that confessions obtained under torture were more likely to be true, and tormented bodies would reveal temporal or metaphysical truths, just as a 'touchstone' revealed whether a sample was gold or not when it was rubbed and scraped.[41] The assumption was that a slave would not spontaneously produce a true statement and that truth was 'generated by torture' (duBois 1991: 36).

The 'reappearance' of the physical body – both for the victim, who becomes aware of physical damage or vulnerability, and for the spectator, who sees hidden parts of the body opened up to the view – has often been a theme in performance art.[42] Tadeusz Kantor reflected on the history of the anatomy lesson as a public revelation of the secrets of the body by stag-ing a 'happening' based on Rembrandt's painting 'The Anatomy Lesson of Dr Tulp'.[43] In the painting, students surround a corpse as Doctor Tulp points to the sinews and nerves of the anatomised arm; a student in the background studies an anatomical text. In Kantor's performance, the participants wore contemporary clothes, surrounding a fully dressed man lying on a table in the centre; Kantor himself held open a reference book. The participants used scalpels to snip open the man's pockets to reveal their contents.[44] Other performance artists have also explored this dynamic of exposing the body: in Yoko Ono's 1965 *Cut Piece*, she offered the audience a pair of scissors to use as they wished; she sat unmoving on the stage, as one after another, individuals snipped away at her clothes, at first tentatively and then more aggressively. In Marina Abramović's six-hour piece *Rhythm 0* (1974), she stood in the same space as the audience alongside a table that held mis-cellaneous objects. A notice by the objects explained: 'There are 72 objects on the table that can be used on me as desired. I am the object. During this time I take full responsibility.' The objects included domestic materials (yarn, paint, wood), foods (bread, olive oil, honey, wine), clothes (scarf, hat, shoes), sub-stances designed for the body (lipstick, soap and perfume), natural objects (flowers, a feather), everyday tools (candle, matches, fork, spoon, comb, pocket knife, scalpel, needle, nails) and more specialised objects (a Polaroid camera, a gun and a bullet). Over the duration of the piece, the interactions became increasingly intrusive and dangerous to the performer.[45]

The body of the performer also reappears for the audience when it seems to be at risk through its perilous position in space, as in aerial performance, trapeze or acrobatics. In both *Drunken Madness* (1981) and *Cuckoo* (1987) by Station House Opera, objects and performers are suspended at height on ropes, in what director Julian Maynard Smith describes as 'an assemblage' rather than a 'made up' world. He comments that 'the stability you normally associate with furniture is taken away, as well as the floor' (Kaye 1996: 195). As in the performances by Ono and Abramović discussed above, the performers are 'subject' to a process rather than being in control of it. Nick Kaye suggests that this leads to a rare equivalence between humans and material objects: as 'both performers and objects are in the air, the performers become in some ways interchangeable with the objects'. As Veltruský suggested, 'a thing and a man can change places … a man can become a thing and a thing a living being' (Veltruský 1964: 90–91). For Maynard Smith, the strength of the Station House Opera approach is that it allows the set to respond to the performer and vice versa. He suggests that it is rare to see the body 'having a two-way relationship with the physical world' in performance: 'Either it's narrative-based theatre or, if you get people hanging up in the air, they do it without any sense of danger. There's no sense of interdependence' (Kaye 1996: 197).

CONSTRUCTING REALITY

If questions of staging violence and eating are never straightforward, it is partly because they heighten the existing fault lines in theories of realism in theatre. Even the banal activity of making a cup of tea or coffee – one of the most common examples of the 'reality effect' at work in soap opera on radio and television – can be problematic. Gay McAuley, a sensitive reader of the object in performance, recalls a production in which the performers made themselves cups of coffee. She describes herself as being 'distracted from the fiction by the mechanics of the set':

> the fact that water had been piped to the sink, that the fridge and kettle were real and were plugged into real power points, registered in my mind and indeed took precedence over the dramatic fiction to the extent that they have remained in my memory while I have forgotten nearly everything else about the production.
>
> (McAuley 2000: 182)

If 'real steam' is a potentially disillusioning force when it appears in classic realism, the following examples suggest that this 'distraction' may sometimes be to the point, and that some dramatists are directing our attention to the material world with a critical purpose.

Caryl Churchill's 1983 play *Fen* portrays the harshness of agricultural labour and domestic violence. In one scene, Angela forces her 15-year-old stepdaughter Becky to drink cups of boiling water as a punishment. Becky drops one cup; Angela immediately fills another from the kettle:

> **Angela**. It's meant to be hot. What you made of girl? Ice cream? Going to melt in a bit of hot? [...] Say sorry and you needn't drink it.
>
> (Churchill 1983: 8)

Potential concern about the actual temperature of the water and the actor's body does not disrupt the spectator's involvement with Becky's experience because the salient characteristics of the drink are so clearly constructed by the dialogue between the two women, just as their relationship is expressed through their relation to the material world: Angela makes a drink that is 'meant to be' too hot to drink. Churchill enjoys playing with the audience's expectations of drama set in rooms that include a kitchen sink – her sense of mischief perhaps accentuated by her long association with the Royal Court, the home of 'kitchen sink drama'. In *Heart's Desire*, a family wait in their kitchen for a grown-up daughter who has just returned from Australia. The action repeatedly resets to the beginning of the scene, a decision that in itself disrupts the audience's desire to see a sequence of events as 'natural' or inevitable. Further, the kitchen is invaded by a series of surprising visitors – armed gunmen, a ten foot tall bird and 'a horde of small children' who 'rush in, round the room and out again'. In the 1997 Royal Court production, the children burst into the room from the kitchen's fitted units – a choice that further dismantled the reality effect of the pine units (Churchill 1997).[46]

The playwright and director Nina Raine has written a very revealing account of the rehearsal process for Churchill's play *Far Away*. She compares the first British production at the Royal Court in 2000, for which she was the assistant director to Stephen Daldry, and Peter Brook's 2002 production of the play in French at the Bouffes du Nord. She discusses the decisions about props in particular detail, noting that these are one of Daldry's strengths: 'He knows how they support, as mini-metaphors, the psychology of a scene. So, for instance, he had little Joan unpacking and unravelling her aunt's sewing kit at the table – as she unravelled explanations from the aunt' (Raine 2002). The play takes place in a near-future of universal war. Joan, as a young adult, is a hat-maker. She makes elaborate hats that are worn in a parade by those who are about to undergo mass execution. Joan says of the hats, 'It seems so sad to burn them with the bodies', a line that, as Raine notes, 'captures the essence of Churchill's blank, poker-faced irony, the affectless surface and the black undertow of laughter'.

In Brook's production, the hats were mere indications of chicken wire and crêpe paper that were swept away after each performance, while the Royal Court invited a milliner into rehearsal to describe the process, and commissioned Philip Treacy to create a hat that was Joan's final achievement. According to Raine, Stephen Daldry had understood that the hats are 'potentially a glorious theatrical gag':

Firstly, he knew that the audience relishes watching something actually being done on stage – rather than faked, or mimed. So Stephen made the actors really paint feathers, hammer nails, soak and steam felt. It was a props nightmare. But he was right – it was very interesting to watch. [...] Secondly, it is a simple gift of a joke that the hat, each time it appears, is successively more elaborate. When Joan produced her final (genuine) Philip Treacy creation, it got a huge laugh every time.

Going beyond the actors simply performing real craft interactions, Daldry explored how they might reveal character through the handling of tools and materials:

'So, they have to bash the felt to get the water in, good. And would she have to sort of struggle with the tubing, manipulate it into shape?'

'Oh yes,' said Susie the hat-maker.

Stephen beamed at Caryl, then, scowling, mimed furious pummelling and yanking, saying Joan's line between gritted teeth – 'It's just if you're going to go on about it all the time, I don't know why you don't do something about it.'

Then, he mimed the other character, Todd, fussily stitching, saying through pursed lips, 'This is your third day.'

Stephen – maybe from his days as a clown in a circus – knew that props can be a great source of comedy. Especially tools. When the two actors were doing their hats, Stephen paid meticulous attention to the symmetry, balance and contrast of their actions – particularly in the scene where they have a heated argument. 'She needs to do something aggressive with a tool' he said musingly. 'He's got his iron – she's got to top that.'

'A drill?' suggested Paul Arditti, the sound designer, who was sitting in on rehearsals that day.

'What would she be drilling?' Stephen countered.

'Doesn't have to be drilling, necessarily' said Paul. 'You can use it to twist or untwist wire very quickly, if you have a hook on the end.'

'Show me' said Stephen.

It worked brilliantly. Stephen finessed it.

'Go like this,' he said to Joan/Kathy. He stood, scowling at Todd/Kevin, holding the drill. 'Check if it works, like this – ' He scowled up at the drill, which he 'bzzd' briefly in the air – 'then, put the wire on, and -'; 'bzzz' – he straightened the wire – eyeing Kevin beadily while he did so, never breaking eye contact. The action expressed all the venting of rage we needed. Also, since the man is on the run in the argument, Stephen matched their actions accordingly. Kathy had to bash things with a hammer – 'but I want Kevin doing something squishy while she's bashing – like rinsing his tea-towel in a bowl'. Kevin's hat was an arrangement of cloth flames, each reinforced with wire. During a particularly tense silence in the scene, Kevin straightened a wilting flame-petal.

'That's right' Stephen said approvingly. 'Get your willy out.'

(Raine 2002)

This account of the rehearsal process is particularly interesting in revealing the way that the craft knowledge of the milliner and the sound designer contributes to the director and actor developing a particular gestural language for the production. The tacit knowledge of a production's aesthetics which members of the technical team deploy is discussed in an article by Nick Hunt and Susan Melrose on the notion of the 'mastercraftsperson':

> Mastery of the performance-technical systems, as a whole, cannot then be fully understood by simple analysis of one thread of the component activities to which it contributes; yet the single 'technicians' must be able to grasp the (operational) whole if they are to intervene effectively in it.
>
> (Hunt and Melrose 2005)

In the case of *Far Away*, the practical experience of using hand tools allows the sound designer to suggest an action that both has a reality in the theatrical action and accords with already established relationships between characters. Rather like Helene Weigel choosing props with her 'net-making, bread-baking/soup-cooking hands' (Brecht 1961: 72), the mastercraftsperson brings their specialist knowledge into performance by operating on several levels at once.

Let's return to the kitchen sink. *The Beauty Queen of Leenane* by Martin McDonagh (1996) contains another scene of a mother and daughter portrayed in conflict over the usually nurturing action of offering a hot drink. Mag praises her adult daughter for her skill in mixing her preferred drink – the invalid food Complan – from powder:

> **Mag**. You do make me Complan nice and smooth. (Pause.) Not a lump at all, nor the comrade of a lump.
>
> **Maureen**. You don't give it a good enough stir is what you don't do.
>
> **Mag**. I gave it a good enough stir and there was still lumps.
>
> **Maureen**. You probably pour the water in too fast so. What it says on the box, you're supposed to ease it in.
>
> (McDonagh 1996: 1–2)

This apparently banal exchange in the opening scene draws the audience's attention to the materiality of the drink, laying the ground for a later scene in which Maureen again prepares Complan for her mother. This time, standing behind her mother's back, she sloshes hot water into the cup and taps the spoon against the side without stirring it, spitefully magnifying the gesture for her own satisfaction and for that of the audience. The spectators are invited to imagine the unappealing lumpy mixture, while the actual contents of the cup are quite irrelevant.

The Beauty Queen of Leenane is full of significant props. Almost all the characters produce material objects as supporting evidence for their conflicting versions of the past: a decaying tennis ball, documents from a mental asylum, a sink that stinks of urine. The play combines banal discussions of afternoon television and the qualities of different kinds of biscuit with Gothic elements such as a love letter carelessly delivered to the wrong person and subsequently burnt. The stage directions specify a richly detailed set, right down to a 'touristy-looking embroidered tea-towel' on the wall that bears the inscription 'May you be half an hour in Heaven afore the Devil knows you're dead'. In the set for the 2010 revival designed by Ultz, whitewashed cottage walls and an old-fashioned cast iron range with a basket of turf and a heavy iron poker to one side evoked the naturalistic tradition of Dublin's Abbey Theatre. But electrical cables ran down the wall and the wooden rocking chair was set against ugly 1970s kitchen units. A long, narrow shelf above the fireplace was crammed with miscellaneous objects coated in thick dust, including small framed photos of children in school uniform, a paraffin lantern, matches and a jar of pens and pencils. A large framed photo of Jack and Bobby Kennedy hung on the wall, with a huge wooden crucifix above it, both covered in cobwebs. In a further twist on the clash between a romantic vision of rural Ireland and its contemporary existence, audience members made their way into the auditorium through an opening in a rough wall of wooden timbers and sheet plastic, like a temporary protection for a new building left unfinished after the collapse of the Celtic Tiger, or for a tumbledown building that the economic miracle had left untouched. Water poured down the plastic so that audience members took their seats shaking droplets of 'real rain' from their hair and faces.

According to the director of the play's first production, Garry Hynes, Irish audiences recognised the visual references to the tradition of the Abbey but 'soon realised that all was not as it seemed'. In the gap between the two realities, 'the black humour of the piece flowed'. But in London, Hynes suggests, audiences failed to recognise the comedy or the tradition, and 'placed the play in the tradition of Ibsen and Strindberg' (Giannachi and Luckhurst 1999: 53). As another commentator puts it, McDonagh's three plays in the Leenane Trilogy [*The Beauty Queen of Leenane*, *A Skull in Connemara* and *The Lonesome West*] are seen in Ireland as painting an 'imaginary, exaggerated picture of the West of Ireland, including plenty of elements which simultaneously underline and undermine its authenticity', but elsewhere, the plays are seen as 'authentic' (Vandervelde 2000: 299).

This misreading can't be entirely attributed to audiences' lack of familiarity with Ireland; the meticulous staging in both productions I have seen contributes to a 'reality effect' that is visceral as much as visual. Early scenes in *The Beauty Queen of Leenane*, like the making of the Complan, present the meaning of material reality as constructed by the characters, with the complicity of the audience, but in the second half of the play, the negotiation is short-circuited. After battling over their memories and versions of reality, the mother and daughter are portrayed in a scene of unambiguous material interaction as Maureen is shown scalding Mag with boiling oil. The stage directions read: '**Maureen** slowly and deliberately takes her mother's shrivelled hand, holds it down on the burning range, and starts slowly pouring some of the hot oil over it, as **Mag** screams in pain and terror' (McDonagh 1996: 47). Catherine Cusack, quoted in the introduction, remembered this moment as one of the most horrifying moments of violence she ever saw on stage.

As Lucy Nevitt cautions, acts of violence 'can be performed in different styles, and perhaps surprisingly, the question of whether they are *realistic* is not a particularly helpful way of approaching stylistic choice' (Nevitt 2013: 18).[47] McDonagh's work has often been included with the group of plays staged at the Royal Court that Aleks Sierz dubbed 'in-yer-face' drama. Reviews of Sarah Kane's *Blasted* (1995) and Mark Ravenhill's *Shopping and Fucking* (1996), emphasised the explicit presentation of sex acts and extreme violence. The productions were more various stylistically than this epithet suggests. Nevertheless, the plays display a shared interest in what Sarah Kane called 'experiential' drama (Sierz 2001: 92), even when they remain broadly within the conventions of realistic theatrical representation in terms of dialogue, fictional setting and continuity of character.[48]

COOKING FOR THE AUDIENCE

Martin McDonagh positions two acts of extreme violence at the end of *Beauty Queen* to resolve questions raised earlier about conflicting accounts of reality. In *Some Voices*, by Joe Penhall (1996), a cookery lesson plays a similar role. Cooking and eating can produce a 'reappearance' of the bodies of spectators and actors similar to that produced by physical violence. Penhall has spoken about the role of food in two of his other plays. *Blue/Orange* (2000), like *Some Voices*, explores the perceptions of a man labelled as mentally ill. During rehearsals, Penhall wanted to cut a moment in which an orange is peeled on stage because he was concerned that it didn't reflect clinical practice. Penhall recalls that Roger Michell, the director, insisted on retaining it because 'it would be a great theatrical moment. And I didn't believe him, but it was. You could smell the zest and see the spray' (Lawson 2011). This physical experience is shared by all three characters (and by the audience), in contrast to the widely differing constructions of reality made by the patient, young psychiatrist and older consultant. In the same interview, Penhall says that his favourite scene in his play *Landscape with Weapons* is a food fight in which the characters throw curry at each other: 'There's something about those purely physical moments'. In *Some Voices* the cooking is 'experiential' in two senses: the spectators directly experience (through smell) the material interaction, and (as the dialogue highlights) the characters' experience of matter is the focus of the scene.[49]

In the play's final scene, Pete teaches his younger brother Ray how to cook an omelette. The chopping and frying of onions, mushrooms and eggs can be both seen and smelt. The scene depends on the performers' real inter-action with the food – if the butter burns or the eggs turn out to be rotten, the audience knows all about it. And the performer must know his materials as well as the character does. Pete knows his eggs, but the eggs control the pace of the scene. The omelette-making is a metaphorical manifestation of the brothers' interaction: in the course of the play, Pete has learned how to 'handle' Ray in a manner appropriate to his idiosyncratic 'grain', and this is embodied in the act of handling complicated raw materials in the real time of the performance. The analogy between Ray's interaction with his brother and his interaction with the material world – confident but not dominating – works on many levels. It provides a model of human relationship to the material world as having the same depth and significance as relationships with other people.

GLAMOUR AND MESS

Tim Crouch's play *The Author* (2009) 'is set in the Jerwood Theatre Upstairs at the Royal Court Theatre – even when it's performed elsewhere' and reflects on the history of representation at that theatre. The four perform-ers are seated among the audience. Three of them play the parts of people working in theatre – two actors and a playwright – and the fourth is a devoted member of the Royal Court audience. He refers enthusiastically to notorious stagings of violent acts – evoking, without naming them, Sarah Kane's *Blasted* and, a generation earlier, Edward Bond's *Saved* (1965). In contrast, the actors and playwright talk about the processes of research and rehearsal, the work done by the stage manager, special effects artist and fight director, and the impact a play's violent subject has on the actors' life outside theatre. These are subjects that are not often thematised within thea-tre (but see Ridout 2006). The actor 'Esther', quoted earlier in this chapter describing audience members' curiosity about stage blood, elaborates on the techniques used:

> I had pouches of stage blood strapped to bits of my body. One famous moment when Vic would hit me in the face and blood would spray from my eye. I had a sponge in my hand, so when I brought my hand up like this – like this, can you see? – I could make the blood spray out. Nobody knew how it was done! It was really shocking and real. The stage was a mess at the end of the show. Poor old stage management spent hours clearing it up at the end. I had to shower for ages to get it all off me!
>
> (Crouch 2011: 191)

There is an ironic contrast between Esther's uncritical comment that the violence was 'real' and her comments about the amount of backstage labour required to create (and clean up after) the image of violence. Dominic Johnson sees *The Author* as an example of contemporary theatre's critique of 'the dominant culture of realist drama from Ibsen to Williams', in particular of visual representation. He notes that the play's 'arduous, ethically uncom-fortable ending' takes place in pitch darkness: 'Relayed in words rather than frank visual content, Crouch's verbal images still graze the mind's eye' (Johnson 2012: 15). In writing a very verbal script that critiques the visual, Crouch is both commenting on the Royal Court tradition and part of it.

Caryl Churchill's play *The Skriker* also suggests the dark side of performance's power to transform everyday reality. The Skriker – a 'shape-shifter and death portent' – is able to effect for her own dark ends the magical transformations we associate with theatre: she makes words into things, by making other people utter coins or toads, and transforms herself into different characters and objects. She magically transports a young woman, Josie, to a lavish feast in a splendid palace among beautifully dressed creatures. The creatures of the underworld press food and drink on Josie, saying in a chant that slips between luxury and violence:

Welcome homesick
drink drank drunk
avocado and prawn cockfight cockup cocksuck
red wine or white wash
champagne the pain is a sham pain the pain is a sham

(Churchill 1998: 269)

Josie is warned by another human girl: 'Don't eat. It's glamour. It's twigs and beetles and a dead body. Don't eat or you'll never get back. Don't drink. It's glamour. It's blood and dirty water' (270). The stage directions for the feast read: '*It looks wonderful except that it is all glamour and here and there it's not working – some of the food is twigs, leaves, beetles, some of the clothes are rags, some of the beautiful people have a claw hand or hideous face.*' The props for this scene have to show both the projected image of beauty and desirability – and at the same time, a repulsive material reality. Here, 'glamour' has a theatrical character, evoking an older usage: 'When devils, wizards or jugglers deceive the sight, they are said to cast glamour o'er the eyes of the spectator' (Oxford English Dictionary). In these examples, we are far from the 'reality effects' of television or film. Instead, the texture of reality is seen as constructed by the characters – but is no less viscerally troubling.[50]

This chapter began by thinking about the problems physical interactions with the body through food and violence cause for performance. 'Esther' refers to the people who have to clean up stage blood, the 'poor old' stage management. Increasingly, theatres offer glimpses of the backstage world through photos and blogs shared on social media. On a recent 'Love Theatre Day' the Young Vic Theatre tweeted photos of backstage areas normally hidden from the public and a list of the ingredients for the stage blood used in their production of *A View from the Bridge*, including black treacle, glycerine and food colouring.[51] A more extended account of a significant prop is given in a blog on the Almeida Theatre's website. Written from the point of view of the stage management team for *Carmen Disruption* by Simon Stephens, it describes the challenges of working with a life-size mechanical bull and large quantities of stage blood. In this production, directed by Michael Longhurst and designed by Lizzie Clachan, the audience entered the auditorium via a door normally reserved for backstage staff. They filed along a dark, narrow corridor, passing the open door to a dressing room where an actor was glimpsed in traditional nineteenth-century costume for the role of Carmen – a ruffled skirt and tightly laced bodice. They stepped up onto the stage through a door in the back wall, crossing the boards to reach their seats. In the centre of the stage, a life-size bull lay on its side, as if felled in a bullfight. Coming up close to the bull, audience members realised that it was breathing, the chest rising and falling gently. The bull was carved by sculptor Stephen Hicklin, and finished by prop-maker Russell Beck, who added a remote controlled actuator, so that stage management could cue the bull's breathing and the movement of a foreleg.

Later in the play, several of the characters describe – from their own points of view – a motorbike crashing into the side of a bridge. The rider's body is described as lying in the middle of the road, 'still as a leather sack full of bones'. As they speak about the crash, black blood – like oil – begins to trickle almost imperceptibly from the bull's mouth. Stage managers experimented with the composition of the stage blood to give it the right degree of viscosity – it needed to 'seep' (Finney 2015). Each performance called for approximately 60 litres of blood, and the mixture had to be washable, since the singer playing Carmen would collapse back, fully dressed, against the bleeding bull. The ingredients under consideration included food colouring, poster paint, milk, golden syrup, fabric softener and washing-up liquid.

Chapter

8

A Scenographic Approach to the Object

In the realist and naturalist approaches to theatre described in Chapter 4, the material reality of the prop is 'looked through' to get at something 'deeper' which is character, or human nature, or 'reality'. Materiality is treated as secondary to human life – thus the object becomes a 'prop' or 'accessory'. As a corollary, the relationship between the human performer and the object is one of 'use' or 'attribute'. The performances discussed in this chapter explore very different kinds of relationship between humans and material things. Here, the object has an independent scenographic role – that is, it is used as part of the 'scenic writing'. The term 'scenography', according to Arnold Aronson, 'implies something more than creating scenery of costumes or lights. It carries a connotation of an all-encompassing visual-spatial construct as well as the process of change and transformation that is an inherent part of the physical vocabulary of the stage' (quoted in Collins and Nisbet 2010: 140). Aronson draws attention to the changes over time that can be experienced by and through the material world of performance.

In contrast to Andrew Sofer's account of a prop's journey through *dramatic* time, the scenographer working with material objects is therefore interested in *stage* time – and also the time encrusted in or embodied by those objects. The prop's journey shapes the performance on an equal basis with other elements such as text and music. Penny Saunders of Forkbeard Fantasy expresses an awareness of the length of time a prop is the focus of attention, and how this varies according to the nature of the prop:

> Props can hang around too long on stage, especially if they are extraordinary. They make an immediate impact that can delight the audience, because they cannot understand how they were done, but leave them there too long and you betray that delight. Ordinary props can stay longer as they work differently on the imagination. They can mellow, be forgotten and then sometimes do something shocking because they have become so familiar.
>
> (quoted in Crawley 2007: 28)

Scenographic approaches have links to both improvised and devised performances and to performance art – which lies beyond the scope of this book. This chapter will focus on the work of Tadeusz Kantor (1915–1990) and Richard Foreman (b. 1937).

Forms of theatre that begin with the material world, including the human body and its movement, are sometimes described as 'physical' or 'visual theatre'. Though the term 'visual theatre' might seem reduplicative, it serves a purpose in making a connection to the visual arts, live art and performance art. In the case of Tadeusz Kantor, both a director and a visual artist, there are strong correspondences between his 'poor theatre' and contemporary art movements including the *informel* and the Italian *arte povera* movement of the late 1960s. In *L'Objet pauvre: mémoire et quotidien sur les scènes contemporaines françaises* [The 'poor' object: memory and the everyday in contemporary French theatre] Jean-Luc Mattéoli describes how a focus on the object in fine art influenced theatre-makers, noting the use of collage by Braque and Picasso and the appropriation of industrially produced objects by Marcel Duchamp: 'The rupture with the ancient system of representation forged in the Renaissance was materialised through the object – whether it was nailed together or glued to a canvas or exhibited in its pure thingness' (Mattéoli 2011: 13).[52] The objects in the work of Picasso, Duchamp and Schwitters are united by their ordinariness – objects that are usually ignored because they are so ubiquitous. Moreover, Mattéoli suggests, the act of choosing such an object is a way of avoiding the cult of the 'hand' of the artist. These artists are performing actions with far less cultural prestige than painting or drawing. Instead, they have made it their practice to 'restore' (like a furniture-maker), 'put together' (like an artisan, or a builder), 'cut out' (like a child), 'glue' (like a graphic artist), or just 'choose' (like a charlatan or a comedian) (Mattéoli 2011: 17). The members of AKHE Russian Engineering Theatre, for example, describe themselves as merely 'operators' of space, light and sound, exploring 'elementary physical laws' (AKHE 2015). Nevertheless, the theatre-makers discussed here do display a recognisable 'hand' in their 'scenic writing'.

TADEUSZ KANTOR: REALITY OF THE LOWEST RANK

In 1944, Tadeusz Kantor mounted a clandestine production of *The Return of Odysseus* in an apartment in occupied Krakow. Kantor writes about the objects used in this first production again and again, as well as quoting them in other performances and preserving or recreating some of them in the Cricoteka archive. They have an emblematic significance, and are used by Kantor to distinguish the 'poor object' from a theatrical prop or abstract work of art.

In his various lists of the objects used in *The Return of Odysseus*, Kantor always describes their physical state – worn, rotten, smeared with mud – as if their form is a temporary coalescence of the formless. These lists make a striking contrast with the list of 72 objects used in Marina Abramović's 1974 piece *Rhythm O*, discussed in the previous chapter. The items on Abramović's list are deliberately generic, without brand names or history.

A stage manager could take the list to a shopping centre and purchase all of the items within an hour. But even the most everyday or generic of Kantor's objects – 'a chair' – is always qualified by description: it is 'simple', 'a kitchen chair' and 'well worn'. This description recalls Brecht's poem in appreciation of the 'knives and forks whose wooden handles/ Have been worn away by many hands' (Willett 1984: 139). The simple kitchen chair, doubtless made of wood, conveys familiarity, domesticity, and also a sense of time, of the generations that have used, misused and looked after the chair.

Other objects used in *The Return of Odysseus* were taken from the street: a cartwheel, a board, a trestle. These wooden objects evoke the closeness of the rural, agricultural life to the sophisticated urban life in Krakow in the 1930s and 1940s. Both trestle and cartwheel are 'smeared with mud'. The board is described as 'rotten', with rusty marks where nails have been pulled out – it might have fallen off a neglected building; in contrast the trestle suggests the energy of building and construction work but is smeared with mud as well as cement and lime. Then there are military-industrial metal objects that are nevertheless dissolving: wire rope and a 'rust eaten' iron gun barrel that has lost its wheels. All these objects are brought into a room that has been bombed, its walls 'full of holes', the floor 'missing planks'. The audience sits on 'parcels' (introducing a key motif for Kantor, that of 'emballage' or wrapping); the parcels are covered with dust and lime from the destroyed walls – in a sense the audience members also seem to be part of the 'debris scattered all over' (Kantor 1993: 73–4).

Writing much later about *The Return of Odysseus*, Kantor said that it would have been 'a wicked pettiness to create papier mâché columns and waves for Odysseus' tragic return. I want to place actors among simple parcels, ladders, and chairs; take their costumes away from them, discard all aesthetic values…' (Kantor 1993: 38). The language of stylised waves was familiar to Kantor since, alongside his direction of the Cricot company he had worked as a designer within the official theatre. Rejecting the tropes conventionally used to represent 'classical Greece' (columns and waves), Kantor places himself in the lineage of Duchamp, referring to all the elements of the performance as potential 'ready mades': space, furniture, actors and text. In 'The Milano Lessons', a manifesto based on a course he taught in Milan in 1986, Kantor contrasts Duchamp's 'found object' with the studiously accurate representation of an object in painting. Through Duchamp's appropriation, a 'different kind of object emerges', an object 'WRENCHED FROM THE REALNESS OF LIFE, BEREFT OF THE LIFE FUNCTION THAT VEILED ITS ESSENCE, ITS OBJECTNESS' (Kantor 1993: 210). By pulling the object out of its everyday context, the artist reveals its 'objectness'. Yet Kantor's appropriations are quite different from the acts by which artists have redefined everyday objects as art objects, such as signing them, placing them on a pedestal or in a vitrine, publishing explanatory texts, manifestos or press releases. In the context of war and genocide, Kantor argues, abstraction and reproduction lost their power and artists appropriated the 'real' instead. But the appropriation is described as a hasty act:

> We had the strength only to grab the nearest thing,
> THE REAL OBJECT,
> and to call it a work of art!

(211)

The objects thus appropriated are not precious or full of personal associations – they are 'poor' objects, broken down and 'about to be discarded'. This lack of function threatens the object's survival, echoing the genocidal discourse of 'useless', 'superfluous' people: a poor object was 'bereft of a life function that would save it':

> An object that was stripped, functionless, a r t i s t i c !
> An object that would make one feel for it pity and affection.

(ibid.)

For Kantor the lack of function is what makes the 'poor object' a 'real object', capable of evoking fellow feeling.

LANGUAGE AS RAW MATERIAL

Kantor's productions of *The Dead Class* and *Wielopole/Wielopole* drew on *l'art informel* of Wols, Jean Fautrier, Georges Mathieu and Jackson Pollock – work he had seen in Paris in 1955. (For a discussion of the *informel* and of Bataille, see Bois and Krauss 1997.) The essential character of matter, its formlessness, is revealed in states of decomposition and disintegration. In a manifesto on the Informel Theatre, Kantor lists verbs that describe 'ways of treating matter' including 'crumpling' and 'crushing', 'kneading' and 'mixing', 'splashing', 'dabbling', 'smearing', 'tearing' and so on. They are also considered as 'physical actions within and without matter' – opening up the possibility of exploring these actions independently of any physical substance, as a gesture that contains a memory (Kantor 1993: 56). In *The Dead Class*, the Charwoman-Death (a lanky woman in black, played by a man) pushes a long row of rotting books from a desk onto the floor: 'cleaning up' becomes an activity of pushing stuff about, speeding the descent of objects into matter, into dust. This figure takes a newspaper from the litter of decaying paper and reads the 'news' of 1914 aloud – the assassination of the Archduke Franz Ferdinand in Sarajevo – 'Well, there's going to be a war'. The past, far from dissolving as its material relics decay, is always present, is the present.

An object that is no longer usable and starts to rot is moving towards the condition of matter. Kantor makes an analogy between 'raw matter' and 'raw speech', in which 'human articulation resembles the remotest, the wildest forms (howling of the pack of dogs) and the cruelest sounds (cracking of bones)' (Kantor 1993: 52). He juxtaposes a list of materials 'at the threshold of becoming matter', such as rags, musty books and worm-eaten wood, with 'the raw matter of speech': 'murmur, stutter, drawl, croak, phonemes, obscene language' and so on (ibid.: 57–8).

Both bodies and objects are equally capable of being inhabited by voices from the past: 'I hold that theatre is a ford across the river. It is a place through which the dead figures from that shore, from that world, cross over into our world and now into our lives.' Kantor suggests as an image for the way in which bodies and objects became inhabited by the past, the dybbuk, a figure of Jewish folklore: dybbuks are 'spirits of the dead who enter into the bodies of others and speak through them' (Pleśniarowicz 1994: 76). The words used in performance gathered from texts by Witkiewicz or Gombrowicz, from an old Yiddish song, from school lessons, Latin quotations and 'Phonetic Blots' resemble found objects:

> The dramatic text is also a 'ready-made object' that has been formed outside the zone of performance and the audience's reality. It is an object that has been found; an object whose structure is dense and whose identity is delineated by its own fiction, illusion, and psychophysical dimension. I treat it in much the same way as I treat other events and objects in the production.
>
> (Kantor 1993: 86)

Words are set loose from their context and become repeated until they become fetishised objects. In *The Dead Class*, the elderly pupils are always descending into gibberish; Klassowicz describes the excited chanting and screaming of the word 'heel' as 'like the Revelation, or the Ascension, of the heel' (Klassowicz 1979: 121). Similarly, in *Wielopole/Wielopole*, the Priest at the wedding urges 'Father' to repeat the words of the service after him: 'But this lifeless dummy can utter nothing but a hideous animal gibber, choking with the effort of remembering the human voice. Thus unfolds the dialogue of the quick and the dead' (Kantor 1990: 37). Objects here are not straightforward 'texts' or 'scores' as they might be for Stanislavski or Brecht. The messages they contain are practically illegible, always on the point of dissolution, past and present smeared together.

BIO-OBJECTS

In *Dainty Shapes and Hairy Apes* (1973), Kantor created what he called 'BIO-OBJECTS', in which the human is fused to an object, the 'quick' to the 'dead': a man with two bicycle wheels grown into his legs, a man with a wooden board on his back, a man carrying doors, a kneeling woman attached to her pew, a woman with a window-frame, a card-player with his table. Bio-Objects reappear in *Let the Artists Die* (1985) and *I Shall Never Return* (1988), and the white-faced actors arranged on traditional school desk-benches in *The Dead Class* form a single Bio-Object, since according to Kantor 'the benches and the pupils make up one organism' (Pleśniarowicz 1994: 94). In binding people to objects Kantor replaced a traditional notion of character with the notion of humans shaped by their objects. 'Without an actor, the object was a lifeless wreck. On the other hand, the actors were conditioned by those same objects; their gestures and actions were influenced by the objects' (Kantor 1993: 391). They can be thought of as reverse prostheses – rather than splints or sticks which support the body, or extend its powers, these objects require the service of the human body – their 'living organ' – to extend their reach (Pleśniarowicz 1994: 67).

In their parasitic relation to the human, these objects resemble dybbuks, the wandering spirits which cleave to already occupied bodies in order to speak. However, they are also like the objects inhabited by dybbuks, for which the possessors are obliged to care. In Kantor's pieces, no-one is released from an object, and no restitution to the unhappy spirit of the object is made. Kantor's constitution of the theatrical subject through a relationship with an object recalls the account given by Ann Rosalind Jones and Peter Stallybrass of clothing in the Renaissance. They write that understanding the significance of clothing in this period requires that we 'undo our own social categories, in which subjects are prior to objects, wearers to what is worn' (Jones and Stallybrass 2000: 2). Just as clothes gave shape both physically and socially to their wearers in the Renaissance, Kantor's objects shape and deform the performers' bodies and give them their names and dramatic functions. Kantor also played with clothing in his *emballage* art work, wrappings which drew on the idea of nomadic peoples or individuals outside society who had a 'passion for packaging their bodies in coats, saddle-blankets, canvas, sunken in the complicated anatomy of clothing, in the arcana of packages, bags, bundles, thongs, strings' (Pleśniarowicz 1994: 23). For Alice Rayner, the prosaic action of wrapping is a comment on the old slur against theatre – that it is 'all surface, all spectacle' (Rayner 2006: 196). If meaning is not hiding in some invisible essence, then it is 'the package that matters because matter is the phenomenon' (197).

Human interactions with objects in performance can produce or release their inherent sound potential. In *The Dead Class*, an old-fashioned cradle which resembles a coffin is brought on stage and is rocked automatically by a motor. During the performance, Kantor places inside the cradle two wooden balls, which clatter in a slightly irregular way as they roll from one side to the other (the sound is amplified). The sound is an echo of the wooden rattles which were traditionally used when bells were silenced during Lent, and therefore associated with a melancholy period. The balls also refer to testicles, to generative powers – an association that is made when, later in the performance, Rozhulantyna takes the wooden balls out of the cradle. Others are shocked: 'you mustn't do things like that. It's barbaric' (Klassowicz 1979: 134). By demonstrating how the sound is produced, Kantor renounces the concealed arts of sound designer, and insists that it is simply the interaction of three wooden objects that makes such a melancholy parody of the heartbeat. The shock at the removal of the balls from the cradle is transmitted to the spectators as the knocking sound is replaced by a hollow creaking. As in his *Anatomy Lesson after Rembrandt*, Kantor here makes a gesture belonging to the Enlightenment tradition (anatomising the body, displaying a mechanism) which nevertheless reinforces the spectators' feeling that something more than lifeless matter lies before them.

RICHARD FOREMAN: ONTOLOGIES OF OBJECTS

Richard Foreman, the founder and artistic director of the Ontological-Hysteric Theater in New York, has written, directed and designed over 50 of his own plays. He reflects intensely on objects in performance, both in his plays and in the essays and introductions collected as *Unbalancing Acts*. In developing his early work, Foreman was fascinated by the idea of alchemy and the material processes undertaken by alchemists – 'stuff' that was 'mixed and remixed or boiled and reboiled' (Kaye 1996: 104). These processes of sublimation, evaporation, mixture and separation were typically repeated hundreds of times on the same sample. Repetition was not seen as failure but as an essential part of the practice: the repetitions were undertaken 'in the hope that at a certain moment, grace, or if you're going to read Jung, the unconscious, or something else, would take over and cause a transformation that you had not purposefully aimed at. You were just creating a space in which this grace might descend' (ibid.). Foreman's discussion here evokes the notions of repetition in rehearsal, but also the interest in material processes found in Kantor's writing. Foreman describes how this translated into the verbal texture of the early plays: 'all the talk was about the physical manifestations, about the physical feelings in the body and things like that'.

Foreman's process begins with writing texts. Each morning he writes half to three pages of dialogue. The dialogue has no indications of characters by name or number – just alternating speeches. He then revisits these texts, looking for a page that seems 'interesting and possible' as a 'key' page, adding others that relate in some way (Foreman 2015). He explains that the connection is intuitive rather than narrative, 'loosely thematic – in a very poetic sense'. Having gathered 40–50 pages in this way, he arranges them

> in search of some possible loose thematic 'scenario' – which again, is more 'variations on a theme' rather than strictly narrative. I look to establish a 'situation of tension' – then imagining how the other pages somehow augment and 'play with' that situation, rather than leading to story and resolution.
>
> (ibid.)

From this loose scenario, he assigns lines to characters. The visual world of the production develops from this script in a similarly associative manner. He flips through the pages of the script and makes sketches, followed by a series of rough scale models of the set in cardboard. Foreman's thoughts turn to props only a few weeks before rehearsal, when he revisits the text and starts to think about how to bring out its buried associations through the material objects on stage:

> Thumbing through the pages, again very casually, I'd say, For this page about the weather, maybe I can use an umbrella? Then I'd think, No, that's boring – better an umbrella at the end of a long stick with a wheel on the bottom. Then I'd go on leafing through the script and imagine one or two things that seemed suggestive for every page. In that way I'd amass a list of props, many of which had no obvious relation to the text, but all of which might add an interesting second level to the scene.
>
> (Foreman 1992: 18–19)

Like the improvisers described in Chapter 3, Foreman works with a reservoir of potentially interesting objects and materials. Many of the props are cut from the final production, but this 'surplus of materials' gives him 'room to play around'. Some of the props, such as the wheeled umbrellas, are produced in multiples to allow for 'choral prop effects'.

For Foreman, the props are a way of making concrete the fleeting associations he finds in his fragmentary texts, and juxtaposing imagery from different levels:

> I know a spectator could never pick up on all the feeling tones and associations packed into [my texts], especially when heard only once, in a single evening's performance. When you read it on the page you have time to allow all the possible associations to hit home, but listening to it whiz past in the theatre is another matter. So I try to help the spectator by adding props and scenic elements – skulls, flowers, globes, mirrors, stuffed animals, crutches, radios, and so on – which suggest the range of possible associations the text continually evokes.
>
> (24)

Bonnie Marranca has described the tableaux of his play *Pandering to the Masses: A Misrepresentation* (1975) as a 'surreal world' that does not conform to the usual physical laws of time and space, with the people who inhabit it moving back and forth in time and slipping easily between indoor and outdoor scenes. The objects 'scattered' here include: 'fruit, an oversized horse and giant pencils, croquet balls, stuffed animals, a pistol, snake and bicycle – all of which have symbolic value in Foreman's psychodrama. These are the symbols of childhood, of violence, of power and fear, temptation and sensuality' (Marranca 1996: 11). Foreman, however, claims that he is not interested in creating striking images that stick in the spectator's mind to be discussed later. Rather, he sees the play as a 'vivid dream' that the dreamer might feel intensely, but find impossible to recall:

> an art that affects you in the moment, but which you then find hard to remember, is straining to bring you to another level. It offers images or ideas from that other level, that other way of being, which is why you find them hard to remember. But it has opened you to the possibility of growing into what you are not yet, which is exactly what art should do.
>
> (24)

The spectator's attention to this kind of play can be compared to the 'free-floating attention' of psychoanalysis, in which the analyst waits for coherence to reveal itself. For those who are looking for coherence, Foreman says, one of his plays 'will appear to be an amorphous cloud of molecular particles, circulating in a seemingly random pattern, like Brownian motion' (27). But this is an image of a shifting world seen through a microscope, in which solid objects are discovered to be made up of atoms with empty space between them: 'I'm trying to function as an atomic physicist of the theater'. (28)

This image of the scenographer as an atomic physicist recalls the principles of materials science, which looks at how the properties of matter change when viewed at different scales. Changes at the microscopic scale can manifest themselves as changes in behaviour at the human scale. As materials scientist Mark Miodownik explains:

> It is this process that our ancestors stumbled upon to make new materials such as bronze and steel, even though they did not have the microscopes to see what they were doing – an amazing achievement. For example, when you hit a piece of metal you are not just changing its shape, you are changing the inner structure of the metal. If you hit it in a particular way, this inner structure changes in such a way that the metal gets harder. Our ancestors knew that from experience even though they didn't know why.
>
> (Miodownik 2013: 9)

Foreman's constellations of objects have an autonomous existence on stage, so that audience members can make their own connections, but he also draws literal connections to support the associations of the written text. In *Pandering*, lengths of string hang from the ceiling and across the space, cutting it into geometrical shapes. Performers move the strings to link objects and performers. In one sequence, for example, Rhoda finds an egg beneath a bottle on a small table. She says: 'Oh. It would hurt less if I put my forehead against the little egg.' She does so, but is not happy with the result. Max holds up a second egg; Rhoda imitates his pose, saying: 'Oh, I understand perfectly. That egg is part of a diagram.' She then hooks her egg onto a string from above. With a loud noise, a projection appears showing the following words:

> Fear enters
> and speaks to Rhoda
> with his soft voice.
> Fear proposes
> a network
> and a joint accomplishment.
>
> (Marranca 1996: 25)

Rhoda makes her egg swing back and forth, 'solving' the problem of fear for Ben, who has been asleep on the floor until this moment. Through the performers' actions, the egg is placed in a dynamic version of the 'diagram' and 'network' mentioned in the text. The gesture of placing the egg against the forehead helps to create an echo between the object and the human, priming the audience to see the characters as figures in a diagram too.

In Foreman's earlier plays, he notes, props were 'simple objects in static situations'. The lamp on the table said, in effect, 'I am a lamp. I go on. I go off. Don't try to do anything with me that you should not do with a lamp' (Foreman 1992: 81). From 1971, Foreman employed a more playful manipulation of objects that sometimes involved changing their function through the way that the performers related to them:

> My new perspective toward the psychic significance of objects allowed me to use the lamp in such a way that the lamp said, 'I am a lamp. But I could also be a projectile that you hurl at your enemy. I could also be something that you can lay on its side and put ketchup on and try tasting to see it if tastes good.' It could be any one of innumerable possibilities.
>
> (Foreman 1992: 81)

John Wright's distinction between 'open' and 'closed' improvisation with objects is useful in thinking about Foreman's move from exploring a series of possibilities for the object to an unfolding of a sequence in which the director or performer asks how the object 'wants' to move and 'What can the object do?' (Wright 2006: 84). Foreman goes on to discuss the idea of 'a world ruled by objects' in which the objects themselves propose new kinds of configuration. This leads the performer to an exploration of the semiotics of shape, usage, relationships between objects and between people and objects. In a world ruled by objects, the lamp could suggest:

> 'I am a lamp, and over there is a bookcase. What are the possible relationships between a lamp and a bookcase? Well, let me, lamp that I am, go over and sit next to a book on a bookcase. Can you read me like you can read a book? Is a book as bright as a lamp?' I'd let my imagination run free: 'I am a lamp. Usually, when

you go to bed at night you take a book and read before you go to sleep. Tonight, try taking me, a lamp, to bed, and hold me in your arms, and look into the light, and tell yourself the story that you see looking into the light.'

(81–2)

The objects that Foreman works with are typically mass-produced objects from the twentieth century. Revealing that his favourite objects are lamps and radios, he invites us to see ourselves in the props on stage:

These objects suggest two opposing sides of the same metaphysical question – are human beings 'lamps' who give of ourselves to illuminate the world, or are we 'radios' who receive information transmitted from elsewhere?

(82)

Foreman's question opens up an intriguing way to think about the objects that directors choose to put on display. Thinking about two of Kantor's favourite objects, we might equally wonder – are human beings 'chairs' who inevitably define every space they enter in terms of its human affordances, or 'umbrellas' who can open up to shelter a small portion of the world?

Chapter

9 Object Theatre

The earlier chapter on Complicite and Improbable describes a move towards 'object animation' in which everyday objects become invested with the illusion of life by endowing them with movement, sound and voice. In contrast, the practitioners of 'object theatre' largely avoid these techniques of animation in favour of investing the object with meaning through storytelling, word play and visual association. They draw on objects of mass production which have been 'charged' by their previous use and yet remain familiar enough to act as conductors of collective imagery. While object theatre is often bracketed with puppet theatre, the genres occupy distinct locations on the spectrum of animation. Like the scenographic prop, an object that appears in object theatre is generally presented as independent of the performer, worthy of attention in its own right, but not endowed with life as it might be in puppetry. Practitioners of object theatre are careful to distinguish their work both from actors' theatre and from puppetry: their focus is on what happens *between* the performer and the object.

'Object theatre' is quite frequently used as a descriptive term in theatre programmes in France, the Netherlands and Germany, but is less familiar in Britain and the United States. One indication of its status might be the programming of a trio of short 'object theatre' performances as part of the programme at the 2011 Charleville-Mézières international puppet festival. The performances were preceded by a playful lecture on the 'théâtre d'objets' for the uninitiated spectator, presented by three members of Bob Théâtre (Rennes). If naturalistic theatre has 'accessoires' (props), they explained, object theatre has 'super-accessoires', everyday objects that become charged with meaning through the performer's gaze or storytelling. It's striking that for this French company, object theatre was assumed to be a concept familiar enough to parody but not so well understood that their explanation was completely redundant.[53]

Object performance can be examined through lenses of both the visual and the performing arts; many of the artists working in object theatre also have practices in the visual arts, including sculpture and installation. In *American Puppet Modernism*, John Bell discusses examples of 'performing objects' ranging from giant puppets in street parades to customised cars. He notes that unlike conventional models of the actor–spectator relationship, in object performance the performer and spectator are both focused on the object, not on each other:

> The dynamics of object performance are similar to the dynamics of painting or sculpture in that the spectator concentrates on some thing designed or designated by another human: yet they are different because of the presence of the performer, who completes the object performance by adding movement, sound, and/or text. With the movement possibilities of her body, and the vocal possibilities of her voice, the performer interprets, frames, and contextualizes the image in front of the spectators, and helps the communal experience of watching performance become one in which our own responses to the chosen objects are provoked.
>
> (Bell 2008: 5)

Director Anna Furse has also discussed this unusual triad in puppetry and object performance, arguing that there is an ethical dimension to the performer's deliberate redirection of the spectator's gaze to a shared object of attention: 'Rather than draw attention to themselves, actor-puppeteers devote their attention to guiding ours outside, leading our attention away from their own bodies via the body itself' (Furse 2008: 21). For Bell, the implications are slightly different. He sees the underlying significance of object performance as metaphysical:

> the performer manipulates the object *in order* to show us how parts of the large and dead material world can be animated by humans. This allows us humans to play with the idea that we have some kind of control over inert matter; or, a bit deeper down, that our playing with objects allows us to come to terms with death.
>
> (Bell 2008: 5)

Despite typically using ready-made objects of mass production, object theatre often explores philosophical and poetic themes that exceed what might be expected of these toys and consumer items.

SOME PRACTITIONERS: AN INCOMPLETE LIST

Object theatre is particularly vibrant as a theatrical form in France, Germany, Belgium and the Netherlands, and in its distinct modern form came into existence in the 1970s and 1980s. It has typically been performed for small audiences, celebrating the diminutive scale of the work and the intimacy this creates, although some productions now make use of live video feeds projected onto large screens above or behind the playing area.

Vélo Théâtre, Manarf and Théâtre de Cuisine (France)

Christian Carrignon claims that the term 'théâtre d'objets' was coined in a kitchen in the south of France in 1980, to describe the work being created by a group of artists that included Charlot Lemoine and Tania Castaing (Vélo Théâtre, founded 1981), Jacques Templeraud (Théâtre Manarf) and Christian Carrignon and Katy Deville (Théâtre de Cuisine). These friends and artistic collaborators were looking for a way to describe the new kind of performance they were making: assemblages of small found objects accompanied by poetic, allusive storytelling. Katy Deville proposed the name: 'théâtre d'objet'. Carrignon recalls:

> We all grimaced because 'theatre' evoked the canonical texts that terrified us, and 'object' was cold, lifeless. But between the grandeur of the word 'theatre' and the littleness of the 'object', there is a precipice. The spectator's poetic energy is needed to bring together the sides of the abyss.
>
> (Carrignon and Mattéoli 2009: 25)

Vélo Théâtre, Manarf and Théâtre de Cuisine all continue to produce work and tour in France and internationally. Carrignon has written a short and revealing book with Jean-Luc Mattéoli, *Le théâtre d'objets* (2009), on his own work and influences. Mattéoli's full length study *L'objet pauvre: Memoire et quotidien sur les scènes contemporaines françaises* (2011) provides an important context for object theatre, considering the history of the object in relation to visual arts and the archaeology of the present, discussing Théâtre de Cuisine and Turak, among others.

TAMTAM Objektentheater (Netherlands)

TAMTAM Objektentheater was founded by Gérard Schiphorst and Marije van der Sande in 1979. They have written that their inspiration comes from found objects:

> Everyone probably has a box or drawer with mostly worthless and broken things. Kept because they might come in handy one day, or because they are souvenirs of special moments. This got completely out of hand with Gérard Schiphorst (1955) and Marije van der Sande (1956) of Dutch visual theatre company TAMTAM Objektentheater. Ever since their youth it was hard for them to throw things away, even if they were old and worn. In their childhood it was a kind of animism, a belief that things have a soul. Later dissatisfaction with over-consumption and overproduction became an important reason to recycle old things. Now they have a large hangar in the former harbour of their hometown Deventer at their disposal for the ever growing collection of found objects.
>
> (TAMTAM Objektentheater)

TAMTAM Objektentheater's performances are typically wordless, with complex soundtracks. *To Have or Not to Have* is set in a long sandbox, with two performers manipulating rusty metal and worn wooden objects, in what the creators describe as a 'medieval arms-race', a 'duel between an impertinent pair of pliers and a tenacious mole trap'.

Gare Centrale (Belgium)

Agnès Limbos founded Gare Centrale in 1984 and has created 11 performances for the company since then. She studied political science and
philosophy before training with Jacques Lecoq from 1977 to 1979. Limbos
has been an influential teacher and director as well as performing widely.
Selections from an essay by Claire Corniquet and Marion Rhéty discussing
the importance of the concept of the 'real object' to Limbos conclude this
chapter.

Peter Ketturkat (Germany)

Peter Ketturkat works both in sculpture and performance. He describes
his move in 1978 from the small village where he grew up to the industrial
region of the Ruhr as a complete change in physical environment that subsequently determined his artistic practice:

> I decided to find a way of transforming the everyday materials and objects I saw
> around me into some kind of artistic experience. It wasn't sentimental nostalgia,
> it was more to do with finding a kind of poetry in this new functional, urban envi-
> ronment, celebrating it even. So ever since then I've been creating theatre shows,
> installations and sculptures out of ordinary household objects, junk materials and
> industrial metals.
>
> (Ketturkat 2015)

Ketturkat has created more than 15 shows, including *Keine Angst vor großen
Tieren!* (*The Crazy Kitchen Crew*), which stars everyday kitchen utensils and
cutlery.

Gyula Molnàr (Hungary/Italy)

Gyula Molnàr, a performer and director of Hungarian origin, long resi-
dent in Italy, has had a significant influence on performers throughout
Europe both through his shows and through his teaching in workshops
and at the Ernst Busch Academy of Dramatic Art in Berlin. His book on
object theatre, *Teatro d'Oggetti* (2009), has been translated into German as
Objekttheater: Aufzeichnungen, Zitate, Übungen but has not yet been translated into English.

Molnàr's *Piccoli suicidi* (*Tre brevi esorcismi di uso quotidiano*) ['Small sui-
cides: three brief exorcisms of everyday use'] was created in 1981. In the first
of these three acts, *Alka-Seltzer (an effervescent tragedy)*, the performer sits
at a table illuminated by a desk lamp. A glass of water stands on the table.
The performer produces a handful of sweets in bright cellophane wrappers.
They giggle and play together. An Alka-Seltzer tablet appears, in grey aluminium foil, and tries to join in, but they reject all overtures. Left alone, the

tablet approaches the glass of water… For performer and scenographer Sean Myatt, this performance

> is one of the clearest and best examples of Object Theatre. Gyula does not disguise or change the nature of the objects but assists them in telling their story. He tells the tale of the sad bullying of an Alka-Seltzer by a group of sweets and its ultimate suicide in a glass of water. It is a perfect example of how the particular expressive qualities of an object give rise to associated meanings: the fizziness of the Alka-Seltzer and its association with headaches link it with depression and death as it sits on the edge of the cup and dissolves itself into the water.
>
> (Myatt 2009: 38)

Myatt performed Molnàr's piece in its entirety as part of his performance lecture *Instinctive Object Ramblings*, a 'series of encounters with people, objects and materials…to illustrate different stages of my professional practice as a puppeteer, object manipulator and designer' (Myatt 2009: 34).[54] In scenarios like these, the performer is not absent but rather builds a complicity with the audience in brief moments of removing the gaze from an attentive involvement in the scene on the table.

Stuart Sherman (United States)

The performance artist Stuart Sherman (1945–2001), a sometime collaborator with Richard Foreman, is best known for his small-scale solo performances under the collective title 'Spectacles'. He used a folding card table as his stage, performing largely wordless scenarios that involved dozens of objects, mostly mass-produced but some specially made. Critic Steven Stern describes him as like a 'high-concept mountebank': 'he would set up a cheap folding table, open a suitcase, pull out his props – toy cars, dollhouse chairs, rolls of masking tape, sheets of newspaper, wind-up teeth – and, with a kind of awkward urgency, he would arrange and position them in cryptic, patterned interactions' (Stern 2010). Sherman performed on the street, in his apartment and in the living rooms of his friends, picking up and repositioning his props at high speed, with a deadpan expression. Sherman described these performances as like sweeping his apartment: 'I didn't become a character, I didn't emphasize anything. It was more in the style of the performance of household chores' (ibid.). While the performances were often wordless, they explored visual-verbal puns and seemed to establish a grammar of objects. Stern describes the experience of watching 'Spectacles' as 'a bit like listening to a speech in an unknown language that somehow, magically, hovers just on the border of comprehension. It's clear there is a logic to the performer's gestures, a coherent grammar and more than that, there is wit' (ibid.).[55]

Paul Zaloom (United States)

Paul Zaloom, a New York-based performer and former member of Bread and Puppet Theatre, puts object theatre techniques to satirical use. His first solo piece, *The World of Plastic* (1978), used found objects including toys, tools and packaging to attack American consumer culture. In *Adventures of White-Man* (2012), the puppet cast is described as drawn from his own collection of 'toy cars, action figures, dolls, wind-up toys, tchotchkes, weird junk, and rubbish' (Zaloom 2015). Toy cars 'zoom' with childish glee and sound effects; plastic G.I. Joe dolls are given heightened, cartoony voices but their rigid bodies can only be jiggled across the toy stage – there is no attempt to create the illusion of independent life. Zaloom wants us to look beyond his props to the story he is telling. He has described himself as 'plonking' his objects on stage but the apparent casualness with which he handles them is deceptive. His hectic energy is like that of a ten-year-old telling himself a story, his thoughts moving too fast for the material world to keep up. As soon as he loses interest in a particular toy, he discards it, seemingly unconcerned about any risk of damage to his props – after all, he can always get another. The dynamic recalls Freud's description of the *fort-da* play of a small child, as Zaloom repeatedly evokes and then rejects the allure of the mass-produced commodity.

Agus Nur Amal (Indonesia)

Performer Agus Nur Amal (b. 1969) uses everyday objects to tell stories in 'a modernized form of a rare southwestern Achenese storytelling genre known as *dangedria*'.[56] After training in modern theatre, Amal researched the *dangedria* form. When asked how he came to incorporate objects into his storytelling, Amal explained that as a child, he was exposed to both traditional storytelling and cinema. When he listened to storytellers, he saw filmic images, and when he came to retell those stories himself, he decided to present the imagery directly to the audience. He sometimes performs from inside a puppet booth made to look like a television:

> Standing in a television-shaped puppet booth, he relates the 9/11 story as object theatre using toys, household items, and handmade props. A cardboard fish transforms into a Boeing 747, a plastic bag becomes flames enveloping the World Trade Center, and a bath ladle and flashlight is a helicopter sent to kill Osama bin Laden. Osama himself is a battery-operated dancing doll in fatigues.
>
> (Cohen 2010: 400)

These interactive 'television' shows are performed to audiences of both adults and children.

What these diverse artists of object theatre have in common is a practical understanding of the semiotics of objects. Like the actor – like Helene Weigel in Brecht's poem – they consider the form, size, colour, age, wear and cultural associations of common objects, searching for the difference in theatrical meaning between a ladle and a slotted spoon, or between a metal dustpan and a plastic dustpan. They would make excellent prop buyers. But their aim is not to support characterisation but to liberate the object's properties and make them visible to others. In this pursuit, they deploy a second level of theatrical semiotics, exploring how movement and the positioning of objects relative to each other and to the stage space creates meaning.[57]

THE ANTECEDENTS OF OBJECT THEATRE

The act of storytelling while showing objects to the audience may go back as far as storytelling itself, to the shadows on cave walls that provided shifting imagery for imaginative interpretation. The eighteenth- and nineteenth-century German *Bänkelsang* was a ballad based on 'true-life' stories, sung in the street or at markets by a performer who stood on a bench (*bänk*) with a placard or painted poster showing scenes from the story.[58] Brecht admired the form for its directness and as a model of the quality of 'showing'. (In Pabst's 1931 film of the Brecht/Weill *Threepenny Opera*, a ballad singer shows a series of poster-sized painted images to the crowd as he sings 'The Ballad of Mack the Knife'.) The Italian *cantastoria* tradition is still extant: the ballad-singers point out individual panels in a composition with a dozen or more panels, like a page of a comic book. These secular forms can be linked to sung interpretations of painted scrolls on religious themes in India, Indonesia and Japan.[59] In the twentieth century, Bread and Puppet Theatre and Great Small Works drew inspiration from these forms for their own *cantastoria*, and have inspired artists working in political theatre such as the puppeteers of the Occupy Wall Street movement.[60] In all these forms, the performer shows unmoving scenes, pointing out details from time to time. It is the spectator's attention that animates the image. The touch of the hand is withdrawn from the object – it may even be held at the length of a pointer or stick.

A famous example of storytelling with props is found in *The Two Gentlemen of Verona*. The clown Launce begins to tell a story like this:

Nay, I'll show you the manner of it. This shoe is my father; no, this left shoe is my father; no, no, this left shoe is my mother; nay, that cannot be so neither; yes, it is so, it is so – it hath the worser sole. This sole, with the hole in it, is my mother, and this my father – a vengeance on't! there 'tis. Now, sire, this staff is my sister, for, look you, she is as white as a lily and as small as a wand. This hat is Nan, our maid. I am the dog – no, the dog is himself, and I am the dog – O! the dog is me, and I am myself; as, so so. Now come I to my father: 'Father, your blessing.' Now should not the shoe speak a word for weeping; now should I kiss my father; well, he weeps on. Now come I to my mother. O that she could speak now like a wood woman! Well, I kiss her; why, there 'tis; here's my mother's breath up and down. Now come I to my sister; mark the moan she makes. Now the dog all this while sheds not a tear, nor speaks a word; but see how I lay the dust with my tears.

(2.3.13–32)

As Frances Teague explains in *Shakespeare's Speaking Properties*, 'we don't know whether Launce simply showed the objects as he named them, or if he gave them movement and sound. His words suggest that he produces a voice for his sister at least: "mark the moan she makes"' (Teague 1991: 30). If some continuity with clown performances into the twentieth century can be assumed, it seems quite likely that Launce did give movement and sound to the props, but without entirely disappearing as a storyteller. For Teague, the shoe becomes a performer 'when it is involved in the stage business of Launce's picking it up to kiss it':

> When the actor says, 'Here's my mother's breath up and down,' the humor of a man kissing his shoe as if it were his mother is heightened by the old comic attitude that all shoes stink. One notes that the property must be recognized by the audience as both mother and as old shoe for this joke to work. While the property does not move independently of the actor, it does operate in much the same way as would a puppet.
>
> (Teague 1991: 31)

Teague cites Bil Baird's definition of a puppet as 'an inanimate figure that is made to move by human effort before an audience' to argue that properties like Launce's shoe are puppets. At the same time, they 'can in some sense be regarded as performers' (ibid.). For our purposes, it is more useful to retain Frank Proschan's term 'performing objects' to describe objects that may be 'created, displayed, or manipulated' (cited by Bell 2008: 2). The small props used in object theatre are almost invariably 'ready-made' rather than created before the audience; they are manipulated in precisely limited ways, closer to techniques of 'display' than to the techniques of puppetry that create an illusion of independent life. What is, however, pertinent in Teague's mention of puppetry is that the audience has a double awareness of the prop, in this case 'as both mother and as old shoe'. In this 'double-vision', the audience's awareness shifts between two states: a process called 'opalisation' by Henryk Jurkowski (by analogy with the way an opal appears to change colour as it is moved in the light) or 'oscillation' by Steve Tillis. Péter Molnár Gál, a designer for the Budapest State Puppet Theatre, characterises it as an unresolved 'double-vision':

> Everything is what it is, plus something else: a recognisable object and a transfigured object at the same time. On the puppet stage a feather-duster may symbolize a fairy prince illumined by glory, but we must never forget that it still remains a feather-duster. While the objects lose their original purpose and become transformed into something else, they still faintly preserve their original character.
>
> (quoted in Tillis 1992: 62)

The process is of particular interest for semioticians because of the play between social and individual meanings, and contemporary practitioners also display sophisticated awareness of this shifting double vision.

Christian Carrignon says that by 'keeping things at a distance, maintaining one's reserve as a storyteller, object theatre is strongly on the side of Brecht, maybe even going further than him' (Carrignon and Mattéoli 2009: 15). The performer wears everyday clothes, neither costume nor 'Sunday best', and adopts a relationship of 'demonstration', rather than identification, towards the character.

PLAYING WITH SCALE AND THE CINEMATIC

As the examples described earlier in the chapter will have suggested, the possibility of playing with scale is a key interest for object theatre practitioners. Jean-Luc Mattéoli says that the 'first function of the object in object theatre is to create a space'. He describes how in *Catalogue de voyage* by Théâtre de Cuisine a single object becomes the whole scenic space:

> A suitcase full of sand is open, facing the audience. On it, there stands a small red tanker truck. The desert is evoked. Theatre is adept at this kind of illusion, but here immensity is suggested by an object on a much reduced scale. 'Littleness,' says Jacques Templeraud, 'is the best way into dreams'. It gives the spectators the feeling of viewing the story from above, in the manner of an establishing shot in film – something theatre does not typically employ, although Christian Carrignon sees it as characteristic of the type of theatre he creates. This feeling is accentuated by the audience's position. Seated on a rake, the audience dominates the tiny stage created by the suitcase, with something like a bird's eye view. The spectator's viewpoint appears to be that of an all-seeing god who can encompass the limits of the desert. The basic principle is that when a small object is set in a space on its own, the spectator's viewpoint undergoes variations based on a cinematographic as well a theatrical model. The littleness of the everyday object is therefore particularly useful for playing with scale.
>
> (Mattéoli 2011: 80)

The stage for object theatre is often a simple table. Sometimes it is recognisable as a wooden kitchen table – thus the stage itself appears to be a found object imported into the theatre space. This allows for a rich layering of time periods and scales.

As Mattéoli suggests, the language of cinema is explicitly employed by Carrignon and other object theatre artists:

> Influenced by the local cinema of our childhood, we pick up a cinematic vocabulary and apply it to theatre. In rehearsal, we talk of wide shots, close ups, flashbacks, point-of-view shots. In performance, we do everything at the same time: acting, framing the shots, editing. We like to show the strings, to show how it's done, and put the backstage onstage. It is a theatre of complicity with and proximity to the audience.
>
> (Theatre de Cuisine website)

As mentioned above, Indonesian performer Agus Nur Amal also cites the influence of cinema on his performance style. Using familiar mass-produced consumer objects (including plastic carrier bags and children's toys), along with a few prepared props or sets made of cardboard (such as an empty television screen or aeroplane window), Amal shifts rapidly between viewpoints. He sometimes takes on a role himself, in this case using the objects as props or costume. He ties a thin red plastic carrier bag over his head, like a headscarf, to become a woman waving goodbye from a plane – in effect, a 'close up', with the performer on the same scale as the audience members. Immediately afterwards, he pulls off the bag, squashing the red plastic down to a small lump of material pinched between his fingers. He moves it across the space, accompanied by the roar of a plane taking off – producing a 'long-shot' of the departing woman.

Amal's performance is embedded in a highly musical storytelling tradition, and he is constantly vocalising inanimate objects (cars, planes) and characters. He cuts between different 'shots' with a rapidity that is hard to achieve in rehearsed performance, let alone improvisation, using singing or sound effects to smooth the transition as he picks up or transforms his props.

In a workshop as part of the first meeting of the Object Theatre Network in Nottingham in 2011, Amal invited students to create a collaborative map of the city using everyday objects placed on the floor. From this 'establishing shot' of the city seen from above, they zoomed in to tell individual stories, using the same objects. Amal had previously used this improvisation as a practical town planning exercise, working with inhabitants of Sumatra in the redevelopment of their city following the tsunami of 2004.[61]

Andrew Sofer has characterised the prop as an object that moves: 'By definition, a prop is an object that goes on a journey; hence props trace spatial trajectories and create temporal narratives as they track through a given performance' (Sofer 2003: 2). In object theatre, the movement of objects to tell a story recalls the etymology of 'metaphor' itself, coming from the Greek *metapherein*, meaning to transfer, or carry across. In object theatre, the 'carrying across' or placement of a small prop can give it a new meaning – can transform a suitcase of sand into a landscape, or a fragile plastic bag into a human being.

THE ASCETIC GESTURE

In general, object theatre performers use a deliberately reduced movement vocabulary. Their handling of objects is practised, rapid and precise but they are not interested in exploring the object's movement potential or giving the audience the illusion that the object is breathing, for example. In their article about the work of Agnès Limbos, Claire Corniquet and Marion Rhéty describe the characteristic movement vocabulary of object theatre. As in chess, objects are 'moved' from one position to another, but the manner of moving them is not highlighted. The change of position is achieved with minimal effort and fuss:

> Picking up, moving, placing: these actions can all be encompassed by the idea of 'repositioning', given that moving an object implies grasping, lifting and replacing it in another position. To be precise, it seems that there is only one means of moving an object. The right gesture is spontaneous yet mechanical. The repositioning is not anthropomorphised: neither walking, nor hopping, nor flying (with rare exceptions, for particular dramatic purposes). Rather, one gently lifts the object, moves it horizontally on or just above the surface (in this case the table) and sets it down. Moreover, there are no adjustments: the start and finish of actions are very clear. The gesture is precise: as in chess, one does not return to a pawn once it has been played.[62]

Corniquet and Rhéty see the 'ascetic gesture' employed by Limbos as a way of discarding any 'encumbrance' that could drown the action and the meaning. As a refusal of acting, it aims to open a space for the object to speak, and is a useful way to characterise the gesture found in the work of artists as diverse as Charlot Lemoine and Stuart Sherman.

Although this 'ascetic gesture' is not the only way of handling objects in object theatre – think of Paul Zaloom's apparently casual, voluble anthropomorphism – for many object theatre artists, a precise but unemphatic 'repositioning' allows the objects of commodity culture to 'speak', to reveal their poetic potential. While Kantor, for instance, sought out the degraded, abandoned or 'poor' objects in which the signs of mass-production had disappeared through dissolution and decay, Agnès Limbos and Christian Carrignon are interested in exploring the characteristics of mass-produced objects. Carrignon writes about the 'children of the Age of Plastic', for whom domestic utensils and toys made of plastic carry an emotional charge:

> These poor objects in plastic belonged to ordinary people, who were perhaps poor but certainly possessed of poor taste. The people I knew, my nearest and dearest, me. These objects touch me because they were bought, loved, forgotten. I touch them on stage: I touch life. They belonged to living people. We are talking about people in object theatre. Nothing else.
>
> (Carrignon and Mattéoli 2009: 16)

OBJECTS AS LINGUISTIC ELEMENTS

The very possibility of handing on or re-creating object theatre scenarios with different performers depends on the fact that they employ mass-produced objects. As with a verbal joke, the performer manipulates shared items (objects, or words) in unexpected ways, rather than drawing attention to a unique interaction with the material. Although the character and rhythm of a specific performer is far from irrelevant – each performer will inflect a scenario differently and audience members will bring their own readings of the material and the performer's physicality – object theatre is not uniquely invested in the body of the performer or a specific designed puppet.

Many of the performers discussing their work describe it in linguistic terms. Agnès Limbos says: 'When I place another object alongside the first, an association of ideas is made in the spectator's mind, just as when you put together the words in a sentence'.

When objects are used like linguistic elements, they can be associated in literal or playful ways, just like words: a number of disparate objects can be combined in sequences (to create phrases that convey a narrative or message); objects can be collected together because they have a resemblance (a collection of elephants of different sizes, made of different substances). In performance, an object can reappear in the same position and aspect (repetition, recurrence), or in a different aspect (evoking transformation, rhyme). Object theatre performers evoke hidden connections, analogies and rhymes between things of the material world. These relationships can be based on form, material, conventional use, sound – or a combination of all of these.

In *There's a Rabbit in the Moon*, by Vélo Théâtre, a tapestry of associations is built up between objects, words and sounds. Some of the objects are mass-produced, such as a die-cast toy car; others are specially made, such as a mysterious dream collecting machine that resembles a beehive of padded calico, strapped to a narrow cart with bicycle wheels. In performance, these objects have equal status with words – or rather, certain words and onomatopoeic sounds are given an object-like status. The connections made between them are loose at first, with echoes and rhymes building up over the course of the performance. A big bass drum standing on one edge represents the full moon but a drum roll is created by Charlot Lemoine rolling his tongue ('*drrrrrrrrrrr*'). We listen to a recording of a song in which a man sings '*mon coeur fait boum*' ('my heart goes boom') and hear about a child who hears his own heart beating, '*boom-boom*'. A pocket watch resembles the bass drum, in miniature, and has a ticking heart of its own. The child is called Pedro – with that *drrrrrrrrrrr* that belongs to the drum-moon in the middle of his name: these disparate things gradually come to belong together.

Carrignon and Lemoine are alert to the possibility that an object's original use may become completely forgotten, therefore burying some of its poetic potential. When a hand-turned coffee mill (*moulin*) could be found in every kitchen, performers could place one on a kitchen table stage to create a landscape with a windmill (*moulin*). But if the object falls out of use and is no longer recognised by spectators, it won't invoke the silent pronunciation of the word 'moulin' (let alone *éolienne*, a modern wind turbine). Bill Brown writes of Claes Oldenburg's sculpture *Typewriter Eraser*, a once-familiar piece of office stationery enlarged so that it towers over viewers:

> The pleasure of looking at the people looking at *Typewriter Eraser*, amused by its monumentality, is inseparable from the pleasure of listening to the child who, befuddled by an anachronistic object she never knew, pleads: 'What is that thing supposed to be?' [...] While the 'timeless' objects in the Oldenburg canon (fans and sinks) have gone limp, this abandoned object attains a new stature precisely because it has no life outside the boundary of art – no life, that is, within our everyday lives. Released from the bond of being equipment, sustained outside the irreversibility of technological history, the object becomes something else.
>
> (Brown 2004: 15)

Brown sees Oldenburg's sculpture as 'staging' obsolescence. There is a constant trembling on the border between the radical potential of the just-obsolete and nostalgia, the 'aha' of recognition and puzzlement at the incomprehensible.

THE REAL OBJECT

In the essay from which the following extracts are translated, Claire Corniquet and Marion Rhéty focus on the objects used in *Troubles*, performed by Agnès Limbos with Gregory Houben.

Corniquet and Rhéty place the work of Gare Centrale in the context of documentary photography, film and writing, comparing her to diverse artists such as the photographer Eugène Atget, film-maker Chantal Akerman and writer Georges Perec:

> Each [of these artists] documents in their own way certain aspects of reality, using different forms of visual support. If object theatre is not usually associated with the practices gathered under the heading of 'documentary', the object theatre performance *Troubles* (2008) by Compagnie Gare Centrale, is an exception, offering a detailed, poetic excavation of daily life by paying attention to the objects that surround us.
>
> The founder of Gare Centrale, Agnès Limbos, is an exponent of contemporary object theatre, a theatrical genre that stages everyday objects, often secondhand ones. Sitting around a small table set on a larger one, Agnès Limbos and Gregory Houben bring us, through *Troubles,* into the life of a couple, of all couples. In this performance, the two actors play with objects, gathering the imaginative worlds attached to them, making the sharing of cliché a condition for receiving the performance. They explore how objects are capable of speaking to us, touching us, beyond verbal language – that is, how the objects that surround us constitute reserves of collective imagery.

Corniquet and Rhéty refer to the object as a 'witness' to the world, material proof that attests to the existence of the real. They cite the work of Arjun

Appadurai (*The Social Life of Things*, 1986) as a way of looking beyond a strictly materialist approach to things, taking into account the various relationships between subject and object, and the changes in status, taste, technique and perception that objects undergo in the course of their existence. These variations are informative about social and human relationships with the material world, but are also revealing of the collective relationship to the past and the process of generating memory:

> In Agnès Limbos's theatre, everything springs from the objects and everything is centred on the object. This article focuses on one aspect of the biography of objects in the particular context of the stage, at the moment when an object that has already done its job, has already 'lived', is seized by a particular social actant, the artist. Where do these objects come from? What do they tell us? Why do they speak to us? Many such questions allow us to access the collective representations, the 'imaginary', shaped by the norms and conventions carried by each individual. Agnès Limbos responds to these questions, not through theoretical analysis of objects, but by staging their poetic qualities.[63]

The authors were particularly struck by the emphasis Limbos placed on the word 'real' in their interviews with her. She says of a specially constructed prop: 'I made a thing but it wasn't a real object, once I started to build it, something didn't work.' She prefers objects that 'have already lived, that I find by chance'. She rarely purchases props and if she does, they usually 'don't work'. Objects for performance, she says, have to be 'charged'.

Corniquet and Rhéty suggest that the use of the expression 'a real object' serves two purposes for Limbos. Firstly, it distinguishes object theatre from puppet theatre: object theatre relies on the manipulation of objects that were not originally intended for theatre. Secondly, it provides a form of legitimation in the context of object theatre as an art defined through its relationship with the mass-produced:

> the term 'object theatre' appeared at the beginning of the 1980s, used by artists with a background in the visual arts who positioned themselves both as part of the flow and in opposition to the invasion of objects of the consumer society, as an 'act of resistance to all forms of obsolescence and demonstrating a desire to speak about human fragility'.

An insistence on defining the object as 'real' seems, however, to raise further questions. As discussed in the previous chapter, the 'poor object' cherished by Tadeusz Kantor was not created for the stage but was 'torn from the reality of life'. Corniquet and Rhéty point out that the material substance of theatre is usually drawn from daily life, and is frequently second-hand – simply 'transferred from the frame of the everyday to that of the stage'. What distinguishes the 'real object' of the theatre of objects (or indeed

Kantor's objects) is that they have already been 'charged' through their 'first owner' or 'first life':

> The term 'charged' suggests the idea of having *already* lived, having *already* been used, having a history – a biography – more often than not unknown to the person who rescues it. As the real object is a form of silent witness to the history of unknown people, it is inevitably linked to collective imagery. Take a suitcase, for example. While a brown leather suitcase often stands as a witness to the journey of migrants through history and/or of the deportation of the Jews, a plastic Samsonite® case brings more playful associations, perhaps of tourism or professional travel. In other words, while an object summons up memories of personal experience, it can also crystalise collective representations varying in character according to the geographical, historical, economic, social and cultural context in which it was – and is – used. The object's 'charge' does not depend solely on its own biographical thread but also on the shared imagery it may carry.
>
> When Agnès Limbos selects objects for the stage, she takes a gamble that her choices 'evoke something' for others and that they make sense to everyone. Thus she departs from the generic use of the object to draw on its materiality, signs – and the symbolism of the represented figure – which lead to the creation of a shared understanding of the object. In this new reading, the 'real object' is not drawn from the imagination of the artist but is something already known and recognisable, and for that reason it is 'inhabited' by meaning and a set of wider significations.

Corniquet and Rhéty set out to consider the intrinsic qualities of the 'real objects' placed on stage by Agnès Limbos before considering the means employed by the artist to create a shared understanding of the objects. They introduce the term 'gleaning' [*glanage*] to describe Limbos's process of acquiring props. Gleaning has a range of relevant associations: originally to do with collecting food that would otherwise be wasted, from fields or street markets after closing time, its meaning has been extended to include picking up objects left in the street. In English, there would be an overlap with practices such as 'foraging', 'scavenging' and 'dumpster diving'.[64] Corniquet and Rhéty cite Agnès Varda's film *Les Glaneurs et la glaneuse* (France, 2000). As well as exploring the reasons that people glean food, furniture and other discarded but useable items in contemporary France (out of necessity, as a protest against waste etc.), Varda makes a powerful analogy between the gleaners she meets and her own work as a film-maker, gathering images and putting them together in a new arrangement to create new meanings. The analogy with object theatre is clear:

> For those who gather abandoned objects, 'gleaning' involves lowering yourself to collect what others consider useless or no longer useful. This recuperation arises from a loss of the object's sense of use and usefulness while at the same time, according to the inclinations of the gleaner, it also provides the object with a new use or purpose. The various reclassifications of the object over time constitute its biography.

As Jean-Luc Mattéoli points out, the poor object has two aspects: it has returned from the brink of existential disappearance and at the same time it is invisible because it is so ordinary. The source of such objects most often mentioned by theatre practitioners is the charity shop. Mattéoli describes the operation of Emmaüs, the charity that works with the homeless in France and sells second-hand goods, including clothes, furniture and furnishings, on three days a week. Some shop there out of need, while others, like Pascal Rome, director of theatre company OPUS (Office des phabricants d'univers singuliers), look for old things, unusual or collectible objects. But it is the weekend, when families go to Emmaüs to browse, that reveals a particular relationship with time:

> The long stroll around a maze of discarded objects acts as a way of escaping from the present, so that one might say it is not about 'finding' as much as 're-finding' something. [...] Thrown up by deaths, house sales, reductions in living space, and a working population that is obliged to move house frequently in the name of 'flexibility', the objects found in Emmaüs speak of the past.
>
> (Mattéoli 2011: 70)

Pamela Howard has also written of charity shops and second-hand warehouses as resources for research, 'places to research and reconstruct daily lives of times past':

> Here are ghosts waiting to be re-incarnated. Shoes waiting to be walked in again, and hats looking for a head. In a furniture repository in Pittsburgh, USA, I saw rows of odd chairs lined up in a storeroom. They had a sense of expectancy as though they were waiting for something to happen in front of them.
>
> (Howard 2009: 83–4)

Corniquet and Rhéty follow Limbos on a similar quest on her daily walk through the city:

> The artists who form the small 'family' of contemporary object theatre to which Agnès Limbos belongs do not glean out of necessity but out of choice. The selection of objects is linked to the creative process which begins outside the theatre or the studio, in the course of the daily work of 'gathering' to which Limbos is committed – albeit with pleasure: in the street, in flea markets, in friends' attics, in charity shops. The point is to recuperate and put on stage objects that have already served their purpose. Agnès Limbos is a gleaner of objects. She rescues that which others have left behind, re-negotiates and re-envisages the usefulness of objects that others consider useless. Her choice of objects is intuitive. It's an intuition relating to the everyday, since she goes out gathering every day. She is open to the idea that every found object 'has a use'. Her practice illustrates the unique perspective of this good-natured treasure-seeker, who looks out for things without searching for them.

A 'found object' [*objet trouvé*] is one onto which Limbos 'stumbles'. As
Corniquet and Rhéty point out, Jean-Luc Mattéoli describes artists as 'falling' (*tombant*) on such objects. The term suggests both the degraded nature
of the objects that occupy a place on the ground, but at the same time their
power to pull the airy conceptualist 'down to earth'.

> In the course of her walks, the artist comes across objects that 'mark' her, that
> she feels 'obliged' to gather up, such as an old red curtain found abandoned by a
> bin that immediately 'spoke' to her. Her perambulations are spontaneous and the
> gleaning is not necessarily defined by a pre-determined theme: 'I make my way
> backwards. I feel as if the object says what I want to say, for me. (...) the theme
> of my piece really emerges from the objects. It's not an intellectual idea.' Room
> is left for the imagination, as the artist says: 'I think that my imagination seizes
> on objects in the street, phrases, words, stories. Everything speaks to me.' To
> choose an object is to be touched by it, or by the images that it evokes. Limbos
> then retraces her steps in order to try to understand and bring out what she
> describes as 'deep, shared, even universal' meanings in the object. To a certain
> extent, the artist feels that the meaning of the object is a matter of 'shared mean-
> ing' or 'common sense'.

This practical approach requires a retrospective creative process, rather like
the approach of the 'bricoleur', as defined by Lévi-Strauss:

> His first practical step is retrospective. He has to turn back to an already existent set
> made up of tools and materials, to consider or reconsider what it contains and, finally
> and above all, to engage in a sort of dialogue with it and, before choosing between
> them, to index the possible answers which the whole set can offer to his problem.
>   (Lévi-Strauss 1966: 18)

Once Limbos has found her theme, a period of research begins, a phase
of obsessional accumulation of similar or adjacent objects. Whether she is
gleaning or searching for an object, her practice involves displacing objects
from one context to another. She enacts a shift of categories as the object
'moves from being an object-tool in an everyday context to an object-actant
in a theatrical context'. Importantly, although Limbos changes the context,
she does not modify the materiality of the object with paint or other additions, 'taking it as it is'. Only rarely does she alter its function:

> 'What does it evoke? What is it telling us?' Agnès Limbos poses these questions
> in order to decide on the meaning given to objects. The word 'evoke' means to
> 'call up' memory or the past – in other words, prior knowledge, in the form of
> mental images produced mainly in response to sight of the object, mental images
> that recall a direct or indirect relationship to the object. As mentioned above in
> the discussion of the real object, such images may be particular to the experi-
> ence of an individual or may be shared, constituting collective images or social
> imagination. The underlying question relates to what it is in the object that allows

for this kind of evocation, or rather, the process by which Limbos manages to give meaning to objects on stage.

As Roland Barthes put it, objects are not only instruments, they also carry meaning. At the same time, objects frequently have several meanings, that is, they don't necessarily mean the same thing to everyone at the same time. The job of the artist is to consider one of the associated meanings and share it with the largest number of people. Agnès Limbos does not reduce the object to a mere prop, carrying meaning and allowing her to tell a story. Rather, she considers history to be at the heart of the object.

The objects in *Troubles* include representations of everyday things (doll's house furniture), images from popular culture (a wolf) and cultural clichés (a yellow New York taxicab). The authors describe how two of these are used in early scenes of the show, drawing on a classic semiotic distinction between icon and index:

Gregory Houben places a miniature plastic wolf on the stage. The figure of the wolf potentially evokes fear and anxiety through stories such as Little Red Riding Hood and the 'big bad wolf' – a fairy tale that comes out of a culturally situated history. But Agnès Limbos does not tell the story of Little Red Riding Hood. Nor does she tell the story of the wolf. By placing a miniature plastic wolf on the stage, she aims to bring out the anxiety stirred by the wolf the object represents. In *Troubles*, the plastic wolf is an icon. […]

The wolf figurine enters the scene – or, rather, it appears behind the bride and groom, who appear not to see it. The staging provokes a feeling of anxiety that is reinforced by howling – the indexical sign of the wolf, confirming its presence – produced by one of the actors. The howl is addressed to the audience and not to the bride and groom who don't hear the sound of the prowling menace. The staging creates a particular situation that allows for a shared image to develop around the troubling presence of the wolf figure. The object is both a carrier of emotion and of intent towards the performed scene.

The miniature yellow car is also an icon because it replaces, by resemblance – in this case by its colour – a New York taxicab. However, this object is also an indexical sign because the object it replaces is the indexical sign of New York City. The yellow cab has become, in Europe, an index of the city, thanks to the widely diffused images in film, television and advertising. As an index of New York City, the yellow cab is part of a semiotic stabilization that leaves no room for ambiguity. In the performance, Agnès Limbos uses it to define the setting of the action. Even if the yellow cab's miniature size allows it to be placed inside a bedroom or a kitchen, it does not leave its usual setting, the city.

If object theatre can use objects like linguistic elements, it also depends upon an understanding of everyday gestures that involve objects. As Limbos says:

When I place one object alongside another, an association of ideas is made in the spectator's mind, just as when you put together the words in a sentence. Beyond that, there is the art of the actor who tells the story of the object.

The account of Stephen Daldry's work with props quoted in Chapter 7 showed how they can be used to support characterisation – in *Far Away*, the unpacking of a tangled sewing box accompanied the unravelling of a complicated lie. In object theatre, the balance between performer and object has shifted. The relationships between objects create metaphors; spoken language is usually minimal, so that words take on an 'object-like' quality too. John Bell has pointed out the resemblance to the dynamics of painting or sculpture; the performer 'interprets, frames, and contextualizes the image in front of the spectators, and helps the communal experience of watching performance become one in which our own responses to the chosen objects are provoked' (Bell 2008: 5). Thus, in *Troubles*, we are a 'long way from traditional theatrical performance in which one incarnates character', as Corniquet and Rhéty write:

> An argument between the man and the woman is represented by a rapid and energetic game with miniature chairs. The woman sulks; the performer places a chair in a corner of the playing area, its back to the table. Her companion does the same, and thus the ballet of chairs develops. To demonstrate the relationship between them, the performers choose conventional gestures: facing, retreating into a corner, turning the back (of the chair). Despite the minimal character of the actions, we understand the conflict. The intention is given by the movement more than the objects. Since the two chairs are identical, our ideas and emotions arise from their movements, which inscribe the space, give it rhythm and charge it with feeling. A map of emotions is temporarily traced on the table (the playing area): the front right-hand edge becomes a 'corner' to which one can retire to let sadness flow freely. The convention is established: when the actress once again moves the chair into the corner, the spectator understands the meaning. Like Christian Carrignon, Agnès Limbos often speaks of 'charging the object'. Naming the fundamental action in this way perhaps serves to avoid the inexhaustible question of whether the object is animate or inanimate. As already mentioned, when objects arrive in the workshop of these artists, they are already charged, by virtue of the wear of the material and their former life – we return here to the biography of objects – something of which we have little or no idea. What is required, then, is to recharge them, that is to say, to make them visible, to bring out a certain expression, a sign, a metaphor.

Although Limbos is working on a deliberately restricted stage and with miniature chairs, the scenario described here, using the placement of objects in space to establish a 'map of emotions', would be quite recognisable to performers working on a human scale, perhaps moving chairs in Ionesco's play of that name.

In puppetry, performers create the illusion of independent life in an object, using voice and expressive manipulation. Whether they work with an object that was originally designed as a puppet or with a found object, they respond to its appearance and movement vocabulary to create characters that are more or less anthropomorphic or zoomorphic. Object theatre, in contrast, is closer to visual art: the objects do not become characters and yet they have a compelling 'liveliness'. Is it correct to say that such objects are at the 'inanimate' end of Veltruský's spectrum of animation? They are clearly 'animated' by the performers' speech, by their positioning in syntactic relationships to other objects and by the restrained touch of the performer. In addition, they bring to the performance the 'charge' of their previous history and the spectator's associations. Thinking about object theatre allows us to consider the various ways in which objects in everyday life are animated through our speech and gesture and through their relationships with other objects. The very presence of two mobile phones on a restaurant table speaks eloquently of the potential connection of this space to other spaces and of the two diners to an infinite number of other people, even before we consider the ways in which people handle their phones, speak about them and into them.

FURTHER READING

The full article by Claire Corniquet and Marion Rhéty is available online in a special issue of the journal *Agôn* devoted to objects: 'L'<<objet vrai>>. Précis des objets dans le théâtre d'objets d'Agnès Limbos, à partir de *Troubles*' in *Agôn 4: L'objet, Dossiers, Objet, mémoire, identité*. http://agon.enslyon.fr/index.php?id=2077. The issue of *Puppet Notebook* 'On Object Theatre' (Winter 2012–13) includes articles by directors and performers including Sean Myatt, Rene Baker and Nenagh Watson. See also Jean-Luc Mattéoli, *L'objet pauvre*: *Memoire et quotidien sur les scènes contemporaines françaises* (2011) for a discussion of the wider context of object theatre.

Chapter

10   Props without Actors

At the far end of the spectrum of animation, when no actors are on stage but props remain, 'the action does not stop'. In fact, Veltruský says, it is then that the 'action force of the object comes to the fore in all its power'. This chapter considers three situations where props appear without actors but retain their theatrical identity, rather than being identified as everyday objects or art objects. In these three contexts, senses other than the visual come to the fore, with the prop activating ideas and feelings through smell, sound and, in particular, touch.

THE PROP IN THE MUSEUM

Arthur Wing Pinero's *Trelawny of the Wells* looks back affectionately at the theatre of the author's youth in the 1860s. A turning point in the plot is the meta-theatrical moment in which props from another production – theatrical relics – melt the hard heart of Sir William Gower, the grandfather of Rose Trelawny's sweetheart Arthur. Sir William is fiercely opposed to his grandson's entanglement with theatre in any form, let alone an engagement to an actress, but comes to Rose's lodgings to look for Arthur. In passing, Rose mentions that her own mother had acted with Edmund Kean. Sir William recalls seeing Kean in his youth: 'A young man then, I was; quite different from the man I am now – impulsive, excitable. Kean!' (Pinero 1936: 72). Rose then takes from her clothes basket some treasured props that had belonged to Kean, explaining: 'the Order and chain, and the sword, he wore in Richard. He gave them to my father; I've always prized them' (ibid.). Sir William puts on the chain and sword. The objects – described by Pinero in a stage direction as 'all very theatrical and tawdry' – have a powerful effect on him. He seems to reinhabit his youth, and his own ambitions to act, in reenacting the role he saw Kean play: '*He paces the stage, growling and muttering, and walking with a limp and one shoulder hunched [...] muttering, 'Now is the winter of our discontent,' etc.* (73). As a result of this moving encounter, Sir William offers to fund a production in which Rose will play a leading role – and which eventually reunites her with Arthur.

Museums and galleries make increasing use of theatrical devices such as storytelling and performance to animate their collections. Designers of museum spaces also consider how elements of the display such as captions, illustrations, video and audio clips can help to frame items of the collection as 'speaking objects'. Margaret Benton of the Theatre Museum, then a department of the Victoria and Albert Museum, wrote in 1997:

> Live performance exists only in the present, a momentary and unrepeatable communication between performer and spectator. Are performing arts museums then not a contradiction in terms, an attempt to preserve the unpreservable, to record the unrecordable? Certainly the shards of performance that make up our collections... can only ever provide a very partial record of the live event. Other museums have to grapple with the problem of documenting and interpreting the ephemeral, but the material vestiges of events rooted in common life-experience have the nostalgic appeal of 'how we used to live' – of past Utopias. Theatre aims to transport people out of the ordinary and into a journey of imagination. Edmund Kean's sword, his death mask or an engraving may fascinate an enthusiast of nineteenth-century British drama, but how can such relics convey the magnetic presence of an actor who once held London audiences in thrall?
>
> (quoted in Bennett 2013: 31–2)

Theatre critic Lyn Gardner seemed to concur, writing after the Theatre Museum's closure as a separate entity: 'I'm not a huge fan of museums. Although I'm well aware that it is heresy to say so, I must confess that I particularly disliked the old Theatre Museum, where the exhibits had the dusty air of something half-forgotten. [...] There are only so many portraits of theatrical knights and the Redgrave family that anyone can stomach in a single viewing' (Gardner 2008).

One of the most successful exhibits in the Theatre Museum's short existence was 'Taking Shape' (May 2001–June 2002). An 'interactive exhibition', curated by Theatre-Rites, it included props from their shows that could be played with and animated by museum visitors.[65] From the promenade performance *Clothworks* came the maze made of tape measures suspended vertically and a humanette puppet with a miniature body and a space for the performer's head was set up in front of a velvet curtain, allowing visitors to take turns to perform for each other. The exhibit did not emphasise the original role of these puppets in Theatre-Rites shows – it simply offered an insight into the techniques used by the company and an opportunity to play.

An exhibition with a similar feel to 'Taking Shape', though with a larger archival component, was curated by Forkbeard Fantasy at the Royal Festival Hall (2011). Many of the exhibits stand alone as automata or arcade style peepshows. Visitors were also able to operate the horse that featured in the performance *Invisible Bonfires*, designed by Penny Saunders. Each of the limbs of this life-size horse is controlled by a rope running up to the ceiling, through a pulley, and down to ground level. In effect, the puppet is operated from above, like a marionette, but by thick cords that are completely unconcealed. Like the horses designed by Handspring for *War Horse*, movement requires the coordination of several puppeteers. The *War Horse* puppets are operated by three puppeteers – two inside, providing the breathing rhythm of the horse, supporting its weight and each moving a pair of legs, and one outside, manipulating head and ears. The Forkbeard horse is operated completely from outside. In the exhibition, visitors became involved in impromptu collaborative work as they tried to coordinate the horse's movements. Families would work together, or unconnected visitors join together to try to reproduce the rhythm of a trot or gallop. The exhibit was unprescriptive about how visitors might interact with it: the horse simply stood on a plinth with its control ropes hanging temptingly.

Susan Bennett offers a critical reading of the current concern with participation, asking whether 'experiential museums merely keep us busy, impelling us, quite literally, to complete their script'. She notes that 'activity... is not the same as agency' (Anna Reading, quoted in Bennett: 59). But the Theatre-Rites and Forkbeard exhibits both seem to offer an unscripted opportunity to engage in the collaborative work that performance involves.

If Lyn Gardner had not mourned the closure of the Theatre Museum, she found much more to enjoy in 'Collaborators', an exhibition of work by UK-based theatre designers in the V&A's new Theatre and Performance galleries. For Gardner, the exhibition's great strength was that visitors were allowed to touch the exhibits. So, for example, they could not only 'gaze' at historically accurate costumes designed by Jenny Tiramani for Shakespeare's Globe, made 'from materials available to Shakespeare and his fellow actors 400 years ago', but could 'actually feel what the lace and embroidery is like and experience the weight of the cloth':

> The exhibition is much more rewarding than simply looking at photographs of a production. The materials and installations from Wildworks' productions – such as *Souterrain* or *The Very Old Man With Enormous Wings* – are displayed in such a way that they are transformed into new works of art. The objects drip emotion.
> (Gardner 2008)

Gardner notes that the crucial contribution that designers make to theatre is often overlooked, and praises the way that this exhibition documents performance and how 'design slips into direction'. Her account emphasises the tactile pleasures but also the sculptural potential of props when displayed inventively. It is worth noting that the exhibition was curated by a theatre designer, Kate Burnett, who clearly understands the importance of the tactile experience for both theatre-makers and audiences.[66]

IMMERSIVE SETS

Theatrical installations for individual exploration described variously as 'immersive', 'site-responsive' or 'site-specific' have been developed by companies including wilson+wilson (founded in 1997 by Louise Ann Wilson and Wils Wilson), Punchdrunk (directed by Felix Barrett and Maxine Doyle and founded in 2000) and dreamthinkspeak (directed by Tristan Sharps). These performances highlight costume, scenography, touch, sound and smell, and raise questions about how audience members interact with the objects on display.

Writing about *House*, a wilson+wilson performance, Louise Ann Wilson emphasises the dialogue between particular sites or spaces and the sceno-graphic elements that the artist brings to them. She always takes audiences on a physical journey to the site of performance:

> In all of my site-specific work, I've taken audiences on a physical journey where they've travelled on foot, or by bus, tram, off-road buggy, pedalo or elevator. Asking people to walk, to make a journey, physically engages them; they have to climb and struggle up narrow stairways or steep mountainsides, squeeze them-selves into a tiny room or a cave along with other participants and performers. *House* encouraged audience members to look inside drawers and behind closed doors, and they found themselves in the same room as the performers; an old man, asleep in a chair in front of the fire, surrounded by the artefacts of his life, providing clues to the rest of the piece. Some just froze, as if they were actually in someone's private space, whereas others were bolder; one person even prodded him to see if he was real.
>
> (Machon 2013: 229–30)

The wilson+wilson pieces take place in locations that may be familiar to audi-ence members – part of daily life – but that are animated in different ways by the expertise of people with specific kinds of craft knowledge: people 'who lived, worked and loved the places which inspired each production – foresters, hoteliers, tea-dancers, 2nd World War veterans, knife-makers, shop assistants, boxers, academics, children, bus drivers, historians, property developers and many more' (Wilson and Wilson).

While wilson+wilson's work often takes place in a landscape setting, or involves a journey curated by the artists, Punchdrunk's work has been building-based. Sometimes these have been disued buildings (*The Firebird Ball* took place in an old factory, Offley Works, *Faust* in a warehouse in Wapping). For the *Masque of the Red Death* (2007), based on stories by Edgar Allan Poe, the company were based in an existing performance space, Battersea Arts Centre, but used all the theatres and public spaces, along with many spaces previously used as offices or for storage. On entering, audience members put on a full length, black velvet cloak and a mask and were then free to wander from room to room. Actors would perform scenes but it was also possible to go into a room and find that it was empty, or to linger in a room after the actors had left. Susannah Clapp's review describes how the scenography appealed to all the senses:

> Camphor and TCP; cloves and oranges; incense and dust. At Battersea Arts Centre the smells alone set you off on a trail. So do the noises – the striking of a clock; the scream behind a locked door; the low hiss in an empty room, like a

record that has reached the end of its song. You can trace a tale through this maze of dusky Victorian corridors by following a hurtling figure – that harlequin, that veiled bride, that distraught dandy. You can bump into mystery and melodrama by moving from what was once a hall and is now a forest of dead trees, to the fragrant cushioned chamber of an opium den... You can stay still, absorbing the give-away detail in a 19th-century drawing-room – the volume of Scott, the suitor's letter to an aunt – and let the stories steal up on you. Whichever route you take, you will end up, after dark passages, swept into an English carnival, a gaudy, golden-lit celebration in a ballroom, the giddiest of pleasures, stalked by the figure of death.

(quoted in McKinney and Butterworth 2009: 193)

Many of the settings were lavishly dressed with lots of props and seemed to have the level of detail of a film set, but theatricality hovered just behind. Swagged lengths of fabric hid inconveniently placed modern fittings, while walls were loosely painted with 'distressed' textures – the scumbling and spattering of theatrical scene painting that is illusionistic at a distance but painterly when seen close up. In a dressing room alongside the recon-structed Victorian music hall, there was a table covered with scent bottles, cosmetics and silver-backed brushes. Were you allowed to touch or just to look? If it had been an installation at a museum, or a display on a market stall, the rules would have been clear. Was the indecision about how far audience members could take part supposed to be part of the experience?

Some audience members report that wearing a mask in Punchdrunk's productions frees them from self-consciousness. I found in *Masque of the Red Death* that I was thrown back into my own corporeality, preoccupied by fear of stumbling or bumping into other people. I felt disconnected from other audience members, and fell into a trancelike, almost 'window shopping' mode of looking. Josephine Machon's largely positive account of her experi-ence also reports the potential for frustration and dissatisfaction in immer-sive performance, as the spectator asks: Have I got the story? Have I missed something? Or even, Have I got enough out of this experience?

I was trapped [...] on one side of the building, enjoying myself, taking the time to experience the side events and the details of the rooms and scenes in which I dwelt, but I was also desperately trying to follow a bigger story, to get over to the other side.

(Machon 2013: 43)

Performer Silvia Mercuriali, herself a creator of immersive performances, acknowledges the paradoxical position she finds herself in as a 'self-con-scious' audience member:

I felt slightly silly because I was wearing a mask, which might have something to do with being a performer and dealing with masks in a very particular way, so suddenly I felt like I was being given a character but one that I didn't know how to move, one that was supposed to roam freely. I know loads of people who loved the fact that they had a mask on, so I know it was my own personal thing. They could hide behind the mask and become invisible, for me the mask made me more visible. [...] I am the worst audience member for any interactive theatre because I get so self-conscious and so scared of fucking it up for them that I cannot enjoy it.

(quoted in Machon 2013: 192)

Her interviews with artists, Machon suggests, foreground 'the idea of immersive practice giving audience-participants permission to behave in an active and sentient manner within these worlds, in a way that more conventional theatre productions – even those that are experiential in form – do not' (100). While it's clear that it's not possible to generalise about immersive theatre, and also that one-to-one experiences can be very different from moving through a building in a masked crowd, these accounts do open up the possibility that such forms could on occasion be *less* physically involving than watching a performance that is framed by a proscenium arch.

An example given by Sue Hill of Wildworks from their production *The Beautiful Journey* suggests how the visual might provoke other sensations, in order to link the 'intimate and epic':

[T]here's a point in the event where a ton of ice is landed, a huge lump of real ice is craned out of the dock and into the space where the audience is. Six hundred members of the audience can't touch the ice but ten children can, and there's a lovely thing which happens where you have this extraordinary image, a crane lifting this huge piece of ice out of the sea, dripping with water and it's beautifully lit and you can see the audience thinking it's a fibreglass prop until the first child puts its hand on it and gasps; something so personal, intimate happens yet the whole audience has the experience of it.

(Machon 2013: 251)

In terms of the spectrum of animation, the lump of ice is a (very large) prop. As in Andrew Sofer's definition of a prop, it is physically moved in the course of the performance, but it is also being 'animated' by the touch of the children (who are, in this moment, 'performers' because they are observed by other audience members).

While the props in Punchdrunk's performances give the illusion of only having been temporarily abandoned by the actors, there is a range of other work that sets objects to work independently, allowing audiences to observe a performance of objects without actors. Such works include *Stifters Dinge*, Heiner Goebbels' piece 'for five pianos with no pianists'; Tim Hunkin's automata and amusement arcade games on Southwold Pier and in the Novelty Arcade, London; Edward Bersudsky's 'Sharmanka Kinetic Theatre'; and the installations created by Michel Laubu of the French company Turak: théâtre d'objets.

As the name suggests, Laubu has affiliations with the *théâtre d'objets*. He makes both performance and installations of uncanny objects. *Appartement témoin*, an installation presented as part of the 2011 Charleville-Mezieres international puppet festival, placed everyday objects in life-size domestic settings, with thin, 'stagey' wallpapered partitions, and motors and fans to give the objects an eerie, jerky life. The mechanisms were largely unconcealed, yet the movement was no less unsettling for the knowledge that the animating breath is provided by an electric fan. The setting was reminiscent of the surrealism in the films of Jan Švankmajer or the Brothers Quay, but with a domestic horror of its own. A triangular scorch mark in the wall of a bathroom suggested an attempted escape by an electric iron which sat – innocently, as it were, in its proper place on the ironing board. It was as if this was how ordinary objects would behave given the chance, if inadvertently left in a configuration that allowed their own charge to circulate.

TOUCH TOURS

Most subsidised theatres now offer one or two scheduled audio-described performances for each of their shows. At these performances, blind and partially sighted members of the audience can listen to a live commentary on the visual aspects of the performance – gestures, expressions, entrances and exits, lighting changes and so on. The commentary is woven in between the spoken dialogue and picked up on individual infrared headset receivers. Audio descriptions in theatre are often supplemented by a 'touch tour' before the performance, allowing audience members to walk the set and handle props, costumes and wigs. Discussion with sighted companions and members of the cast and crew plays an important role in contextualising the objects both in terms of everyday life and their subsequent use in the performance. The experience of participants in touch tours offers some intriguing hints about the importance of the non-visual senses in performance.

   In a production set in a specific historical period, the touch tour may provide an understanding of the form and materials of objects no longer in common use such as Elizabethan ruffs, Victorian hooped skirts, or mechanical typewriters. As in Lyn Gardner's comments about the 'Collaborators' exhibition, the weight and texture of reproduction or vintage costumes is sometimes the focus. At other times, ingenious mechanisms and trick props are the point of interest. A hands-on exploration may be the only way to convey to a blind audience member the scale, shape and texture of custom-made props, particularly the outsize props and exaggerated silhouettes of pantomime.

   Along with the audio describers, company members including actors, stage managers and members of the wardrobe team typically attend a touch tour. The dialogue between company members and participants is not a one-way transmission of technical knowhow or historical research. Depending on the nature of the piece, there often is a three-way – and frequently intergenerational – exchange.[67]

Mike Leigh's 2011 play *Grief* is set in 1957, in a suburban home built in the 1930s, its inhabitants emotionally frozen since the end of the Second World War. The set, designed by Alison Chitty, was meticulously detailed, with period furniture and household items sourced by stage management from antique shops and auctions. On the polished walnut sideboard, there was a silver tray with glasses, cut-glass decanters and a soda syphon. In the kitchen area, there was a hostess trolley complete with a spherical chrome teapot, china cups and saucers, sugar bowl and tongs and a cake stand.

At the touch tour for *Grief*, older participants became involved in a dialogue about the props that was full of reminiscence. One recalled, 'We had a tea set with a pattern just like this'. A sighted participant handed her companion a small object: 'Here, feel this, do you remember these? Sugar tongs! Who uses those now?' These tiny details of pattern may be invisible to most of the (sighted) audience but, like the unseen set bedroom, used by an actor when 'upstairs', they help the company create a physical and emotional reality. The gesture that accompanies the picking up of sugar cubes with tongs conveys a whole social world – the tongs may be invisible to the back row, but the gesture is reflected in the actor's whole body. Leigh's rehearsal practice may be unusual in British theatre but it shows the potential of working with real props in devising and rehearsal.[68]

At the other extreme in mood and physicality from *Grief*, the touch tour for the musical *Top Hat* returns us to the realm of circus skills, Vakhtangov and Meyerhold. In one scene the dancer playing Jerry Travers – the character created by Fred Astaire in the 1935 film – uses a hat stand as a dance partner. Rather like a circus performer, the dancer and object are in a 'symbiotic relationship' (Pleśniarowicz 1994: 181–2). For a blind or partially sighted audience member to have a feeling for the dancer's skill and grace during the live performance, it is essential that they handle the hat stand for themselves. This points up how much the visual experience of sighted audience members is conveyed to muscular memory through kinaesthetics. A translation into words alone would struggle to produce the same emotional quality.

Most of the scenes in *Top Hat*, designed by Hildegard Bechtler, take place in a luxurious London hotel. The touch tour primarily gives a tactile understanding of objects that are unfamiliar, no longer used, perhaps difficult to describe. For example, participants might sit on a 'conversation piece', a round sofa found in the hotel lobby, or on a winged leather clubman's chair with a small shelf attached for a glass, or trace the art deco design on a lacquered sideboard. Although such objects may be unfamiliar to a contemporary audience, a sighted spectator may register them as part of a 'general impression' of the period, taking in materials such as lacquer, watered silk, brass and so on without consciously identifying them. Without the opportunity to handle such objects, a blind theatregoer might not be aware of how the material world of the musical differs from a modern hotel, missing out not only on an understanding of how characters are distributed in space but also on the sensual pleasures of the piece.

There are also specific props that are used by the dancers, such as the two types of cane used by chorus members. At the touch tour, participants are encouraged to experiment with the canes, feeling the difference between the lightweight blonde bamboo cane with a curved handle, and the heavier, silver-topped black cylindrical cane, and testing the sound that they make on the stage floor. The prop here could be regarded as an accoutrement, the fashion accessory it would have been originally, but its sound properties are exploited by the choreography. The touch tour anticipates this use to some extent, but thereby allows blind audience members to make independent interpretation of the soundscape during the performance, hearing the difference between a dancer swishing a cane over the floor, or tapping it lightly on the boards.

A brass ashtray on a stand moves from scene-setting to active participant, when Jerry Travers takes a handful of sand from the ashtray and sprinkles it on the floor in order to perform a 'sand dance'. This might be a reference to the 'Egyptian' vaudeville act performed by American comedy trio Wilson, Keppel and Betty in the 1920s and 1930s, but Travers mentions the folkloric 'Sandman' figure, who sprinkles sand into the eyes of children to bring on sleep. In the 1930s, sand was put on the floor to amplify the sound of a soft shoe shuffle – a delicate, smooth tap dance. Travers performs his sand dance to mollify his downstairs neighbour, trying to sleep in the room below. What is significant from the props point of view is that Travers (or rather, Astaire, in the first place) rethinks an unnoticed object (so common in the 1930s that it would be merely part of the set-dressing for any grand hotel room), picking out an ignored part of its materiality (the sand usually serves only to extinguish cigarettes) and using it to transform the hotel room for a different kind of performance.

He performs a similar transformation on a heavy brass hat stand – rocking it forwards and back, setting it spinning on the circumference of the heavy base, catching and releasing it in time to the music, playing with it as a 'dance partner'. We delight equally in the playfulness of this apparently spontaneous appropriation of the everyday, and in the dancer's skill in charming a heavy, lifeless object into graceful motion. The dancer's virtuoso control of the object depends on rehearsal, on a muscular memory of its weight, centre of balance and so on. It would be potentially disastrous to swap one hat stand for another.

A bald verbal account of this action – 'Jerry dances with the hat stand' – gives us no access to the play of weight and timing, the sense of a dialogue between the man and object. We might imagine from words alone that he is skipping around a hat stand, or lifting it into his arms and waltzing round the room. Similarly, it will be obvious without thinking about it to a sighted spectator that a rectangular hat stand with four wooden feet would not perform in the same way; and nor would a spindly aluminium hat stand on a lighter base. Handling the object at the touch tour, feeling its weight and being invited to rock it to just the point before it overbalances allows blind audience members to participate in the kinaesthetic experience.

The insights gained from touch tours draw attention to the existence of spectators' whole body physical responses to objects. Nicholas Ridout has said that a 'post-show tour of inspection' of the objects in *Stifters Dinge* 'is a privilege of which the modern theatre's dominant conventions usually need to deprive us so as to preserve the mysteries of the world backstage, where once the lights are off them the actors will always turn out to be disappointingly real and the machinery of illusion flat' (Ridout 2012). But is this so? Some users of audio description experience the touch tour as disillusioning, but for most the tour offers a mixture of pleasures related to the tactile: appreciation of the craft skills of prop-makers, or of the original makers of objects that have been found; sensual/sculptural pleasure in fabrics, wood, metal and other materials; nostalgic pleasures akin to those of the heritage museum, but also opportunities to engage the tactile memory of use.

The props in these examples taken from museum displays, immersive sets and touch tours differ from other kinds of objects that might be 'on display'. Their intimate association with performance means that their history of use and potential future animation are always highlighted. Props without actors stand at the far end of the spectrum of animation. Even when they are not touched directly, they emphasise the embodied nature of the spectator's interaction with props.

FURTHER READING

On props in museums:

Susan Bennett's *Theatre and Museums* (2013) is a very good short introduction to the issues around participation and interactivity. See also: *Performing Heritage: Research, Practice and Innovation in Museum Theatre and Live Interpretation*, edited by Anthony Jackson and Jenny Kidd (2011) and Helen Chatterjee (ed.), *Touch in Museums: Policy and Practice in Object Handling* (2008).

On immersive sets:

In *Immersive Theatres* (2013), Josephine Machon offers a useful survey of contemporary British practice, with interviews with a range of practitioners and a theoretical context that draws on Jacques Rancière and Nicolas Bourriaud on 'the emancipated spectator' and relational aesthetics, and Juhani Pallasmaa, Doreen Massey and Gaston Bachelard on space. See also Claire Bishop, *Installation Art: A Critical History* (2005) and Nicholas Ridout's discussion of *Stifters Dinge*, Heiner Goebbels' piece 'for five pianos with no pianists' (Ridout 2012).

On touch:

Constance Classen, *The Book of Touch* (2005); Peter Dent, *Sculpture and Touch* (2014); Elizabeth Pye, *The Power of Touch* (2007).

Chapter

11   The Props Cupboard

Articles for the general public on the work of theatre props departments often feature a long list of miscellaneous items, marvelling at the sheer multifariousness of the collection, and its power to evoke past eras and past performances. An article published in the *New York Sun* on 25 February 1912 describes the property department of the Metropolitan Opera House:

> In charge of the property department is a master of properties, who has to look after an insignificant total of about 20,000 objects! These range all the way from so trivial a thing as a single feather to whole sets of expensive furniture. The feather does duty in various operas in which a quill pen is needed, as in 'Tosca,' where it is used to write the unhappy singer's passport before she assassinates Scarpia.
>
> The opera house property department has enough furniture to fill a hotel. There are over 100 side chairs, as those without arms are called; about forty arm chairs and fifteen sofas, not counting various settees, benches and wooden stools. In the same category are about fifty tables, several screens, hatracks, a cheval glass, chests and so on. [...]
>
> The opera house is pretty well fixed to repel an attack, for in the property master's department there are about 500 swords of all shapes and sizes, 350 helmets, 100 breastplates, 8 full suits of armor, scores of spears, a lot of guns and even some big sticks [that] belong to the giants in the Ring.
>
> (*New York Sun* 1912)

Alice Rayner describes the prop store as 'both an archive of past productions and a promise of possible ones', with objects in a signifying limbo, 'neither fully in the world nor yet onstage' (Rayner 2006a: 75). This peep into the props cupboard will look at just one prop – the skull. Although it is atypical in many ways, the skull has become the emblematic prop or, as Aoife Monks puts it, the 'theatrical object *par excellence*'. The image of Hamlet holding a skull is often used to signify the play, and acting more generally. Lezlie C. Cross discusses the way that words animate this particular object: 'The Gravedigger's words give the skull a name, an identity, a history. Hamlet's words animate the skull further, reimagining the living man's body: his back, his lips, his "gibes" and "gambols"' (Cross 2014: 64). Depending on the production, the skull is sometimes also animated by gesture, by Hamlet's gaze into the empty eye-sockets, or turning the head outwards, as if Yorick was taking in the audience.

Cross traces one particular Yorick skull that belonged to Horace Howard Furness, a 'collector of Shakespeareana'. Furness, who was an editor of Shakespeare's works, had among his collection a pair of gloves that were believed to have belonged to Shakespeare, having passed through the hands of actors David Garrick and Fanny Kemble before reaching Furness. In 1876 he was given a skull with visible evidence of its provenance: it had been signed by the actors Charles Kean (1811–1868, the son of Edmund Kean), William Macready (1793–1873) and John Philip Kemble (1757–1823) among others, and tradition had that it had been lent to Henry Irving in 1884 and to Edwin Booth the following year. Cross describes Booth's super-stitious refusal to keep a skull among their stage properties. His father had toured with a skull but after his death Edwin replaced it with a papier mâché version. On tour, the company had to furnish themselves with a skull in the towns and cities where they played, usually borrowing one from a local physician, but sometimes substituting 'a carved turnip or loaf of bread' (Cross 2014: 67). The skull is now in a museum at the University of Pennsylvania:

> Local Philadelphia lore – from the nineteenth century to today – claims that the Furness skull was once the head of John 'Pop' Reed, a stagehand at the Walnut Street Theatre. Reed willed his skull to the theatre upon his death with the express wish that it become Yorick in productions of Hamlet.
>
> (69)

Unfortunately the chronology doesn't fit what is known of the skull's his-tory, but the legend persists. Determined to identify the first 'owner' of the skull, Horace Howard Furness even turned to spiritualists. The trope of the skull donated to theatre turns up again in England in the late twentieth cen-tury, as Aoife Monks discusses in the following essay.

'A HUMAN SKULL'

Aoife Monks

In the newly curated theatre galleries of London's Victoria and Albert (V&A) Museum sits a human skull that is missing most of its teeth. Its cranium is signed with names, in blue felt tip marker, and it is surrounded by the paraphernalia of the stage – scripts, photographs, costumes. This is the skull that played Yorick in the 1980 Royal Court production of *Hamlet* starring Jonathan Pryce, famous for his depiction of a Hamlet possessed by the ghost of his father. The skull, the V&A online catalogue tells us, was signed by the cast and entered as a raffle prize at the end of the production. In an oddly Dickensian twist, it was left in a cardboard box on the doorstep of the Theatre Museum like a foundling, noted by the gnomic statement in the museum's catalogue: 'given anonymously.'[a]

This skull makes the peculiar nature of theatrical objects visible in its shift-ing status as body, human remains, theatrical property, raffle prize, and finally, museum artefact. The skull arrives at the V&A having travelled through a series of 'regimes of value' in Arjun Appadurai's term,[b] shifting from self to thing, from commodity to gift, from theatrical metonym to membership of a collection. The skull is itself imprinted by these moves, moving from flesh to bleached bone, from toothed to toothless. Indeed the V&A catalogue notes: 'Jonathan Pryce is depicted holding the skull [...] when the skull appears to have had more teeth. Some were obviously lost during the production'.[c] The skull teeters between the status of character and object on-stage and then goes from being a reus-able theatrical property to becoming a historical artefact by being signed by the performers, rendering it useless for future *Hamlets*. It goes from being a prize to a gift – an anonymous one – and then finally takes its place in the museum as a singular object that is worthy of our attention by virtue of its specific performance history. And now the skull takes on the qualities of the illustrative and the instruc-tive, staring out endlessly from its glass case.

Here, in the story of this skull, we see the theatrical object *par excellence*, an object that is the perfect metonym. In a museum that must offer us the exemplary stand-in, this Royal Court skull substitutes for theatrical skulls more generally, just as theatrical skulls so often stand in for the theatre itself. After all, the image of an actor addressing a skull has taken on the sheen of inevitability in its depiction of 'acting' in portraits, photographs, and parodies. Yorick, perhaps even more than Hamlet himself, condenses the grand narrative of Western theatrical history into the forlorn, singular object of the human skull. The signed skull reveals the metonymical habits of the theatre itself.

Perhaps this is the great attraction of skulls for the theatre – their shifting, uncanny, theatrical state – after all, they're not *exactly* objects. Skulls personify our ambivalent relationship to bodies, functioning simultaneously as objects and as the remains of selves. The Royal Court skull was 'somebody' or 'somebody's'; it was once a self, or owned by a self, and was then owned by a theatre, employed by an actor, and is now the possession of a museum. Its murky status as a *property* makes visible the dialectical relationship between subjects and objects; it makes concrete the frailty and fragility of subjectivity. The skull stands as a memento mori not only for our impending deaths but also for the precariousness of our selves.

As Andrew Sofer points out, this ambivalent state may be why Yorick so often threatens to upstage Hamlet by taking on a chattering, staring persona of his own. The skull emerges as a character onstage, Sofer argues, and turns Hamlet into an object, a decaying body that is Yorick's prop.[d] The status of the skull as a character emerged most recently in the story of Andre Tchaicowsky, whose donation of his skull to the theatre after his death in 1981 led to a tabloid scandal in 2008, when he finally appeared in the role of Yorick with David Tennant in the Royal Shakespeare Company's [RSC] production of *Hamlet*.[e] This scandal gave Tchaicowsky's skull a similar status to the celebrity actor onstage, disrupting the illusion with alternative and competing histories, narratives, and personae. Tchaicowsky's skull became an object that *objects*, resisting its total incorporation into the fictional narrative.

In this, there may be something specific about the skull's status as relic that differentiates it from other theatrical objects, resisting illusionary incorporation through its disruptive status as a [no]body. As Alexandra Walsham argues, 'A relic is ontologically different from a representative or image: it is not a mere symbol or indicator of divine presence, it is an actual physical embodiment of it.'[f] The relic proposes an ontological challenge to the status of theatre as a representational art, continually insisting upon its own distinctive history. In this, skulls exemplify Bert O. States' claim that objects are always in danger of slipping from their semiotic moorings and piercing the image onstage with the assertion of their own claims to agency and subjectivity. As he argues:

Theatre ingests the world of objects and signs only to bring images to life. In the image, a defamiliarized and desymbolized object is 'uplifted to the view' where we see it as being phenomenally heavy with itself. [...] One feels the shudder if its refusal to settle into the illusion.[g]

However, States suggests that it is in the tension between the semiotic and the phenomenal qualities of theatrical objects that the pleasures of theatre emerge – what we witness is the theatrical apparatus displaying its virtuoso power to incorporate those objects that stretch its limits within the frame of representation.[h] Skulls, then, might be seen as the exceptions that prove the rule for their capacity to test the theatre's ability to make images from the things of the world.

Furthermore, the Royal Court skull, in how it displays its performance history through its many signatories, stands as a literal embodiment of the intertextual powers of performance; the ways in which the material things of the stage (properties, costumes, actors) are continually reformed and remoulded by their re-uses and recycling. Jonathan Pryce might not actually be marked by his performance of Hamlet but, as I have argued elsewhere, it is certainly the case that he has retained a ghostly air in the reception of his subsequent work.[i] The skull becomes a literal example of the ways in which performance makes its mark, but is at the same time *too* marked for further theatrical employment. The signed skull is rendered useless, redundant for the theatre's art of turning stuff into image, becoming instead an autonomous art-work or artefact. In Arjun's term, the skull's 'semiotic virtuosity' has been delimited by those signed names, by the heavy imprint of its theatrical past, and it is taken out of circulation to become exemplary of the ways in which all objects are formed and reformed by their performance history.[j]

In this, finally, the Royal Court skull stands as a memento mori for the loss of performance itself. After all, what else do those glass cabinets at the V&A contain than bodily remains; the relics of performances? The skull mutely confronts us with the thing that is absent, the theatrical event that is irretrievable. And yet, as Rebecca Schneider has recently argued, performance remains,[k] and it does so in the museum through the debris of skulls, photos, costumes, and scripts. As Barbara Hodgdon has suggested this debris retains a fascination as much for what it refuses to tell us, for its uncanny muteness, as for its revelation of performances past.[l] The carefully ordered taxonomies of things in their display cases remain, but their stories are necessarily incomplete and now framed by the shorthand of the museum: 'Height: 13.0 cm approximately, Width: 15.0 cm approximately,

Depth 20.0 cm approximately; [...] Materials: Bone; Categories: Entertainment & Leisure.'[m] This signed skull, with its missing teeth, its tenderly and jokingly signed cranium, its staring eye sockets and its half-remembered performance; this is an object characterized most of all by the stories it refuses to tell us.

Aoife Monks (2013) 'Objects' in *Contemporary Theatre Review* 23:1, 53–4. Reprinted by permission of Taylor & Francis Ltd, www.tandfonline.com.

Chapter

12 Conclusion

Props are paradoxical things: essential for many kinds of performance, but often disparaged; theorised as empty signs but nonetheless resolutely material; objects taken for granted as part of common-sense reality and also objects which can fascinate spectators, in which we can 'lose our gaze'. Many people involved in performance have deeply held feelings about props – makers, actors, directors, spectators – but particular examples are not widely discussed outside technical handbooks and the unrecorded dialogues in the workshop. In all these respects, props embody the complicated position of materiality in performance and, as the discussion in previous chapters has shown, decisions made about props inevitably reflect the broader attitudes to materiality expressed by a production.

Stage managers, prop buyers and makers call on craft knowledge about an incredible range of materials – metals, plastics, wood, fabric, plaster, paints, glues. They need to know how materials behave under conditions of repeated – sometimes heavy – use, how they combine, and how they will appear from a distance, under stage lights. Materials scientist Mark Miodownik emphasises the importance of this kind of 'empirical understanding of materials', the knowledge employed by craftspeople. As he puts it, we know materials 'with our hands as well as our heads' (Miodownik 2013: 10). This understanding calls for knowledge that goes beyond the technical: a material that might be perfectly adequate from the point of view of its behaviour and cost will be useless in performance if it doesn't look right. Miodownik wonders about the psychology of materials, our 'sensual and personal relationship with stuff':

> We love some materials despite their flaws, and loathe others even if they are more practical. Take ceramic, for instance. It is the material of dining: of our plates, bowls and cups. No home or restaurant is complete without this material. We have been using it since we invented agriculture thousands of years ago, and yet ceramics are chronically prone to chip, crack and shatter at the most inconvenient times. Why haven't we moved to tougher materials, such as plastic or metal for our plates and cups? Why have we stuck with ceramic despite its mechanical shortcomings?
>
> (Miodownik 2013: 9–10)

This musing on materials will be familiar to anyone working with props. Why does it matter so much – to the actor, to the director – that *this* cup and not that one is used in the performance? Why does one maker prefer to work in wood and another in foam plastic? Why does one spectator – or participant on a touch tour – lose herself in contemplation of a particular prop, while others are indifferent to it? Ceramic, the substance Miodownik chooses as exemplary of our emotional attachment to specific materials, is one that pertains to the 'cup and saucer', the objects particularly associated with questions about everyday reality on the stage. Those questions were not raised for the first time in relation to nineteenth-century 'cup and saucer drama', but the discussions about realism initiated in that period are still resonating today.

Realism is still the dominant mode of much drama but even within canonical naturalist or realist drama, there are moments in which playwrights draw our attention to materiality – in *A Doll's House*, for example, Nora's tarantella dress has to be found and mended for a performance within the play. The very title of Ibsen's play is a metaphor for making models of an idealised reality: in the world of children's make-believe and theatre alike. Nora's departure makes clear that there are other models, other ways of living. She seems to leave not only the fictional house in which she has been living, but also the 'house' of the theatre – to bang shut not a set door made of light wood, but one of the heavy exit doors that leads to the street. In contemporary theatre, both designers and directors can be alert to these moments of excessive materiality, 'the depth charges' laid by the so-called naturalist playwrights, and can invite the audience to reflect on them. The space of attention that opens up around the prop can be created with light, with sound, with an actor's gesture – and it can involve any or all of the artists that make the performance.

Beyond the 'realist' frame, this study has considered the ways that theatre-makers have engaged directly with materiality – with objects and with raw materials. The materials that threaten to overturn the illusion of realist theatre – children, animals, running water, fire – are key to the work of many performance artists and theatre companies from Welfare State International to Societas Raffaello Sanzio. If 'real steam' can be taken as emblematic of the aspects of 'reality' that could not be seamlessly incorporated into the realistic stage picture, what is performance struggling to 'digest' now? I will end by discussing two areas of difficulty for contemporary theatre: the apparently immaterial digital world and, at the other extreme, questions about the material world on a global scale.

AN OBJECT THAT FITS IN THE HAND

While there is a drive to represent the multiple interlinked worlds of the web and social media, digital realities still seem to pose a problem for theatrical representation. How can performance involving real human bodies represent the way in which one person can inhabit several worlds at once? In

1997, Patrick Marber's *Closer* (1997) was hailed as innovative in putting chat rooms onto the stage. The first production showed two characters meeting in an online chat room, with their typed dialogue projected onto screens above the characters' heads. Yet Vicki Mortimer's design did not neglect the physical 'stuff' that continues to pile up in the sign economy. Props accumulated on the stage, rather than being taken away between scenes:

> I wanted to give it a London root, but most of all I felt it was crucial in the staging to make it clear that there are echoes beyond the given consequences of any scene. So, for example, though there is furniture it's not naturalistic, and the way it is moved to the back of the stage and stays there throughout makes it clear that everyone's regrets, words and actions remain – they are always there.
>
> (quoted in Saunders 2008: 73)

Both digital and theatrical realities have changed in the years since the first production of *Closer*, with virtual realities now more numerous and elaborated than the simple lines of text in a chatroom. But, as Matt Trueman comments, theatremakers have 'struggled to place our online lives onstage' while avoiding clichés. Jennifer Haley's play, *The Nether* (2014), portrays a virtual world of the near future which offers physical as well as visual stimulation. The play implies that games of make-believe in the virtual world might have consequences in real life. Designer Es Devlin describes the virtual reality depicted in the play, the 'Nether', as 'the absolute apogee of coding': 'Its world needs to be ultra-real, not techy, but we need to see the process that built it.' By projecting the image of an object onto the surface of the same object in three-dimensional reality, she was able to produce a sense of 'glitching and fragmentation': images go out of focus or flash to reveal the wireframe of coding beneath (Trueman 2014b). By presenting both 'virtual' and 'real world' settings through digital projections, Es Devlin suggests an equivalence between them. Projections are widely used to 'illustrate' an absent reality; here, they were also used to constitute the immediate reality.

Encountering an unfamiliar prop in *Pomona* by Alistair McDowall (2014) suggested how objects might lead spectators into another reality. In Georgia Lowe's design for the Orange Tree Theatre production, a character wears a mask that entirely covers her head in the form of a giant octopus. She moves in the same space as two unmasked, apparently human characters, a bearded man and a young woman. The masked figure wears a modern outfit, a T-shirt, short skirt and trainers. The octopus head recalls H. P. Lovecraft's character Cthulhu but this mythological figure is not named in the opening scene. The bearded man instructs the girl to give the masked figure an object from a bag. It was an object I didn't recognise: a purplish polyhedron that looked as if it was made of hard plastic, but seemed – from the way they handled it – heavier than you might expect. There were some symbols on each of the faces. The man repeated his instruction, and another polyhedron was produced and given to the strange creature. Was it some kind of food?

She didn't eat the objects, simply placed them carefully on the ground beside her, and yet there was a kind of hunger or addiction in her wordless demand for another, and yet another. I imagined at first that the polyhedron was specially made for the strange world of this play. Back at home, I recalled the discussion of role playing games – 'RPGs' – in the play, and found that dozens of designs of 'RPG dice' are available for sale: in wood, plastic or metal, varying in colour and number of facets, and decorated with numbers or runes.

A small material object, a hand prop that costs a few pounds, can serve as metonym of a larger world. I have never handled a polyhedron die like the one in *Pomona*, but hundreds of thousands of people know it as a prop for playing RPGs. Maybe they turn it over in their hands for luck, pick it up for its tactile pleasures between games. I had understood the object physically – through the characters' attitude towards it – through the performance without knowing what it 'was' in the 'real world'. The directorial decision that none of the characters would roll the die or otherwise give a clue to its 'real world' function kept its meaning open. The writer of *Pomona*, Alastair McDowall, has compared theatre to graphic novels, citing Scott McLeod's theory of comic books: 'A comic is two panels and a space in between; everything that happens exists in that gap. You fill in the blanks. It's the same with theatre: it's all created, not on stage or in the audience, but somewhere in the air in between them' (Trueman 2014a). With the polyhedron, as with the whole play, I had to work out the connections between spoken elements and actions shown – they were not congruent. That process continued beyond the time in the theatre. This view of the theatrical reality as constructed by an audience's imagination acting in the 'gaps' between words and objects continues to offer an alternative to the dominance of realism.

OBJECTS TOO LARGE TO HANDLE CLEVERLY

If the digital world is infinitely malleable, at the other extreme there is increasing awareness of the impact of human manipulation of the material world. Geologists have proposed that human activity has had such an impact on the Earth's climate, geological and biological state that it defines a new era, the Anthropocene (McKie 2016). Theatre struggles to represent realities beyond the human scale, such as the global scale of climate change, the extra-planetary scale of space exploration or the microscopic scale of antibiotic resistance and nanotechnology. Yet it is clear that these scales do have an impact at the human scale, where we spend most of our time and energy. To work on these non-human scales, theatre-makers have made use of non-realist approaches such as projections and animations, and non-realist use of everyday objects and raw materials. Equally significant in indicating a more ecological model of performance are the improvisatory approaches that ask actors to discover the inherent qualities of objects, their material properties and inclinations. Enrique Pardo's suggestion that performers should practice working with materials that are 'too large to control cleverly' (Pardo 1988: 170) is one tactic to discover a way of handling the material world without manipulating it, following and listening rather than directing and exploiting.

Designers, prop-makers and stage managers tacitly and explicitly negotiate between material and immaterial values – practical questions of the health and safety of materials, costs, longevity and so on, as well as affective-aesthetic questions. Making these discussions more explicit enables all the artists and craftspeople involved in theatre-making to explore a full range of aesthetic possibilities. Further, it might enable artists and craftspeople to contribute to a wider debate about defining human relationships to matter, both through their art, and through their engagement in wider society. This account has shown that realism – whether of the cup and saucer or of the kitchen sink variety – has only been a part of the story of representing matter in performance. As ideas from ecology and the 'new materialism' are filtering through to performance studies, props will become an increasingly important focus of attention. Looking at how a particular prop moves along the spectrum of animation in performance is a way of thinking analogous to new materialism's consideration of the agency of non-human objects in a non-hierarchical assemblage. It is an approach that draws on the craft knowledge of people – makers, actors, stage managers, directors – who think intensely, with hands and head, about the properties of objects and materials. At the same time, for those who look and think about theatre primarily from the auditorium, the spectrum of animation provides a way to identify the distinct attitudes to matter that are embodied in performed interactions. Props have been intrinsic to performance since long before Aristophanes lampooned the actor Dikaiopolis for his helpless desire for all kinds of picturesque hand props including a beggar's cane, a 'little goblet with a broken lip', and some withered greenery for his 'little basket'. While props will continue to be needed in many diverse types of performance, it seems likely that we will come to speak less of 'props' – as private possessions, frivolous accessories, semi-invisible supports for the actor's work – and more of 'objects' and 'things' as they perform alongside humans in an ecological scenography.

Notes

1. For a sample of the various discussions that arise from Heidegger's notion of 'the thing', see the selection of readings in *The Object* (2014), a volume in the series of 'Documents of Contemporary Art' published by the Whitechapel Gallery, which includes Appadurai, Lacan and Latour on 'things'.
2. Veltruský draws on the work of other semioticians of the Prague School including Otakar Zich and Jindřich Honzl (see Honzl 1976). Important work relating to props was also done by Petr Bogatyrev and Jan Mukařovský, whose interest in folk theatre and puppets allowed them to think about the deliberate production of meaning through materiality, something that is particularly relevant to props. See Elam (1981) and Aston and Savona (1991) for further accounts of theatre semiotics, and Bogatyrev (1976).
3. Theories of language are becoming more 'lexical' and less 'grammatical' according to Kress and van Leeuwen:

   > More and more linguists, particularly in areas such as corpus linguistics and 'formulaic language', now conceive of people's knowledge of language not in the way Chomsky did, as a small, economical set of rules that can generate an infinite number of linguistic utterances, but as a vast, maze-like storehouse of words and collocations of word, of fragments of language, idioms etc. (Kress and van Leeuwen 2001: 113)

4. 'According to a scheme employed in physiology, the body's sensory powers can be divided into three categories. Introception refers to all sensations of the viscera, that is, the internal organs of the body. It is usually distinguished both from exteroception, our five senses open to the external world, and proprioception, our sense of balance, position, and muscular tension, provided by receptors in muscles, joints, tendons, and the inner ear' (Leder 1990: 39).
5. The jarring reference to 'primitives' to some extent reflects usage at the period of the translation.
6. See Chapter 4 of *Stanislavsky in Focus* by Sharon Marie Carnicke (1998).
7. The effect of this delay is discussed by Jean Benedetti, 1999. *An Actor's Work*, Benedetti's translation and editing of *An Actor Prepares* and *Building a Character* brings the two parts together in one unified volume (2008).
8. Stanislavski's account of the imagined contents of Ranevskaya's handbag might be compared with Winnie's handbag in Beckett's *Happy Days*. In both cases, the objects refer to other places, to the past. Ranevskaya's possessions are coherent with what we know of her character – for example, her romantic misadventures in France are nicely evoked by the presence of the novel – but the objects in Winnie's handbag seem to express a gap between the character and her possessions. She struggles to make out the words on a brush – the letters have lost their sense, rather as the objects have become cut off from their original context. While it might be feasible to extend the list of Ranevskaya's possessions indefinitely,

it would not be fruitful to imagine further objects in Winnie's handbag in an attempt to 'build up' a sense of her character. The objects in *Happy Days* appear as 'things' in themselves, rather than as 'accessories' belonging to an owner.

9. The term 'to mime' is not used, perhaps because of its association with comedy, and the commedia-influenced pantomime, perhaps because while Stanislavski was searching for 'truth', mime evokes notions of the counterfeit, mere 'mimicry'. But there's no question that counting money (or Boleslavsky's exercise in pouring tea, among many other examples) involves mime. Later in the twentieth century, practitioners such as Decroux set out to reclaim the word 'mime' from these 'low' associations.

10. Regrettably, the translator notes that he has omitted from this list 'certain exercises relating to specific aspects of Soviet life in the 1930s' (Stanislavski 2008: 681).

11. 'Many – possibly even *most* – of the finest American actors to emerge in the second half of the last century had some connection to Strasberg, and he prided himself on his connection to them. Strasberg's impact on the American theatre – and on film acting – cannot be overstated' (Malague 2012: 31).

12. Uta Hagen mentions the psychologist Jacques Palaci when explaining her use of the term 'trigger object'; similarly, Lee Strasberg has been described as 'a Behaviorist, a Pavlovian' (Mekler 1987: 132).

13. Jean Benedetti suggests that the character of the narrator in *An Actor's Work on Himself* is a composite of Stanislavski himself and Vakhtangov (see Stanislavski 2008).

14. In October 1917, on the day of the declaration of peace, Vakhtangov came across a worker fixing a broken streetcar wire. His ideas about the Revolution changed on seeing the man at work: 'The worker's hands revealed it to me. *The very way* these hands worked – *the very way* they picked up and replaced the tools, and how calmly, confidently and earnestly they moved – this caused me to see and understand that the worker was fixing *his own* wire, and that he was fixing it *for himself*. Only *master's* hands can work like this. This is the meaning of the revolution. I am convinced, I know, that the worker who now owns the state, and who is now a *master* in it, will be able to fix everything that was destroyed. He will do more than "fixing"; he will also *build*. He will now be building for himself' (quoted in Malaev-Babel 2013: 146).

15. Vakhtangov directed the Habima production of Anski's play *The Dybbuk* which was to have a great influence on Tadeusz Kantor's spatial ideas (see Pleśniarowicz 1997).

16. This tradition was little known outside the Soviet Union until the 1990s. In the 1960s and 1970s, Grotowski and Eugenio Barba attempted to re-invent biomechanics by working from photographs and written descriptions. In the 1990s, Russian acting teachers Alexei Levinski and Gennady Bogdanov, who both had a direct link with Meyerhold's teaching through studying with Nikolai Kustow – a former student and colleague of Meyerhold – began to lead workshops on biomechanics in Britain and Germany. For a full account see Pitches 2003.

17. The account in this and the following paragraphs draws on a video documenting a week-long workshop that Levinski led at the Centre for Performing Arts in Wales in October 1995 (Levinski 1996).

18. As part of a puppetry workshop, actor and puppeteer Steve Tiplady led the following exercise with sticks to develop concentration and collaborative work: Each actor has a light rod or dowel about five feet long. They work in pairs, bringing the

sticks together to form an inverted 'V', leaving a gap of an inch between the ends. They maintain this distance while moving slowly round the room, alternating the lead. The actors share an objective measure of their concentration. As the aim is to maintain a gap, rather than to lead or follow 'well', responsibility is shared and it is often hard to say who is leading at any particular moment. As a second stage, the actors use two sticks each. Each leads with one stick and follows with the other. Peripheral awareness is heightened and focus is split. These exercises are particularly useful for puppetry, where manipulators might need to use their hands independently at different tempi and in collaboration with other puppeteers. The exercise can be extended so that groups of three or four work together to maintain two gaps, or a whole company focuses on a single gap.

19. The acting teacher Lenard Petit was a student of Chekhov's student Deirdre Hurst du Prey. He elaborates Chekhov's descriptions of the 'building blocks of the universe' by blending the elements:

> Earth is much more than wet clay; it is also sand, or gravel, or heavy stone. Each image delivers a new yet related movement experience. If we put a bit of air in the earth then it is easier to move through, or we could come to a complete halt and crack our way through the stone. The earth could mix with water to result in mud or fertile land. The mud could freeze or become baked with the heat of fire into a hard cracked or brittle medium to move through.
>
> Water flows, but objects in it float lazily upwards, resting upon it, supported and influenced by the nature of the flow. Water can also rise in a flood or ebb away. Tiny streams trickle and they also swell with rain. The water can be supportive or crushing. Waves move with tremendous force taking things with them either to arrive or be swept away. They also crash violently on a beach with weight and force. There are currents and whirlpools, etc. (Petit 2010: 45–6)

Petit goes on to expand the element of water to include all fluids, each with their specific movement quality – blood, oil, honey – and suggests how the element of air might be subdivided into gusts, gales, breezes and whirlwinds – with movement direct or indirect, fast or slow.

20. This paragraph and the following four draw on a longer discussion of the shoe in performance in Margolies 2003.

21. See the discussion in Murray and Keefe 2007, especially pages 129–37. Although there are programmes with titles referring to 'physical' or 'visual' theatre within drama schools, as well as full-time courses at schools such as École Internationale de Théâtre Jacques Lecoq (1956–present), the Desmond Jones School of Mime and Physical Theatre (till 2004), and the London International School of Performing Arts, much teaching in this area is through shorter courses or workshops.

22. McDermott carried out research in the Michael Chekhov archives at Dartington, and is credited with being one of the key people to revive British interest in Chekhov's teaching.

23. From personal notes on workshop.

24. A number of Improbable's shows have since used Sellotape, most spectacularly Julian Crouch's outdoor show, *Sticky*. As McDermott has pointed out (in an interview with the author), not all sticky tape is the same. On tour, members of the company scoured street markets, testing rolls of tape for the precise combination of stickiness and tearability. Audience members will be all too familiar with the frustrating search for the starting point on a roll of tape – one seems to wrestle

with a hostile material, capable of hiding or even reabsorbing a torn end. The process threatens to go on forever – and no sooner is a loose end teased away from the roll, than it shreds and is lost again. The performers risk this most frustrating of material encounters on stage.

25. The design by Ian McNeil for the 2014 production of *A Doll's House* directed by Carrie Cracknell set the apartment on a revolve, with rooms exposed to view in a way that made them feel toylike. His design for Stephen Daldry's 1992 revival of *An Inspector Calls* (1946) famously placed the actors inside another 'doll's house', an Edwardian building perched above a bombed landscape. The house was eventually blown open, as if by the social revelations contained within Priestley's play.

26. For Chekhov's ecological concerns, see *Reading Chekhov* by Janet Malcolm (2001) and '"There Must be a Lot of Fish in that Lake": Towards an Ecological Theater' by Una Chaudhuri (1994).

27. Japanese Kabuki theatre distinguishes between 'real articles used in daily life (*hommono*) and items created specifically for the stage (*koshiraemono*)' (Hart 2013: 4).

28. The internet has also enabled the direct exchange of set items, props and materials between theatre companies that might not otherwise know of each other. The British message board Set Exchange www.set-exchange.com was set up to reduce waste and help share resources. It operates on the Freecycle model, with members posting their offers and wants. Companies including the Royal Court, Manchester Royal Exchange, the Royal Opera House, Glyndebourne and the National Theatre have been involved, along with smaller commercial and fringe venues. The advertisements make enjoyably surreal reading: '3 pieces of giant broccoli. About 2.5m tall and 1.7m wide. Made from polystyrene scrimmed with idenden & painted, chicken wire and foam rubber. Can be carried between 2 people. Could work for The Borrowers, Alice in Wonderland or panto! To go asap.'

29. The acting editions of plays published by Samuel French conventionally provide a Furniture and Property plot for the convenience of stage managers. The props lists can be as evocative of their period as photographs of contemporaneous productions. Noel Coward's 1943 play *Present Laughter*, for example, requires a grand piano, a soda syphon and decanters of both whisky and sherry. The plot is suggested in compressed form by the dial telephone, the two separate breakfast trays, wire letter tray, and handbag containing a cigarette case and lighter.

30. Stage manager Peter Maccoy notes that the cast 'are the people who have to use the props and furniture, so their involvement is important and they must always be given the option to try out and veto any prop that they have to use. A prop may need to have a specific function or be used in a particular way; the performers need to be able to practise with this and, if they are unable to make it work properly, it may need to be changed. It is far better that this happens during the rehearsal period than during the tech' (Maccoy 2004: 209).

31. A prospectus for an undergraduate course in prop-making gives an idea of some of the skills demanded:

> You will develop skills in research, analysis, collaboration, design interpretation, as well as strong technical drawing skills and an understanding of colour theories and working to scale. You will also cultivate a broad understanding of period styles and aesthetics.

Year 1: sculpting, mould making, casting, fibre glass and plaster work, vacuum forming, paint effects, construction, design interpretation, welding and polystyrene carving. Also: text analysis and research skills.

Year 2: body padding, advanced mould making, silicone and resin work, advanced sculpting, fabrication and model making. Also: design interpretation, time management, self-management and budgeting.

(Adapted from Central School of Speech and Drama's online prospectus 2014)

32. A notable example of this cross-over is the work of the theatrical designer James Thornhill, who was invited to decorate the Great Hall (now known as the Painted Hall) at Greenwich Hospital in 1708: on the walls, he used theatrical decorative techniques to create grooved pillars and *trompe l'oeil* low relief sculptures of naval paraphernalia.
33. See, for example, the work of Catherine Malabou, which reflects on phenomenology and neuroscience, often with reference to the performing arts.
34. It remains difficult, even on an industrial scale, to recycle all plastics into desirable objects. There are technical reasons for this – the mixture of plastics in a typical object (there might be four different types forming one shampoo bottle) makes them tricky to separate for recycling; in addition, there is a diminishing return, as plastics always move down the scale towards dull colours and less sophisticated materials, from clear drinks bottles to fleece fabrics and thence down towards bin-bags, plant-pots and aggregate for road-building.
35. 'Humans have made enough plastic since the second world war to coat the Earth entirely in clingfilm' (McKie 2016). Aside from the rapid disappearance of sites for landfill, both forms of 'disposal' pose hazards to health – landfills can pollute rivers and the water table with toxic run-off (including biological hazards from nappies, clinical waste); incinerators produce variable quantities of airborne pollution, of which the most hazardous are the dioxins produced when plastics are combusted. Some so-called 'biodegradable' plastics merely break down into small particles of plastic, and no research has been done on how these particles might affect the eco-system, or whether they continue to leach chemicals into the soil, while 'microbeads' of plastic have been added to cosmetics and cleaning products that are also washed into rivers and seas. Research has revealed the enormous volume of plastic that is floating in the sea, with estimates of the size of the so-called Great Pacific Garbage Patch alone ranging from 700,000 square kilometres (about the size of Texas) to more than 15,000,000 square kilometres. Unlike organic debris, which biodegrades, the plastic simply disintegrates into ever smaller pieces. The microscopic plastic pieces form a soup in upper levels of the water, acting as a sponge for other environmental pollutants, and are consumed by wildlife.
36. Carolin Karrer's comparative study of the materials used in theatres in Norway and Britain includes an interview with Anthony Barnett of the props department of the Royal Opera House which also refers to the importance of personal preference in choice of materials: it's not just a question of availability or cost but also the background and experience of the maker. Karrer notes that in Norway there is no equivalent of the British theatrical supplier, Flints, and so fibreglass has to be purchased from boat builders. Norwegian prop-makers, in general, are fine artists rather than being specifically trained in theatre construction and methods

of casting in fibreglass and resin. Karrer found that many materials which are standard in UK workshops are not available in Norway, including Jesmonite, Idendend and Rosco Foamcoat.

37. When paper was made of costly cotton and linen, the growing demand led to legislation and systems all over Europe to ensure that no rag would be wasted. Rags were even collected at the end of church services (Rudlin 1990: 92). Renewed interest in sustainability is leading to the development of new materials such as an alternative to MDF made of discarded tomato vines.

38. See Bobby Baker's *Drawing on a Mother's Experience* (1988) and *Kitchen Show* (1991). See also 'The Performativity of Matter' by Zoe Laughlin, in which she demonstrates the properties of unusual materials. Laughlin trained as a scenographer and is now a Creative Director of the Institute of Making www.instituteof making.org.uk.

39. See Nicholas Ridout, *Stage Fright, Animals, and Other Theatrical Problems* (2006) for more about the irruption of the real into the theatre, with chapters on stage fright, embarrassment, animals on stage, labour and laughter.

40. Drew Leder is unusual in considering the contribution of these techniques to phenomenology (Leder 1990).

41. 'The Ancient Greek word for torture is "basanos". It means first of all the touchstone used to test gold for purity; the Greeks extended its meaning to denote a test or trial to determine whether someone or something is real or genuine. It then comes to mean inquiry by torture' (duBois 1991: 7).

42. Materials scientist Mark Miodownik traces his interest in materials to the violent experience of being stabbed with a razor blade as a school student: 'This tiny piece of steel, not much bigger than a postage stamp, had cut through five layers of my clothes, and then through the epidermis and dermis of my skin in one slash without any problem at all.' As a result, he began to notice steel in the world around him – a staple, the family car, a soup spoon: 'Then a million questions poured out. How is it that this one material does so much for us, and yet we hardly talk about it? It is an intimate character in our lives – we put it in our mouths, use it to get rid of unwanted hair, drive around in it – it is our most faithful friend, and yet we hardly know what makes it tick' (Miodownik 2013: 2–3).

43. *The Anatomy Lesson after Rembrandt*, Kunsthalle, Nuremburg, 1968; Foksal art gallery, Warsaw, 1969.

44. Several of Kantor's other happenings from this period involved wrapping or revealing the body. Photographs of *A Small Cosmetic Operation* show the naked model at first reading aloud from a text but then progressively bandaged to remove the possibility of moving her legs, hearing, speaking, seeing or moving at all (Pleśniarowicz 1997: 180–3).

45. See Biesenbach 2010 for the full list of objects. Frazer Ward writes: 'It began tamely. Someone turned her around. Someone thrust her arms into the air. Someone touched her somewhat intimately. The Neapolitan night began to heat up. In the third hour all her clothes were cut from her with razor blades. In the fourth hour the same blades began to explore her skin. Her throat was slashed so someone could suck her blood. Various minor sexual assaults were carried out on her body. She was so committed to the piece that she would not have resisted rape or murder. Faced with her abdication of will, with its implied collapse of human psychology, a protective group began to define itself in the audience. When a loaded gun was thrust to Marina's head and her own finger was being

worked around the trigger, a fight broke out between the audience factions' (Ward 2012: 120).

46. See also *Our Father* by Charlottte Keatley (2012) in which a kitchen sink floods as a reservoir breaks, a wider environmental catastrophe bursting through the walls of the domestic.

47. Nevitt's short book *Theatre & Violence* (2013) discusses the 'in-yer-face' playwrights of the 1990s in a wider philosophical context.

48. Kane explained that the night she saw *Mad* (directed by Jeremy Weller, Edinburgh 1992), she 'made a decision about the kind of theatre I wanted to make – experiential' (Sierz 2001: 92). Weller's production altered conventional relations between stage and audience, fiction and reality in several ways; the audience was seated on the stage and the performers stated that they were relating their own experiences of mental illness, and were not just playing a 'role'.

49. These paragraphs draw on a longer discussion of this scene in 'Smelling Voices: Cooking in the Theatre' in *'On Smell': Performance Research* vol. 8, issue 3 (Margolies 2003a).

50. Elaine Aston discusses *The Skriker* and *Far Away* in the context of Timothy Morton's concept of 'dark ecology' in Aston, 2015.

51. Tweet from the Young Vic Theatre, 18 November 2015.

52. This and subsequent translations from Mattéoli are my own.

53. While there are important overlaps between object theatre and the 'toy', 'model' or 'paper' theatres, both in terms of practitioners working across these fields and the aesthetic and practical issues they confront, these latter forms are outside the scope of this book.

54. *Piccoli suicidi* has also been re-staged by Carles Cañellas of Rocamora Theater, Barcelona.

55. Robin Deacon, a British artist born in 1973, has re-enacted Stuart Sherman's scenarios in the frame of the art gallery. Deacon's film *Spectacle: A Portrait of Stuart Sherman* (2013) includes some archive footage of Sherman and an interview with the maker of some of his key props. See www.robindeacon.com.

56. Matthew Isaac Cohen describes Agus Nur Amal as 'a Jakarta-based comical storyteller, puppeteer, performance artist, and media personality, born in Aceh, Indonesia, and trained in modern theatre at Institut Kesenian Jakarta (IKJ, or Jakarta Arts Institute). Agus has been active in peace campaigns in Jakarta and Aceh since 1999 and assumed national prominence as a television commentator in the wake of the 2004 tsunami. His stock in trade is a modernized form of a rare southwestern Acehnese storytelling genre known as *dangedria*, which he researched after graduating from IKJ. Agus performs under the nom de stage of PM Toh, after the most famous *dangedria* artist in living memory, now deceased, who took his own stage name from a bus stop' (Cohen 2010: 400).

57. See also Sean Myatt and Daniel Watt (2012) and Rene Baker (2012) in the 'object theatre' issue of *Puppet Notebook*. Baker trains actors and puppeteers in working with objects – demonstrating, for example, how to distinguish between objects as puppets, objects as equal partners with actors, and objects as props. She writes of her workshop 'From Prop to Protagonist': 'Objects have a language; they speak of culture and context.' One technique used in the workshop is the interview. Participants present an everyday object, and members of the group ask questions, at first to the curator and then directly to the object: 'It works best

if the curator doesn't try to animate the object or pretend it is a character, they simply hold the object in their hand, look at it, and say whatever comes to mind. Humans tell one side of the cultural story and objects tell another. Objects are often worried about cleanliness and being handled correctly. They are quick to point out the difference in a man's and woman's touch. They talk about society and its codes' (Baker 2015).

58. Tom Cheeseman suggests that *Bänkelsang* could be translated as 'shocking ballad picture show' (Cheeseman 1994).

59. Ali Momeni, a contemporary Iranian projection artist based in the United States, cites an ancient Persian tradition as the inspiration for his visual storytelling in public spaces.

60. The scenes are often painted on fabric suspended from poles for easy changes, or made into 'crankies' – painted on long sheets of paper with the scenes changed by turning a handle (or 'cranking').

61. See the accounts by Myatt and Watt (2012) of workshops by Charlot Lemoine, Paul Zaloom and Agus Nur Amal.

62. Corniquet and Rhéty (2012); this and following translations are my own.

63. 'L'imaginaire' is a term used by Sartre and Lacan, usually translated as 'the imaginary'.

64. The French penal code enshrines the right to *glanage*, the gathering of crops such as wheat or potatoes from the ground after the main harvest has been made, making a distinction from the *grapillage* of fruit from trees and bushes. See www.jeunes-ecologistes.org/blog/2013/12/le-glanage.

65. The roles that are credited in creating the exhibition could equally belong to a performance, and many of the artists who work regularly with Theatre-Rites on live performances were involved, including designer Sophia Clist.

66. A film made for the Victoria and Albert Museum by Donatella Barbieri and Netia Jones explores the designer's phenomenological experience of costume (see Barbieri 2012 for an account of the research and a link to the film).

67. Muriel Bailly has written about her experience of the conversations provoked by hands-on sessions in museums: 'Handling sessions are characterised by smaller groups than those attending traditional gallery tours. The intimacy of the session and the public's direct experience with the object (or the related topic) means that visitors share a lot more of their personal stories. The session becomes a conversation where the staff delivering the session learn from the participants as much as the other way around. [...]Because the engagement is punctuated by visitors' personal stories, the possibilities are endless, as well as unpredictable. No two sessions are the same. You need to be ready to hear what people have to say, and sometimes it can be very emotional...' (Bailly 2015).

68. Jacqueline Riding, a research advisor on Leigh's film *Mr Turner,* notes that 'Mike Leigh's film-making process is intensive and collaborative, with character, action and dialogue gradually emerging from months of research, discussion and improvisation – and he told us that this method is broadly the same whatever the subject'. The research process for *Mr Turner* took place over six months of rehearsals, and a four-month shoot. Actors had lessons in topics such as oil painting, traditional wet shaving and daguerreotype photography (Riding 2014).

NOTES TO 'A HUMAN SKULL' BY AOIFE MONKS

a. See the V&A online catalogue, 'Skull' http://collections.vam.ac.uk/item/ O138197/skull/ Accessed 10 October 2011. The story of the skull's arrival at the theatre was related to me by Kate Dorney, the museum's Curator of Modern and Contemporary Performance.

b. Arjun Appadurai, 'Introduction: Commodities and the Politics of Value' in *The Social Life of Things: Commodities in Cultural Perspective*, ed. by Arjun Appadurai (Cambridge: Cambridge University Press, 1986), pp. 3–64 (p. 15).

c. V&A, 'Skull'.

d. See Andrew Sofer, *The Stage Life of Props* (Ann Arbor: University of Michigan Press, 2003), pp. 89–117.

e. See Simon de Bruxelles, 'At last, for Yorick, Bequeathed skull stars in Hamlet'. *The Times*, 26 November 2008.

f. Alexandra Walsham, 'Introduction: Relics and Remains' in 'Relics and Remains', *Past and Present*, 206 (suppl 5 2010), 9–36, p. 12.

g. Bert O. States, *Great Reckonings in Little Rooms: On the Phenomenology of Theatre* (Los Angeles. University of California Press, 1985), p. 37. For further discussion of the phenomenological qualities of stage objects, see Alice Rayner, *Ghosts: Death's Double and the Phenomena of Theatre* (Minneapolis: University of Minnesota Press, 2006), pp. 73–110.

h. Ibid., pp. 19–48.

i. See Aoife Monks, *The Actor in Costume* (Basingstoke: Palgrave Macmillan, 2010), p. 128.

j. See Appadurai, 'Introduction', p. 38.

k. See Rebecca Schneider, *Performing Remains: Art and War in Times of Theatrical Reenactment* (London and New York: Routledge, 2011).

l. See Barbara Hodgdon, 'Shopping in the Archive: Material Memories' in *Shakespeare, Memory and Performance*, ed. by Peter Holland (Cambridge: Cambridge University Press, 2006), pp. 135–68 (p. 165).

m. V&A, 'Skull'.

Bibliography

Adam, Barbara and Kathleen Sullivan (2000) 'Pluto, the Invisible Presence of Time-Transcending Technologies'. Paper given at 'Between Nature' conference, Lancaster University, July 2000.

Ainslie, Sarah (2010) *Complicite rehearsal notes: a visual essay of the unique working methods of the company*, London: Complicite.

AKHE (2015) www.akhe.ru/eng/about.html Accessed 19 November 2015.

Asendorf, Christoph (1993) *Batteries of Life: On the History of Things and Their Perception in Modernity*, Berkeley and Los Angeles: University of California Press.

Askegaard, S. and A. F. Firat (1997) 'Towards a Critique of Material Culture, Consumption and Markets' in Susan Pearce (ed.) *Experiencing Material Culture in the Western World*, London: Leicester University Press.

Aston, Elaine (2015) 'Caryl Churchill's "Dark Ecology"', in Carl Lavery and Clare Finburgh (eds) *Rethinking the Theatre of the Absurd: Ecology, the Environment and the Greening of the Modern Stage*, London: Bloomsbury.

Aston, Elaine and George Savona (1991) *Theatre as Sign System*, London: Routledge.

Bachelard, Gaston (1994) *The Poetics of Space*, Boston, MA: Beacon Press.

Bailly, Muriel (2015) 'Handling Collection: Challenges' http://blog.wellcomecollection.org/2015/08/04/handling-collection-challenges/ Accessed 13 August 2015.

Baker, Rene (2012) 'Shifting Focus: The Performer's Task in a Theatre of Objects' in *Puppet Notebook* Winter 2012–13, 16–18.

Baker, Rene (2016) 'From Prop to Protagonist' https://littleangeltheatre.wordpress.com/2016/01/11/from-prop-to-protagonist-by-rene-baker/ Accessed 24 January 2016.

Banham, Martin (ed.) (1995) *The Cambridge Guide to Theatre*, Cambridge: Cambridge University Press.

Barad, Karen (2003) 'Posthumanist Performativity: Towards an Understanding of How Matter Comes to Matter' in *Signs* vol. 28, no. 3, 801–31.

Barbieri, Donatella (2012) 'Encounters in the Archive' in *V&A Online Journal* Issue No. 4 Summer 2012 www.vam.ac.uk/content/journals/research-journal/issue-no.-4-summer-2012/encounters-in-the-archive-reflections-on-costume Accessed 1 December 2015.

Barker, Clive (1977) *Theatre Games*, London: Methuen.

Barker, Clive (1989) 'Games in Education and Theatre' *New Theatre Quarterly* vol. 5, no. 19, 227–35.

Barthes, Roland (1977) 'The Grain of the Voice' in *Image – Music – Text,* London: Fontana.

Barthes, Roland (1982) *Camera Lucida: Reflections on Photography*, New York: Hill & Wang.

Barthes, Roland (1984) 'The Reality Effect' in *The Rustle of Language,* trans. Richard Howard, Berkeley and Los Angeles: University of California Press.

Baudrillard, Jean ([1968] 1996) *The System of Objects*, London: Verso.

Baugh, Christopher (2010) 'Brecht and Stage Design: the *Bühnebildner* and the *Bühnenbauer*' in Collins and Nisbet (2010).

Begley, Varun (2012) 'Objects of Realism: Bertolt Brecht, Roland Barthes, and Marsha Norman' in *Theatre Journal*, vol. 64, no. 3, October 2012, 337–53.

Bell, John (ed.) (2001) *Puppets, Masks, and Performing Objects*, Cambridge, MA: MIT Press.

Bell, John (2005) *Strings, Hands, Shadows: A Modern Puppet History*, Detroit: Detroit Institute of Arts.

Bell, John (2008) *American Puppet Modernism: Essays on the Material World in Performance*, New York: Palgrave Macmillan.

Benedetti, Jean (1999) *Stanislavski: His life and art* (3rd edition), London: Bloomsbury.

Benjamin, Walter (1970) *Illuminations*, London: Jonathan Cape.

Benjamin, Walter (1985) *The Origin of German Tragic Drama*, London: Verso.

Bennett, Jane (2010) *Vibrant Matter: A Political Ecology of Things*, Durham, N.C.: Duke University Press.

Bennett, Susan (2013) *Theatre and Museums*, Houndmills, Basingstoke: Palgrave Macmillan.

Biesenbach, Klaus (2010) *Marina Abramović: The Artist Is Present*, New York: Museum of Modern Art.

Bloomer, Jennifer (1996) 'The Matter of the Cutting Edge' in K. Rüedi, S. Wigglesworth, and D. McCorquodale (eds) *Desiring Practices: Architecture, Gender and the Interdisciplinary*, London: Black Dog Publishing.

Bogatyrev, Petr (1976) 'Semiotics in the Folk Theater' in *Semiotics of Art: Prague School Contributions*, ed. Ladislaw Matejka and Irwin R. Titunik, Cambridge: MIT Press.

Bois, Yves-Alain and Rosalind E. Krauss (1997) *Formless: A User's Guide*, New York: Zone Books.

Booth, Michael R. (1980) 'Introduction' to T. W. Robertson, *Six Plays*, Ashover, Derbyshire: Amber Lane Press.

Bossonet, Felix (1978) *The Function of Stage Properties in Christopher Marlowe's Plays*. Vol. 27. The Cooper Monographs on English and American Language and Literature, "Theatrical Physiognomy Series", Bern: Francke.

Braun, Edward (1995) *Meyerhold: A Revolution in Theatre*, London: Methuen.

Brecht, Bertolt (1961) *Poems on the Theatre*, tr. John Berger and Anna Bostock, Middlesex: Scorpion Press.

Brecht, Bertolt (1987 [1957]) *Brecht on Theatre*, tr. John Willett, London: Methuen.

Brown, Bill (2004) 'Thing Theory' in Bill Brown (ed.) *Things*, Chicago: University of Chicago Press.

Bruster, Douglas (2002) 'The Dramatic Life of Objects in the Early Modern Theatre' in Harris and Korda (2002).

Buck-Morss, Susan (1989) *The Dialectics of Seeing: Walter Benjamin and the Arcades Project*, Cambridge, MA: MIT Press.

Burchill, Fraser (2001) Interview with author.

Burkett, Ronnie (2010) 'Papier mâché rediscovered' in *Puppet Notebook* 18.

Burnett, Kate (ed.) (2007) *Collaborators: UK Design for Performance 2003–2007*, London: The Society of British Theatre Designers.

Candlin, Fiona and Raiford Guins (eds) (2009) *The Object Reader*, Milton Park, Abingdon, Oxon: Routledge.

Carnicke, Sharon Marie (1998) *Stanislavsky in Focus*, London: Harwood Academic Publishers.

Carnicke, Sharon Marie (2000) 'Stanislavsky's System: Pathways for the Actor' in Hodge (2000).

Carrignon, Christian (2006) *Le théâtre d'objets: mode d'emploi*, Séminaire « Le Théâtre contemporain et le Théâtre d'objet », 14, 15 et 16 mars 2005 à Dijon, Collection l'édition légère, carnet n°2, Pôle National Ressources Théâtre Bourgogne.

Carrignon, Christian and Jean-Luc Mattéoli (2009) *Le théâtre d'objet: A la recherché du théâtre d'objet*, Paris: Editions THEMAA.

Central School of Speech and Drama (2014) www.cssd.ac.uk/study/undergraduate /ba-hons-theatre-practice/ba-hons-theatre-practice-prop-making Accessed 29 July 2014.

Chatterjee, Helen (ed.) (2008) *Touch in Museums: Policy and Practice in Object Handling*, Oxford: Berg.

Chekhov, Anton (2012) *Three Sisters (in a new version by Benedict Andrews)*, London: Oberon Books.

Chekhov, Michael ([1953] 2002) *To the Actor*, London: Routledge.

Chekhov, Michael (2005) *The Path of the Actor*, London: Routledge.

Churchill, Caryl (1983) *Fen*, London: Methuen.

Churchill, Caryl (1997) *Blue Heart*, London: Nick Hern Books.

Churchill, Caryl (1998) *Plays: 3*, London: Nick Hern Books.

Clarke, Laurie Beth, Gough, Richard and Daniel Watt (eds) (2007) *On Objects: Performance Research*, vol. 12, no. 4.

Classen, Constance (2005) *The Book of Touch*, Oxford and New York: Berg.

Cohen, Matthew Isaac (2010) 'PROMISED PARADISE by Leonard Retel Helmrich; Agus Nur Amal' *Asian Theatre Journal*, vol. 27, no. 2 (FALL 2010) 400–402.

Collins, Jane and Andrew Nisbet (2010) *Theatre and Performance Design: A Reader in Scenography*, Milton Park, Abingdon, Oxon: Routledge.

Connor, Steve (2011) *Paraphernalia: The Curious Life of Magical Things*, London: Profile Books.

Cook, Dutton (1878) 'Stage Properties' in *Belgravia, vol. 35*. 1878: 287–9.

Corniquet, Claire and Marion Rhéty (2012) 'L'objet vrai. Précis des objets dans le théâtre d'objets d'Agnès Limbos, à partir de Troubles' in *Agôn 4: L'objet, Dossiers, Objet, mémoire, identité* http://agon.enslyon.fr/index.php?id=2077 Accessed 21 May 2013.

Coward, Noel (1943) *Present Laughter*, London: Samuel French.

Cranz, Galen (1998) *The Chair: Rethinking Culture, Body and Design*, New York: W.W. Norton & Company.

Crawley, Greer (2007) 'A Landscape of Possibilities' in Burnett (2007).

Crease, Robert P. (1993) *The Play of Nature*, Bloomington and Indianapolis: Indiana University Press.

Cross, Lezlie C. (2014) 'The Linguistic Animation of an American Yorick' in Schweitzer and Zerdy, *Performing Objects and Theatrical Things*, Basingstoke: Palgrave Macmillan, 63–75.

Crouch, Tim (2011) *Plays One*, London: Oberon Books.

Curry, J. K. (ed.) (2010) 'The Prop's The Thing: Stage Properties Reconsidered', *Theatre Symposium*, vol.18.

Dartnell, Guy (2001) Interview with the author.

Davies, Gill (2004) *Stage Source Book: Props*, London: Methuen.

Davy, Kate (1981) *Richard Foreman and the Ontological-Hysteric Theatre*, Ann Arbor, MI: UMI Research Press.

De Beauvoir, Simone (1976) *The Prime of Life*, New York: Harper & Row.

De Certeau, Michel (1984) *The Practice of Everyday Life*, Berkeley and Los Angeles, University of California Press.

Decroux, Etienne (1978) *Words on Mime*, Claremont, CA: Pomona College Theatre Department.

De Grazia, Margreta, Maureen Quilligan and Peter Stallybrass (1996) *Subject and Object in Renaissance Culture*, Cambridge: Cambridge University Press.

Dent, Peter (ed.) (2014) *Sculpture and Touch*, Farnham, Surrey: Ashgate.

Dessen, Alan C. (1995) *Recovering Shakespeare's Theatrical Vocabulary*, Cambridge: Cambridge University Press.

DeVoe, S. S. (1971) *English Papier Mâché of the Georgian and Victorian Periods*, London: Barrie & Jenkins.

Dickinson, G. (1925) *English Papier-mâché: Its Origin, Development and Decline*, London: The Courier Press.

DuBois, Page (1991) *Torture and Truth*, New York: Routledge.

Easterling, Pat (2005) 'Agamemnon for the Ancients' in Macintosh et al. (2005).

Eddershaw, Margaret (1996) *Performing Brecht: Forty Years of British Performances*, London: Routledge.

Elam, Keir (1980) *The Semiotics of Theatre and Drama*, London: Routledge.

Erickson, Jon (1995) *The Fate of the Object: From Modern Object to Postmodern Sign in Performance, Art, and Poetry*, Ann Arbor: University of Michigan Press.

Finney, Simone (2015) 'The Care and Keeping of your Mechanical Bull', 15 May 2015 www.almeida.co.uk/the-care-and-keeping-of-your-mechanical-bull Accessed 17 March 2016.

Fleck, H. R. (1943) *Plastics: Scientific and Technological*, London: English Universities Press.

Foreman, Richard (1992) *Unbalancing Acts: Foundations for a Theater*, New York: Pantheon Books.

Foreman, Richard (2015) website of the Ontological Hysterical Theater www.onto-logical.com Accessed 1 November 2015.

Foster, Hal (1996) *The Return of the Real*, Cambridge MA: MIT Press.

Fox, John (1990) 'Commissions and Audiences' in Tony Coult and Baz Kershaw (eds), *Engineers of the Imagination: The Welfare State Handbook*, London: Methuen Drama.

Fried, Larry K. and May, Theresa J. (1995) *Greening Up Our Houses*, Drama Publishers.

Furse, Anna (2008) 'Committed to the Other: The Ethics of Puppetry', *Puppet Notebook* 13, 20–21.

Gardner, Lyn (2008) 'A Theatre Exhibition with Feelgood Factor' *The Guardian*, 28 April 2008 www.theguardian.com/stage/theatreblog/2008/apr/28/atheatre-exhibitionwithfeelgood Accessed 1 November 2015.

Garner, Stanton (1994) *Bodied Spaces: Phenomenology and Performance in Contemporary Drama*, Ithaca, NY: Cornell University Press.

Garrett, Ian (2014) 'Kudzu' in Wallace Heim and Eleanor Margolies (eds) *Landing Stages*, London: Crinkle Crankle Press.

Giannachi, Gabriella and Mary Luckhurst (1999) *On Directing*, London: Faber and Faber.

Gordon, J. E. (1976) *The New Science of Strong Materials*, Harmondsworth: Penguin.

Govier, Jacquie (1984) *Create Your Own Stage Props*, London: A & C Black.

Hagen, Uta (1973) *Respect for Acting*, New York: Macmillan.

Hagen, Uta (1991) *A Challenge for the Actor*, New York: Macmillan.

Hall, Edith, Fiona Macintosh and A. Wrigley (eds) (2004) *Dionysus since 69: Greek Tragedy at the Dawn of the Third Millennium*, Oxford: Oxford University Press.

Hardwick, Lorna (2005) 'Staging *Agamemnon*: The Languages of Translation' in Macintosh et al. (2005).

Harris, Jonathan Gil (2002) 'Properties of Skill: Product Placement in Early English Artisanal Drama' in Harris and Korda (2002).

Harris, Jonathan Gil and Natasha Korda (2002) *Staged Properties in Early Modern English Drama*, Cambridge: Cambridge University Press.

Harrison, George W. M. and Vayos Liapis (eds) (2013) *Performance in Greek and Roman Theatre*, Leiden: Brill.

Harrod, Tanya (2015) *The Real Thing*, London: Hyphen Press.

Hart, Eric (2011a) 'Categories of props' www.props.eric-hart.com/features/categories-of-props Accessed 15 February 2015.

Hart, Eric (2011b) 'Real objects versus constructed props' www.props.eric-hart.com/reprints/real-objects-versus-constructed-props/ Accessed 21 February 2015.

Hart, Eric (2011c) 'A place to buy thunder' www.props.eric-hart.com/reprints/a-place-to-buy-thunder-1898 Accessed 25 February 2015.

Hart, Eric (2013) *The Prop Building Guidebook*, New York and London: Focal Press.

Hatley, Tim (2001) Interview with author.

Haydon, Andrew (2012) 'Three Sisters – Young Vic' 27 September 2012 http://postcardsgods.blogspot.co.uk/2012/09/three-sisters-young-vic.html Accessed 30 November 2015.

Heidegger, Martin (1971) *Poetry, Language, Thought*, New York; London: Harper and Row.

Herbert, Jocelyn (1981) in Richard Findlater (1981) *At the Royal Court: 25 Years of the English Stage Company*, Ambergate, Derbyshire: Amber Lane Press.

Herbert, Jocelyn (1993) *A Theatre Workbook*, London: Art Books International.

Highfill, Philip Jr. (1966) 'Rich's 1744 Inventory of Covent Garden Properties', *Restoration and Eighteenth Century Theatre Research* vol. 5, no. 1, 7–17.

Hodge, Alison (ed.) (2000) *Twentieth Century Actor Training*, London: Routledge.

Hoheisel, Tobias (2012) 'Period. Question Mark?', Annual Gordon Craig lecture, Society for Theatre Research/Central School of Speech and Drama. In conversation with Judith Flanders.

Holt, Michael (1994) *Stage Design and Properties*, London: Phaidon Press.

Honri, P. (1985) *John Wilton's Music Hall*, Hornchurch, Essex: Ian Henry Publications.

Honzl, Jindřich (1976) 'Dynamics of the Sign in the Theater' tr. Irwin Titunik, in Matejka and Titunik (eds), *Semiotics of Art: Prague School Contributions*, Cambridge: MIT Press.

Howard, Pamela (2009) *What Is Scenography? Second Edition*, Abingdon, Oxon: Routledge.

Howes, Philip and Zoe Laughlin (2012) *Material Matters: New Materials in Design*, London: Black Dog.

Hristic, Jovan (1995) '"Thinking with Chekhov": The Evidence of Stanislavsky's Notebooks' in *New Theatre Quarterly* XI, no. 42: 175–83.

Hudek, Anthony (2014) *The Object*, London and Cambridge, MA: Whitechapel Gallery and the MIT Press.

Hunt, Nick and Susan Melrose (2005) '*Techne*, Technology, Technician: The creative practices of the mastercraftsperson' in *Performance Research* vol. 10, no. 4, 70–82.

Ingold, Tim (2000) *The Perception of the Environment: Essays on Livelihood, Dwelling and Skill*, Abingdon: Routledge.

Innes, Jocasta (1976) *The Pauper's Homemaking Book*, Harmondsworth: Penguin.

Innes, Christopher (2000) *A Sourcebook on Naturalist Drama*, London: Routledge.

Jackson, Anthony and Jenny Kidd (eds) (2011) *Performing Heritage: Research, Practice and Innovation in Museum Theatre and Live Interpretation*, Manchester: Manchester University Press.

James, Thurston (1987) *The Theater Props Handbook*, White Hall, VA: Betterway Publications.

James, William (1884) 'What is an Emotion?' *Mind*, 9, 188–205. http://psychclassics .yorku.ca/James/emotion.htm Accessed 3 November 2015.

Jencks, Christopher and Nathan Silver (1973) *Adhocism: The Case for Improvisation*, London: Secker & Warburg.

Johnson, Dominic (2012) *Theatre and the Visual*, Houndmills, Basingstoke: Palgrave Macmillan.

Jones, Ann Rosalind and Peter Stallybrass (2001) *Renaissance Clothing and the Materials of Memory*, Cambridge: Cambridge University Press.

Jurkowski, Henryk (1988) *Aspects of Puppet Theatre*, London: Puppet Centre Trust.

Kantor, Tadeusz (1993) *A Journey through Other Spaces: Essays and Manifestos, 1944–1990 / Tadeusz Kantor; Edited and Translated by Michal Kobialka; with a Critical Study of Tadeusz Kantor's Theatre by Michal Kobialka*, Berkeley; London: University of California Press.

Karim-Cooper, Farah (2012) 'Props' in Stuart Hampton-Reeves and Bridget Escolme (eds) (2012) *Shakespeare and the Making of Theatre*, Basingstoke: Palgrave Macmillan, 88–101.

Karrer, Carolin (2014, unpublished thesis) 'How do prop-making materials used in Norway differ from those used in the UK?'

Kaye, Nick (1996) *Art into Theatre*, Amsterdam: Harwood Academic Publishers.

Kazan, Elia, J. E. Bromberg and Lee Strasberg ([1935] 1984) "Outline for an Elementary Course in Acting". *TDR* vol. 28, no. 4 (Winter 1984): 34–37.

Keatley, Charlotte (2012) *Our Father*, London: Methuen.

Klassowicz, Jan (1979) '*The Dead Class* Scene by Scene' in *Gambit* vol. 9, no. 33–34, 107–136.

Knowles, Ric (2004) *Reading the Material Theatre*, Cambridge: Cambridge University Press.

Kolb, Justin (2011) '"To me comes a creature": Recognition, Agency, and the Properties of Character in Shakespeare's *The Winter's Tale*' in Wendy Beth Hyman *The Automaton in English Renaissance Literature*, Farnham: Ashgate, 45–60.

Kolesnikov, M. (1991) 'The Russian Avant-Garde and the Theatre of the Artist' in N. V. N. Baer (ed.) *Russian Avant-Garde Stage Design 1913 –1935*, London: Thames and Hudson.

Kress, Gunter and Theo van Leeuwen (2001) *Multimodal Discourse*, London: Arnold.

Lakoff, George and Mark Johnson ([1980] 2013) *Metaphors We Live By*, Chicago and London: University of Chicago Press.

Law, Alma and Mel Gordon (1996) *Meyerhold, Eisenstein and Biomechanics: Actor Training in Revolutionary Russia*, Jefferson, NC and London: McFarland & Co.

Lawson, Mark (2011) 'Joe Penhall: Regrets? Too few to mention' *The Guardian* 29 November 2011 www.theguardian.com/stage/2011/nov/29/joe-penhall-interview?newsfeed=true Accessed 1 December 2015.

Leabhart, Thomas (1989) *Modern and Post-modern Mime*, Basingstoke: Macmillan.

Leabhart, Thomas (ed.) (1993) *Words on Decroux*, Mime Journal 1993/1994, Claremont, CA: Pomona College Theatre Department.

Lecoq, Jacques (ed.) (1987) *Le théâtre du geste: mimes et acteurs*, Paris: Bordas.

Leder, Drew (1990) *The Absent Body*, Chicago: University of Chicago Press.

Levinski, Alexei (1996) *Meyerhold's Biomechanics: a workshop*, Exeter: Arts Archives [video].

Lévi-Strauss (1966) *The Savage Mind*, Chicago: University of Chicago Press.

Maccoy, Peter (2004) *Essentials of Stage Management*, London: A & C Black.

Machon, Josephine (2013) *Immersive Theatres*, Basingstoke: Palgrave Macmillan.

Macintosh, Fiona, Pantelis Michelakis, Edith Hall and Oliver Taplin (eds) (2005) Agamemnon *in Performance 458 BC to AD 2004*, Oxford: Oxford University Press.

Malague, Rosemary (2012) *An Actress Prepares: Women and 'The Method'*, Abingdon, Oxon: Routledge.

Malaev-Babel, Andrei (2011) *The Vakhtangov Sourcebook*, Abingdon, Oxon: Routledge.

Malaev-Babel, Andrei (2013) *Yevgeny Vakhtangov: a critical portrait*, Abingdon, Oxon: Routledge.

Malone, Edmund (1790) *The Plays and Poems of William Shakespeare*, London: J. Rivington & Sons, vol. 1, part ii, 302–4.

Margolies, Eleanor (2003) 'Were Those Boots Made Just For Walking?: Shoes as Performing Objects in Everyday Life and in the Theatre' in *Visual Communication*, vol. 2, no. 2, 169–88.

Margolies, Eleanor (2003a) 'Smelling Voices: Cooking in the Theatre' in *'On Smell': Performance Research*, vol. 8, no. 3, 11–23.

Margolies, Eleanor (2014) 'Return to the mound: animating infinite potential in clay, food, and compost' in Dassia N. Posner, Claudia Orenstein and John Bell (eds) *The Routledge Companion to Puppetry and Material Performance*.

Marker, Frederick J. and Lise-Lone Marker (1989) *Ibsen's Lively Art: A Performance Study of the Major Plays*, Cambridge: Cambridge University Press.

Marranca, Bonnie (ed.) (1996) *The Theatre of Images*, Baltimore, ML: Johns Hopkins University Press.

Martínez, Ana (2011) 'Scenographies behind the Scenes: Mapping, Classifying, and Interpreting John Rich's 1744 Inventory of Covent Garden' in Joncus, Berta and Jeremy Barlow (2011) *'The Stage's Glory': John Rich, 1692–1761*, Newark DE: University of Delaware Press.

Mason, Felicity (1993) *The training sessions of Michael Chekhov: a summary of basic features*, Exeter, Arts Archives [video].

Mattéoli, Jean-Luc (2011) *L'Objet pauvre: mémoire et quotidien sur les scènes contemporaines françaises*, Rennes: Presses universitaires de Rennes.

McAuley, Gay (2000) *Space in Performance: Making Meaning in the Theatre*, Ann Arbor: University of Michigan Press.

McDermott, Phelim and Julian Crouch (2000) 'The Gap' in Anthony Dean (2000) *Puppetry into Performance*, London: Central School of Speech and Drama.

McDonagh, Martin (1996) *The Beauty Queen of Leenane*, London: Methuen.

McKie, Robin (2016) 'Plastic now pollutes every corner of Earth' *The Guardian*, 24 January 2016 www.theguardian.com/environment/2016/jan/24/plastic-new-epoch-human-damage Accessed 26 January 2016.

McKinney, Joslin and Philip Butterworth (2009) *The Cambridge Introduction to Scenography*, Cambridge: Cambridge University Press.

Meikle, James L. (1990) 'Plastics in the American Machine Age' in Penny Sparke (ed.) *The Plastics Age: From Modernity to Post-Modernity*, London, V & A Publications.

Meikle, James L. (1997) *American Plastic: A Cultural History*, New Brunswick: Rutgers University Press.

Mekler, Eva (1987) *The New Generation of Acting Teachers*, New York: Penguin.

Mekler, Eva (1989) *Masters of the Stage: British Acting Teachers Talk About Their Craft*, New York: Grove Weidenfeld.

Melrose, Susan (1994) *A Semiotics of the Dramatic Text*, Basingstoke: Macmillan.

Merleau-Ponty, Maurice (1968) *The Visible and the Invisible*, Evanston, IL: Northwestern University Press.

Merleau-Ponty, Maurice (1976) *Phenomenology of Perception*, tr. Colin Smith, London: Routledge & Kegan Paul.

Miller, Arthur (1988) *Plays: One*, London: Methuen.

Miller, Daniel (2008) *The Comfort of Things*, Cambridge: Polity Press.

Miller, Daniel (2010) *Stuff*, Cambridge: Polity Press.

Miodownik, Mark (2013) *Stuff Matters*, London: Penguin.

Mitter, Shomit (1992) *Directors in Rehearsal*, London: Routledge.

Moi, Toril (2006) *Henrik Ibsen and the Birth of Modernism: Art, Theater, Philosophy*, Oxford: Oxford University Press.

Monks, Aoife (2013) 'Objects' in *Contemporary Theatre Review*, vol. 23, no. 1, 53–54.

Mossman, Susan T. (ed.) (1997) *Early Plastics*, London: Leicester University Press.

Motley (1975) *Theatre Props*, London: Studio Vista.

Murray, Simon and John Keefe (2007) *Physical Theatres: A Critical Introduction*, Abingdon: Routledge.

Myatt, Sean (2009) 'Instinctive Object Ramblings' in Eleanor Margolies (ed.) (2009) *Theatre Materials: What Is Theatre Made Of?* London: Centre for Excellence in Training for Theatre, Central School of Speech and Drama, 34–9.

Myatt, Sean and Daniel Watt (2012) 'From Frozen Sponges to Plastic Bags: A Developing Network', *Puppet Notebook* 22, Winter 2012–13, 19–22.

Nevitt, Lucy (2013) *Theatre and Violence*, Houndmills, Basingstoke: Palgrave Macmillan.

New York Sun, February 25, 1912, page 16 www.props.eric-hart.com/reprints/20000-objects-in-opera-property-room-1912/ Accessed 21 February 2015.

Norman, Donald A. (1998) *The Design of Everyday Things*, London: MIT Press.

Oxford Shakespeare, The (1998) *A Midsummer Night's Dream*, ed. Peter Holland, Oxford: Oxford University Press.

Paavolainen, Teemu (2012) *Theatre/Ecology/Cognition: Theorizing Performer-Object Interaction in Grotowski, Kantor, and Meyerhold*, New York: Palgrave Macmillan.

Pardo, Enrique (1988) 'The Theatres of Boredom and Depression', *Spring* 1988, 166–76.

Pearce, Susan (1992) *Museums, Objects and Collections: A Cultural Study*, Leicester: Leicester University Press.

Penhall, Joe (1996) *Some Voices* and *Pale Horse*, London: Methuen.

Petit, Lenard (2010) *The Michael Chekhov Handbook: For the Actor*, Abingdon and New York: Routledge.

Petroski, Henry (1989) *The Pencil: A History*, London: Faber and Faber.

Pinero, Arthur Wing (1936 [1898]) *Trelawny of the 'Wells'*, London: Samuel French.

Pitches, Jonathan (2003) *Vsevolod Meyerhold*, London: Routledge.

Pitches, Jonathan (2007) 'Tracing/Training Rebellion: Object work in Meyerhold's biomechanics' in *'On Objects': Performance Research* vol. 12, no. 4. 97–103.

Pleśniarowicz, Krzysztof (1994) *The Dead Memory Machine: Tadeusz Kantor's Theatre of Death*, tr. William Brand, Kraków: Cricoteka.

Pleśniarowicz, Krzysztof (1997) *Kantor: Artysta końca wieku*, Wrocław: Wydawnictwo Dolnośląskie.

Powers, Sarah (2010) 'Helen's Theatrical Mechane: Props and Costumes in Euripides' *Helen*' in *Theatre Symposium* 18.

Pye, Elizabeth (ed.) (2007) *The Power of Touch: Handling Objects in Museum and Heritage Contexts*, Walnut Creek, CA: Left Coast Press.

Raine, Nina (2002) 'Peter Brook and Stephen Daldry' in *Areté* 08, Spring/Summer 2002 www.aretemagazine.co.uk/08-spring-summer-2002/peter-brook-stephen-daldry/ Accessed 18 August 2015.

Rayner, Alice (2006) 'Presenting Objects, Presenting Things' in David Krasner and David Z. Saltz (eds), *Staging Philosophy: Intersections of Theater, Performance and Philosophy*, Ann Arbor: University of Michigan Press, 180–99.

Rayner, Alice (2006a) *Ghosts: Death's Double and the Phenomena of Theatre*, Minneapolis, University of Minnesota Press.

Rebellato, Dan (1999) *1956 and All That: The Making of Modern British Drama*, London: Routledge.

Rebellato, Dan (2009) 'When we talk of horses or, what do we see when we see a play?' *Performance Research* 14 (1), 17–28.

Reeves, David (1959) *Furniture: An Explanatory History*, London: Faber and Faber.

Riding, Jacqueline (2014) 'Impressions of Mr Turner: a film researcher's view from books to screen' in *The Guardian*, 31 October 2014 www.theguardian.com/film/2014/oct/31/mr-turner-making-mike-leigh-film Accessed 1 December 2015.

Ridout, Nicholas (2006) *Stage Fright, Animals, and Other Theatrical Problems*, Cambridge: Cambridge University Press.

Ridout, Nicholas (2012) 'On the Work of Things: Musical Production, Theatrical Labor, and the "General Intellect"' in *Theatre Journal* 64, 389–408.

Robertson, T. W. (1980) *Six Plays*, Ashover, Derbyshire: Amber Lane Press.

Rogerson, Margaret (ed.) (2011) *The York Mystery Plays: Performance in the City*, York: York Medieval Press.

Rosenfeld, Sybil (1973) *A Short History of Scene Design in Great Britain*, Oxford: Basil Blackwell.

Rudlin (1990) *Making Paper*, Vällingby, Sweden: Rudins.

Samuel, Raphael (1994) *Theatres of Memory*, London: Verso.

Sartre, Jean-Paul (1969) *Being and Nothingness*, London: Routledge.

Saunders, Graham (2008) *Patrick Marber's Closer*, London: Continuum.

Schumann, Peter (2001) 'What, At the End of This Century, Is the Situation of Puppets and Performing Objects?' in Bell (2001).

Schweitzer, Marlis and Joanne Zerdy (2014) *Performing Objects and Theatrical Things*, Basingstoke: Palgrave Macmillan.

Senelick, Laurence (ed.) (1992) *Wandering Stars: Russian Emigré Theater, 1905–1940*, Iowa City: University of Iowa Press.

Serres, M. (1985) *Les cinq sens*, Paris: Hachette.

Serres, Michel and Latour, Bruno (1995) *Conversations on Science, Culture and Time*, Ann Arbor: University of Michigan Press.

Shields, David (2010) *Reality Hunger*, London: Penguin.

Sierz, Aleks (2001) *In-Yer-Face Theatre*, London: Faber and Faber.

Sofer, Andrew (2003) *The Stage Life of Props*, Ann Arbor: University of Michigan Press.

Solga, Kim (2015) *Theatre & Feminism*, Basingstoke: Palgrave Macmillan.

Stanislavski, Constantin ([1936] 1980) *An Actor Prepares*, translated by Elizabeth Reynolds Hapgood, London: Methuen.

Stanislavski, Constantin (2008) *An Actor's Work*, translated and edited by Jean Benedetti, Abingdon, Oxon: Routledge.

States, Bert O. (1985) *Great Reckonings in Little Rooms: On the Phenomenology of Theater*, Berkeley: University of California Press.

Stern, Steven (2010) 'Stuart Sherman', *Frieze* 129, March 2010 www.frieze.com/issue/review/stuart_sherman/ Accessed 13 August 2015.

Stewart, Ena Lamont ([1947] 1983) *Men Should Weep*, London: Samuel French.

Stow, John ([1598]) *The Survey of London*, Dent: London.

TamTam Objektentheater (2015) www.tamtamtheater.nl Accessed 1 November 2015.

Taplin, Oliver (1993) *Comic Angels and Other Approaches to Greek Drama through Vase-Paintings*, Oxford: Clarendon Press.

Taylor, Paul (2012) 'Review: Three Sisters, Young Vic, London www.independent.co.uk/arts-entertainment/theatre-dance/reviews/three-sisters-young-vic-london-8139210.html (Monday 17 September 2012) Accessed 20 November 2015.

Teague, Frances (1991) *Shakespeare's Speaking Properties*, Lewisburg: Bucknell University Press.

Theatre de Complicite (1994) *The Three Lives of Lucie Cabrol*, London: Methuen.

Theatre de Cuisine (2015) www.theatredecuisine.com Accessed 1 November 2015.

Thomson, Peter (1992) *Shakespeare's Theatre* (second edition), London: Routledge & Kegan Paul.

Thomson, Peter (2000) 'Brecht and actor training: On whose behalf do we act?' in Alison Hodge (ed.) *Twentieth Century Actor Training*, 98–112.

Till, Nicholas (2010) '"Oh, to make boards to speak!"' in Collins and Nisbet (2010).

Tillis, Steve (1992) *Towards an Aesthetics of the Puppet: Puppetry as a Theatrical Art*, New York: Greenwood Press.

Toller, Jane (1962) *Papier-mâché in Great Britain and America*, London: G.Bell & Sons.

Tordoff, Rob (2013) 'Actors' Properties in Ancient Greek Drama: An Overview' in Harrison and Liapis (2013).

Trotter, David (2000) *Cooking with Mud: The Idea of Mess in Nineteenth-Century Art and Fiction*, Oxford: Oxford University Press.

Tufnell, Miranda and Chris Crickmay (1990) *Body, Space, Image*, Alton: Dance Books.

Trueman, Matt (2014a) 'Alistair McDowall' www.theguardian.com/stage/2014/apr/26/alistair-mcdowall-rules-theatre-anything Accessed 26 February 2015.

Trueman, Matt (2014b) 'The Nether' www.theguardian.com/stage/2014/jul/22/the-nether-online-paedophilia-computer-game-theatre-royal-court Accessed 28 February 2015.

Vandervelde, Karen (2000) 'The Gothic Soap of Martin McDonagh' in Eamonn Jordan (ed.) *Theatre Stuff: Critical Essays on Contemporary Irish Theatre*, Carysfort Press, Dublin.

Van Leeuwen, T. (1999) *Speech, Music, Sound*, Basingstoke: Macmillan.

Veltruský, Jiři ([1955] 1964) 'Man and Object in the Theater' in *A Prague School Reader on Esthetics, Literary Structure, and Style*, Washington, D.C.: Georgetown University Press.

Vendrovskaya, Lyubov and Galina Kaptereva (eds) (1982) *Evgeny Vakhtangov*, translated by Doris Bradbury, Moscow: Progress Publishers.

Vervain, Chris and David Wiles (2001) 'The Masks of Greek Tragedy as Point of Departure for Modern Performance' in *New Theatre Quarterly*, XVII, 254–72.

Walton, J. Michael (2005) 'Translation or Transubstantiation' in Macintosh et al. (2005).

Ward, Frazer (2012) *No Innocent Bystanders: Performance Art and Audience*, Lebanon, NH: University Press of New England.

Watson, Lyall (1990) *The Nature of Things: The Secret Life of Inanimate Objects*, London: Hodder & Stoughton.

Wiles, David (2004) 'The Use of Masks in Modern Performances of Greek Drama' in Hall, Macintosh and Wrigley (2004) 245–63.

Wiles, David (2007) *Mask and Performance in Greek Tragedy: From Ancient Festival to Modern Experimentation*, Cambridge: Cambridge University Press.

Wiggins, Martin with Catherine Richardson (2012) *British Drama 1533–1642: A Catalogue*, vol. 1 Oxford: Oxford University Press.

Willett, John (1984) *Brecht in Context*, London: Methuen.

Willett, John (1986) *Caspar Neher: Brecht's Designer*, London: Methuen.

Williams, David (2005) 'Simon McBurney' in Mitter, Shomit and Maria Shevtsova (eds) (2005) *Fifty Key Theatre Directors*, Abingdon: Routledge, 247–52.

Williams, Richard and Chris Vervain (1999) 'Masks for Menander: Imaging and Imagining Greek Comedy', in *Digital Creativity*, vol. 10, no. 3, 180–82.

Wilson, Andy (2003) *Making Stage Props: A Practical Guide*, Marlborough, Wiltshire: Crowood.

Wilson+Wilson www.wilsonandwilson.org.uk Accessed 21 February 2015.

Wright, Elizabeth (2009) *Narratives of Continuity & Change: British Theatre Design 1945 – 2003, An Oral History* [Thesis].

Wright, John (1998) Interview with the author.

Wright, John (2006) *Why Is That So Funny?* London: Nick Hern Books.

Wulf (2000) 'Understanding Age and Wear Effects' in *Proptology* http://home.eol.ca/~props/index.html#toc Accessed 1 November 2015.

Wynne, Brian (1996) 'And May the Sheep Safely Graze' in Scott Lash, Bronislaw Szerszynski and Brian Wynne, *Risk, Environment and Modernity: Towards a New Ecology*, London: Sage.

Index